Pathways to Positive Parenting:

Helping Parents Nurture Healthy Development in the Earliest Months

Jolene Pearson

Washington, DC

Published by

ZERO TO THREE
1255 23rd St., NW., Ste. 350
Washington, DC 20037
(202) 638-1144
Toll-free orders (800) 899-4301
Fax: (202) 638-0851
Web: http://www.zerotothree.org

Cover and text design and composition: K Art and Design, Inc.

10 9 8 7 6 5 4 3 2 1
Printed in the United States of America

ISBN 978-1-938558-56-6

Suggestion citation:
Pearson, J. (2016). *Pathways to positive parenting: Helping parents nurture healthy development in the earliest months.* Washington, DC: ZERO TO THREE.

Table of Contents

Part 4—The Pathways

Part 5—Appendices

Part 6

Acknowledgments

My first professional position was in the newly created Minnesota Early Childhood Family Education (ECFE) program, a universal access program designed to provide information and support to parents of children from birth to 5 years old. I immediately discovered I needed to learn much more about working with parents and infants. Thus began my search for this information.

My search led me to enroll in the infant and toddler master's program at Wheelock College in Boston, MA. There I met Linda Gilkerson, who has remained an inspiration to me all these years later. Linda was my adviser and also one of my professors. Linda connected me to an incredible internship at the Child Development Research Unit where Dr. Berry Brazelton was then director. I had the opportunity to see Brazelton demonstrate the amazing capabilities of newborns through the Neonatal Behavioral Assessment Scale. I was hooked! Brazelton also taught me about the opportunities and vulnerabilities of working with parents during this time of family formation. Others who contributed to deepening my knowledge at this time were John McCarthy, Heidi Als, and Carey Halsey.

Upon my return to Minnesota, Joann O'Leary invited me to join her in her exciting work at Abbott Northwestern, where she had created the "Infant as a Person," a postpartum education program. It became obvious there was a need to provide training and support to other professionals who could expand these types of programs in their communities.

Pathways began as a training guide for my colleagues in Minnesota's ECFE program in 2000. In 2006, *Pathways*'s Christopher Watson invited me to develop *Pathways* as an online course at the University of Minnesota's Center for Early Childhood Development. In 2009, *Pathways* was adapted for use by Part C Early Intervention personnel. Many thanks are owed to Karen Anderson for her dedication to making these courses come alive.

I am deeply grateful to many colleagues who have shared in the work: Barb White, Renee Torbenson, Melaine Faulhaber, Karen Riecsh, Kathy Morris, Jude Schaff, Jean Mendenhall, Jane Bromaghim, Sara Wille, and Leah Butzler and Jennifer Brown Guiney. Also thanks to Betsy Dadabo, Scott Strand, Donna Wiemann, and Dawn Braa, who made important technical contributions to this text. Finally, I am deeply grateful to all of the parents who have shared their experiences with me and the babies who have taught me so much.

What began as a search for information turned into an incredibly rewarding journey because of the many passionate and knowledgeable people it has brought into my life.

Foreword

Being born is among the most important transitions a person will face, and it creates an immense challenge for those who experience it, especially the newborn and his parents. According to noted pediatrician Dr. T. Berry Brazelton, the birth of a child represents a unique developmental touchpoint during which professionals can help parents adapt optimally to their new roles. New parents are eager to promote their infant's growth and development. Getting off to a good start is crucial to both parents and children in reaching their highest potential as humans.

Pathways is an important and practical manual for those with clinical roles in working with parents and newborns. It guides professionals in providing information and support to families from the first days of their new baby's life to the first months at home. Dr. Pearson's training guide and curriculum, an outgrowth of her vast clinical experience with parents and newborn babies, is supported by solid developmental, behavioral, and psychological theory.

For more than 25 years, Dr. Pearson has been a certified Neonatal Behavioral Assessment (Brazelton) examiner and taught "Infant as a Person" classes as a powerful way to demonstrate a full-term newborn's many capabilities and facilitate the acquisition of positive parenting skills by hundreds of new parents each year. In a clear, easy-to-read format, Dr. Pearson writes passionately and specifically about ways to engage parents and babies in learning about one another. She presents this process through eight key vantage points, or "Pathways":

1. The Transitioning Baby
2. The Sleeping Baby
3. The Social Baby
4. The Crying Baby
5. The Oral Baby
6. The Dexterous Baby
7. The Strong Baby
8. The Premature Baby

Within each Pathway, the author discusses materials to use, sample questions to ask, descriptions of how to demonstrate the Pathway, developmental context, implications, and parent care. In each section, she provides the reader with ample useful references.

As a Brazelton trainer since 1981 with first-hand knowledge of Dr. Pearson's extensive clinical experience and innovative ideas about parents and newborn infants, I find *Pathways* to be an incredibly creative adaptation of the Neonatal Assessment Scale that is meticulously faithful to its underlying concepts. *Pathways* is a significant publication and a must for all professionals who care for and about newborn infants and their parents.

—**John T. McCarthy, MD**, New York University Child Study Center

Jolene Pearson has been my friend and colleague for more than 25 years as we have worked together with parents and their newborn babies. The Pathways Training Guide and Curriculum addresses a broad spectrum of questions, thoughts, observations, feelings, and concerns of the many new parents with whom we have worked. This book is an outcome of years of experience in using the Brazelton Neonatal Behavioral Assessment Scale (NBAS) in a group setting and working with individual families. Consulting with one another, we were able to successfully adapt the NBAS to meet the needs of many families and use it in a group setting in a hospital environment. The format has proven to be an excellent one for educating parents about newborn development, providing them with anticipatory guidance, connecting them to community resources, and giving them a facilitated opportunity to learn from each other as well as from their own baby.

The strength of this training guide and parent education curriculum is the concrete way Jolene has taken the important developmental behaviors of the newborn and put them into "So What?" practical guides. For the less-experienced educator, she has created protocols for using a Teaching Teddy and developed a series of Teaching Photographs. She has carefully delineated three levels of facilitation based on the skills and experience of the educator wishing to use this training guide and curriculum.

Jolene has incorporated ways to acknowledge and support the reciprocal relationship between the parent and baby. The curriculum also acknowledges the intense disequilibrium of the postpartum period for both the parent and baby. Jolene provides information on how to use this time of transition as a teachable moment. To have omitted either the concepts of the reciprocal relationship or the intensity of disequilibrium would have missed the meaning of the lived experience of the transition from pregnancy to postpartum.

Getting to know newborns and their parents from a developmental perspective is an adventure. If you are able to use this curriculum in a group setting you may find it challenging at first. Whether you work in a group setting or a one-to-one situation, in the role of educator you must train yourself to observe the baby and tune into the parent at the same time. It is critical that you complete all of the background readings and study the protocols fully before attempting to do this work. The birth of a child is a very special time in the life of families. They are open to learning and at the same time very vulnerable. Being a part of this special time for the family is a privilege. Enjoy the information and all you will learn.

—Joann M. O'Leary, PhD, MPH, MS, IMH-E® (IV)

Part 1
Pathways Framework

Introduction

Nurturing a child and developing a relationship with a child are two of the most intense and important tasks people may be called upon to do in their lifetime. It takes information and practice to develop parenting skills and time and support to adjust emotionally to parenthood. Parents need to feel competent in their roles in order for children to reach their highest potential. The attention and care that a parent gives an infant is not just enjoyable for the infant; it is essential for that child's healthy development (Swain, Lorberbaum, Kose, & Strathearn, 2007).

For the child, these initial experiences in life shape how he feels about who he is, teach him what to expect from others, and model how he should interact with others. Basic human capacities such as trust, intimacy, and the give-and-take of communication begin to be established in the first year of life. The extent to which these qualities are developed sets the stage for future successes or challenges (Beeghly & Tronick, 2011). How do parents help their tiny baby become the individual he has the potential to be?

Successful parenting provides protection and emotional organization and encourages learning and exploration (Beckwith, 1990). Early parent–infant interactions must be in the context of a stable, nurturing, and attentive relationship in order to have a positive effect on the child's development (Greenspan & Greenspan, 1985; Pawl, 1995). Stimulating experiences alone are not enough to support a child's future competency in development. The critical role parents play in their child's early development cannot be replaced or underestimated (Leach, 1995).

Parents develop in stages that parallel their baby's development (Brazelton & Cramer, 1990; Eagan, 1985; Gaziano & O'Leary, 1998). There are predictable times when parents will benefit from specific information, insights, and support (Brazelton & Nugent, 1995). Parenting skills can be enhanced through learning opportunities, especially in the newborn period (Brazelton & Nugent, 1995; Bromwich, 1997). The newborn period can be an especially opportune time to promote a positive parent-child relationship (Barnard, Morisset, & Spieker, 1993; Blackburn & Kang, 1991; Brazelton & Cramer, 1990; Brazelton &

Nugent, 1995). *Pathways* is developed around important information that is needed by parents of young infants. The information alerts parents to the capabilities, individuality, and developmental needs of their new baby, while at the same time supporting parents as they develop their skills. For those with an interest in learning about or comparing other parent education/intervention models using these concepts, see Appendix E. Educators who have used *Pathways* have found it can help parents become knowledgeable and sensitive caregivers to their infants. This is critical because sensitive and responsive parenting promotes secure attachment (Ainsworth, Blehar, Waters, & Wall, 1978; Erickson & Kurz-Riemer 1999; Greenspan & Benderly, 1997). Secure attachment has been found to be linked to desirable outcomes such as a child who is cooperative, persistent, a good problem solver, and socially competent (Erickson, Sroufe, & Egeland,1985; Gudsnuk & Champagne, 2011). *Pathways* focuses on the informational needs of parents. *Pathways* gives professionals dynamic ways to impart important information about infant care and development and demonstrate support to new parents.

What Is *Pathways*?

Parents of newborns and infants are especially open to learning, and many new parents are actively seeking information. What do we teach them? How do we teach them? *Pathways* is an educator's guide to educating and supporting new parents. *Pathways* provides information to share with parents, training in creative and effective ways to teach parents, and materials proven to engage parents. *Pathways* has inspired the development of programs for new parents and has enhanced the training of professionals already working with new parents. *Pathways* is a compilation of important information about infant development, stages of parent growth, best practice information, and innovative strategies for imparting information and providing support to new parents.

The information, ideas, and teaching strategies you will find in this book have been used successfully in a variety of settings by a diverse group of professionals for more than 10 years. (A brief history of the development of *Pathways* is found in Appendix F.) *Pathways* has been found to complement and enhance the knowledge base and skills of professionals from backgrounds such as early childhood education, early intervention, parent education, occupational and physical therapy, nursing, and social work. This volume was born out of a need to "fill in the gaps" for a variety of professionals by providing information regarding early infant development and an understanding of the growth of parents. *Pathways* provides strategies for working with parents and infants steeped in infant mental health principles.

Pathways guides professionals in developing an approach to parent education that reflects respect for the tremendous transition parents go through when a new baby joins the family. It provides professionals with up-to-date information to share with parents based on recommendations endorsed by the national organizations representing best practices. In addition, *Pathways* uses innovative teaching strategies, such as the *Pathways* Teaching Photographs and a Teaching Teddy, that educators can incorporate into their practice. This guide will be useful to professionals (from a variety of disciplines) who find themselves working with parents of newborns and very young infants.

Through *Pathways*, educators will learn to provide the kinds of information and support that nurtures the parent–infant relationship. Nurturing the parent–infant relationship is at the heart of infant mental health and is the foundation for infant mental health practice. Infant mental health is the healthy social and emotional development of a child from birth to 3 years old. It begins with the care and nurturing provided by parents that can be enhanced by the information and support offered by professionals.

Pathways informs and describes how infants communicate their needs and wants in various states of consciousness and with behavioral cues. In addition, *Pathways* provides information and resources on important topics such as postpartum depression (PPD), Safe to Sleep, tummy time, breastfeeding, and coping with crying. Educators who complete the self-training Infant Observation Guide (see Appendix B) will enhance their ability to identify infant states of consciousness and identify cues. The infant observation activities, Teaching Photographs, and Teaching Teddy (demonstrations that are part of *Pathways*) provide dynamic ways for parents to learn. Each activity has been field tested and proven to be effective.

Endorsements From Professionals Who Have Studied and Used *Pathways*

> Pathways *is a wonderful guide to teaching parents with newborns about their baby's development, reading their cues and offering support with positive parenting skills. The clear instructions that are presented in the manual have helped me become more comfortable and more confident in teaching parents. The way it is organized makes it convenient to use. It is helpful having the photographs for each pathway and the instructions on demonstrating with a Teaching Teddy. I look forward to becoming more experienced in educating parents using* Pathways. —Elizabeth Asturia, occupational therapist, Birth to Three Early Intervention

> *I believe that the concepts I learned regarding SIDS, "back to sleep," tummy time, and postpartum depression should be essentially learning points for anyone working in this field. I think these are hot topics in the field of child development, and it was good to learn what they are and how they can be addressed when working with families. Prior to this course, I had a general understanding of each of these things; however, I was not sure how to present the information to parents in a sensitive way.* —Jen Ishaug, home visitor, Early Intervention

> *The* Pathways *curriculum provides a wealth of information about the parent–child relationship and newborn development. I think that all parents benefit from the* Pathways *curriculum because the facilitator can gear discussions or present information based on the needs or circumstances of the parents while considering the time allowed*

for the session or visit. Families appreciate the visuals that accompany the information being presented. I use the Pathways *photos and Teaching Teddy at each visit. The* Pathways *curriculum provides families with practical and effective strategies that can be applied immediately and support the growth and development of their new baby.* —Leah Butzler, parent educator, Early Childhood Family Education

I have used the Pathways *curriculum in my work as a family educator and as an infant massage instructor. The teaching photos are a valuable tool that I use during each session. I find that parents are drawn to the photos and often comment how helpful they are. The* Pathways *Teaching Photographs have also been helpful when sharing this information with other professionals.* —Renee Torbenson, licensed parent educator, lactation educator, and certified infant massage instructor

I have been using Pathways *for 13 years. I have been able to use it in multiple settings in my work. I have used it one on one and with small groups at a busy city hospital, and with parenting groups that have included moms, dads, and grandparents. I currently use it in my job working with teen moms who are pregnant or have a newborn baby during their weekly parenting classes. The moms love to learn about what their baby can do and how to help them through the first few months of life. My students are able to "get" the information they are given and then share it with the people who are supporting them. Many of my students have a lot of misinformation about newborns, and they can use their interactions at home with their baby to teach others what they have learned.* —Melanie Faulhaber, early childhood educator and licensed marriage and family therapy associate

The Pathways *curriculum offers clear guidelines and practical suggestions for training staff to work with parents of newborns. It has proven to be a valuable tool in developing shared understanding necessary for collaborative relationships between early childhood education and medical staff. What an excellent resource!* —Mary Scott, MSN

Benefits of Using *Pathways* With Parents

- Provides helpful information and practical ideas that capture parents' attention. Parents can immediately apply what they have learned.
- Provides important, up-to-date information on topics about which new parents need information, such as Safe to Sleep, tummy time, and the stress of coping with a crying baby.
- Highlights the newborn's ability to communicate, alerting parents to the importance of reading and responding to their baby's cues.
- Dispels misconceptions such as responding to a parent's concern about spoiling the baby or letting an infant become too "attached" if held too much.

- Promotes positive infant mental health by acknowledging the capacity of infants to feel and relate to others and the importance of early experiences.
- Encourages parents to pay attention to their own well-being as they take on their new role.

Training Guidelines for *Pathways* Educators

Pathways is designed to enhance the work of professionals by helping them:

- Learn to identify specific newborn behaviors and capabilities that highlight the infant's competencies, individuality, and developmental needs.
- Promote a positive parent–infant relationship and the infant's social and emotional development by alerting/guiding parents in reading and responding optimally to their infant's cues.
- Facilitate a learning process that empowers parents to be informed and active learners about their infant's behavior and developmental needs as well as their own needs as parents.
- Stimulate a thoughtful approach to parenting and interest in parent education and support programs sponsored in the community.
- Integrate current best practice information into parent education.

Role of the Educator

The intention of this curriculum is to educate and empower parents while acknowledging the importance of the relationship they are developing with their child.

This curriculum illuminates important information to share with parents of young infants as well as critical methods to facilitate such learning. *Facilitation* can be defined as approaching parents at an opportune time to provide additional information and insights or sensitive observations that enhance the parents' knowledge about their baby and themselves as parents. The facilitation process involves assessing parents' current knowledge and perceptions and discerning what additional information or insights would be beneficial to share with them.

Much of parenting is intuitive and need not be "taught." Babies are born with a range of behaviors designed to draw their parents to them (Beckwith, 1990; Brazelton & Cramer, 1990; Emde, 1980). Professionals should take great care not to obstruct the intuitive and natural attachment competencies a parent and baby bring to one another during the newborn period.

Each *Pathways* session develops its own tone and course of discovery based on the uniqueness of the participants. Every parent and baby offers the educator a dynamic opportunity to foster education and support.

Competencies for the *Pathways* Educator

The art of using this curriculum, whether in a group setting or in a one-to-one session, depends on the educator's ability to:

1. Identify/interpret/demonstrate the language of the newborn by observing and discussing the baby's states of consciousness and behavioral cues.
2. Meet and engage parents in a respectful and empowering manner that acknowledges the adult learning process and stages of parent development.
3. Embrace a process of facilitation in which the educator must be willing to be fully focused and yet totally flexible in order to utilize the most teachable moments.
4. Offer parents up-to-date best care practice information.

In Welcome Baby Levels 1 and 2, educators will utilize the comments and observations of parents along with observations of the infant to create teachable moments. Welcome Baby Level 1 facilitation protocols call for the utilization of a teddy bear, to model interaction and positioning, and teaching photographs, to illustrate educational concepts rather than direct interaction with the newborn.

In all three levels of facilitation, educators will find the Teaching Teddy, Teaching Photographs, and Welcome Baby Level 1 protocols useful in teaching. Using these allows the educator to master the content and attend to facilitation while gaining experience in directly observing and interacting with infants.

Suggestions for focusing on spontaneous infant behaviors are included, but Welcome Baby Levels 1 and 2 educators are purposely not directed to attempt to alter the baby's state of consciousness. Facilitation of babies from one state of consciousness to another takes practice and skill and should be undertaken only by Neonatal Behavioral Assessment Scale (NBAS)-certified individuals when using *Pathways* at Welcome Baby Level 3. (For descriptions of infant states of consciousness, see Appendix A). An exception might be helping a crying baby become calmer —when a parent needs assistance. All educators using *Pathways* will be directed to work directly with a crying baby in order to demonstrate techniques to calm a baby.

The Welcome Baby Level 3 educator can use the comments and observations of parents along with her own observations of the infant. She must also focus on the participants and engage in group process to create the desired mutual learning environment. In addition, the Welcome Baby Level 3 educator will generate the content and teachable moments through administration of adapted items from the NBAS and use her NBAS skills in helping the baby move between states of consciousness.

How to Begin Using *Pathways*

Welcome Baby Levels 1 and 2

- Read and study this guide, taking time to explore recommended resources.
- Create a set of teaching points to accompany the Teaching Photographs (see Appendix G for directions for creating teaching points).
- Engage in a series of observations to learn about infant states of consciousness, state-related behaviors, and infant capabilities by observing 8–10 babies and complete the Infant Observation Guide for each of these encounters (see Appendices B and C).
- Practice the art of listening and reflecting with both parents and your colleagues.
- Practice using the Teaching Teddy and Teaching Photographs as described in each Pathway.

Welcome Baby Level 3

- The Welcome Baby Level 3 educator will benefit by studying the protocols for Welcome Baby Levels 1 and 2 and becoming familiar with the use of the Teaching Teddy and Teaching Photographs as an enhancement to the administration of NBAS items.
- In each pathway are suggestions for the educator who has achieved reliability in the administration and scoring of the NBAS and is comfortable in administering the NBAS in front of parents.

Part 2
Parents

The Developing Relationship Between Parent and Infant

The term *attachment* indicates the formation of an emotional bond with others during early infancy. John Bowlby was a British psychiatrist known for his work with infants, in which he described his attachment theory as a biodirectional process in which babies and parents interact with one another and form emotional bonds (Bowlby, 1969/1982). Attachment is the foundation for healthy development. Attachment and bonding are often spoken of interchangeably, but there is a difference.

Erickson and Kurz-Riemer (1999, p. 55) made a helpful delineation between bonding and attachment: "Bonding is often used to describe a relatively brief experience during the first moments or days of the baby's life, when many parents feel those first rushes of parental instinct and nurturing love." On the other hand, Erickson and Kurz-Riemer described attachment as a "relationship that develops gradually over weeks and months as the baby and adults engage in repeated interactions, adapting to each other's unique ways."

Erickson and Kurz-Riemer (1999) go on to make this important statement about the securely attached child: "Research has shown secure attachment develops from the child's experience with a caregiver who is consistently responsive to the child's cues and signals" (p. 56). The child has learned to trust that the caregiver will be there to meet her needs. And, importantly, the child has learned to trust in her own ability to solicit that care. Experience tells the child that "when I give a signal, it counts. I have the power to see that my needs are met" (Erickson & Kurz-Riemer, 1999, p. 59). This statement has extremely important implications for *Pathways*. This is because parents play a vital role in helping their baby adjust to new experiences. A newborn enters the world experiencing many new and often overstimulating sensations (Barnard et al., 1993; Nugent, 1985). Some of these are external in terms of sights, sounds, and feelings. Others are internal from feeling hunger, gas, or even lack of the secure boundary once provided by the uterus. A sensitive, responsive parent or caregiver must tune in to the baby in such a way as to identify the individual ways this particular baby likes to be held, talked to, comforted, and wrapped. Through *Pathways* information and strategies, educators will demonstrate and inform parents about the importance of responding sensitively to the baby based on recognizing the infant's state of consciousness and reading the baby's cues.

Responding to the baby's cues is the way in which a parent enters into a relationship with a baby (Barnard et al., 1993; Beckwith, 1990). Within *Pathways* are opportunities to discuss individuality and model sensitive interactions. *Pathways* demonstrates how to "speak" the language of the newborn through reading the baby's cues, respecting the baby's state of consciousness, and intentionally responding (Brazelton & Nugent, 1995; Nugent, 1985). For example, when parents are able to help their babies calm down and become focused, parents begin to feel a sense of achievement (Brazelton, 1992). If a baby is crying all the time, the baby cannot take in new information. The baby must first be helped to become calmer. A baby who is in a quiet alert state can use his visual and auditory capabilities to learn about the world.

Pathways focuses on affirming and supporting the parent–infant dialogue. Interweaving parents' comments and linking them to the process of attachment is key in the *Pathways* approach. By listening carefully to the parents' descriptions of their experiences, *Pathways* educators will often be able to affirm the ways in which the parents and baby are communicating with one another (Cardone & Gilkerson, 1989; Mercer, 1986).

Another *Pathways* approach is to assist the parent in problem solving when the parent is challenged, confused, or exhausted. *Pathways* validates the "learning as you go" nature of being a parent; in turn, due to the individuality of each baby, parents may need different approaches. In these ways *Pathways* supports the developing relationship between the parent and infant. Keep in mind that parenting is first and foremost a relationship—in which knowledge is a guide. The *Pathways* facilitation includes information as well as ways to demonstrate sensitive and responsive interactions with very young infants.

Parents Develop in Stages Too

Parenting is a relationship like no other. The intensity of this relationship is not something for which one can prepare by simply reading or hearing from another person's experience. It is through experiences such as caring for the baby while being totally sleep deprived, or witnessing the baby's first smile, that a parent can sense the importance of the journey she has undertaken. The parent will never be the same person as before the baby was born (Eagan, 1985; Kitzinger, 1995; Mercer, 1986). In the days and weeks that follow the birth of a new baby, parents can benefit from support and guidance (Boukydis, 2012; Brazelton & Cramer, 1990; Gerber & Johnson, 1998; Hotelling, 2004).

The driving force of growth in a parent is the child's need for nurturing. In caring for the baby, a parent learns more about the baby as a person with individual needs, likes, and dislikes. In meeting the needs of the baby, parents grow too (Galinsky, 1987). They learn to stretch beyond themselves and become responsible for another human being. The information contained within this curriculum can provide parents with both important information and helpful insights as they develop as a parent—and get to know their baby.

The respectful, thoughtful approach of the educator should model attuned and attentive interactions with both babies and their parents.

The *Pathways* educator must be knowledgeable and sensitive to the vulnerability and disequilibrium experienced by new parents. Written in 1987, Ellen Galinsky's book *The Six Stages of Parenthood* provides a timeless, important, and insightful framework for gaining an understanding of the developmental stages of becoming a parent. Galinsky conceptualizes stages when the parents' emotional and intellectual energy is focused on a major psychological task that corresponds with the child's development. Galinsky developed her theory based on the concept that new parents have formulated images of whom they should be and how they should act in response to the various developmental stages their child moves through. Within this theory of parental growth and development, each stage comprises parenting tasks that parents must deal with and come to terms with along their parenting journey. The stages are presented chronologically and focus on the task of parenting along with the myriad emotions parents—especially new parents—experience: joy, pleasure, guilt, anguish, fear, and uncertainty. Those working with parents should become as knowledgeable about parent growth and development as they are about child development. This understanding of the growth and development of the parent can increase the educator's insights into ways to support and inform new parents.

Parents in Galinsky's "nurturing stage" are learning to care for their dependent child in unexpected and profound ways. During this stage, parents often put their own needs on hold and grow and mature, thus changing their sense of self. The following section provides excerpts from the relevant section of Galinsky's (1987) book, and shares how those called upon to work with new parents can use the *Pathways* to meet the needs of parents in this stage.

The Developing Parent

This section is intended to provide a conceptual framework describing how new parents may begin to get to know their newborn and themselves as parents. Also highlighted are insights for ways in which the educator should be sensitive and mindful in interacting with parents during this time of transition.

The Birth: Images and Realities

> *It is important for the parents to tell their birth story as a way of reconciling the actual birth from the imagined birth . . . and [as] part of the process of forming an attachment with the new baby.* (Galinsky, 1987, p. 55)

Prelude questions suggested in *Pathways* encourage parents to:

- Talk about their birth experience.
- Process their experience by sharing it with an attuned listener.

Through listening to the parents tell their birth story, the educator gains key insights into the parents' perceptions. This helps the educator decide what may be important to share with this particular parent. As the educator listens, she learns the answers to the following questions:

- Was the birth experience what the parent expected, or did it depart dramatically from her expectation?
- Was the caregiving during the labor and birth perceived as supportive, or did parents feel abandoned or fearful?
- Was there a support person/spouse/partner present in labor?
- Was there concern about either the baby's or the mother's well-being during the labor or at birth?

The educator's attentive listening to this personal and intense experience builds rapport. The educator gains important insights into how to place emphasis on particular information, such as a demonstration of a position or handling technique, or when validation of a specific observation would be beneficial to a parent. Listening to parents is as important as providing information. Through listening, you will understand what is important to the parent. It gives you an understanding of what they already know or do not know. Listening can help you guide your conversation with the parent in dynamic ways versus beginning by sharing information.

The New Baby: Images and Realities

> *Seeing the child for the first time is a moment equal to that of the birth, it is etched in parents' memories.* (Galinsky, 1987, p. 55).

Educators should refrain from labeling an infant's behavior, because new parents are in the process of reconciling the image of the real baby with the imagined baby (Brazelton & Cramer, 1990; Slade & Cohen, 2009). It is important that professionals refrain from comments that may reflect their personal and idiosyncratic perceptions of the baby. For example, about a baby who cried lustily before a feeding: "You've got a real feisty one on your hands!" What might that mean to the parent? Positive? Negative? How might these kinds of comments influence the parent's perception of their baby? Educators should attempt to limit their comments about the baby to ones that are reflective of the baby's state of consciousness, cues, or behaviors (Boukydis, 2012). It is best to avoid comments that may attribute particular personality or character traits to the infant. By attending to the baby's states and signals one is honoring what the baby brings to the relationship, as opposed to making assumptions or interrupting the parent's image-forming process. Brazelton and Cramer (1990) pointed out that when the baby is born, the mother must create a new bond. They believe that some of these "formidable" tasks include adapting to a new being, mourning the loss of the imaginary child, and "adapting to the characteristics of a specific baby" (p. 30). Extraneous comments may not help this important process and could be harmful.

The educator may honor and acknowledge images and realities the parent may be working through by inquiring, "Have you given your baby a name?" rather than "What is the baby's name?" There are several reasons why parents may not have named their child after the birth. For example, parents may have wished or perhaps been told during an ultrasound that they were having a girl and instead discovered at birth the baby is a boy.

Is This Child Really Mine?

> *I had expected to love my child, to have this feeling. . . . This is my child, I'm his father. It was all there in pieces, but the gestalt didn't occur.* (Galinsky, 1987, p. 62)

Educators do not need to touch or hold the baby in order to be effective. The educator should always ask permission to touch or hold the baby. As simple as this may sound, observation of hospital practice reveals that this occurs infrequently: Countless personnel interact with the baby, and few ask the parents' permission. Asking permission acknowledges that they, the parents, are in charge of their baby. The materials and techniques found in *Pathways* provide innovative strategies for beginning a conversation and relaying important information that do not involve direct interaction with the baby. (How to use the *Pathways* Teaching Photographs and Teaching Teddy in each Pathway will be described in detail.)

New parents are often regarded as experts about their own baby or are told they are experts. Although this is true, parents may not feel this or realize that their observations make them experts. Therefore, **asking questions about the baby in the hours, days, and weeks after birth should be done with care.** Posing questions to the parent should be done in such a manner that the parent will have a way to answer and not be put on the spot. Parents often enjoy sharing details about what they have observed about their baby. As parents share their thoughts and observations they confirm what they have learned. Parents are experts about their experiences, perceptions, and observations and will be able to competently share them with an interested listener. The experienced educator may be able to use what the parents say to highlight a point in a Pathway or open a Pathway's discussion based on what parents share. By listening, the educator might also discover the parent has some gaps in his knowledge of current best practice infant care, or may have concerns that should be addressed. Only through carefully listening to parents can educators know where and how to join the conversation or which information may be important to highlight.

Affinity/Dissimilarity

> *Another important ingredient in early attachment is feeling that parents have an affinity with or dissimilarity to the baby.* (Galinsky, 1987, p. 63)

The educator should suspend her own commenting and allow the parents to process and share their thoughts and perceptions. Parents may spontaneously report that the baby looks just like either the mother or father or someone else in the family. The baby's personality or behaviors may remind them of someone in the family. These can sometimes be painful associations as well as positive ones. It is important to simply listen for the information, neither probing nor offering your observations of how, to you, the baby might look. Listening and observing are preferred over speaking or providing "teaching" when just getting to know the parent and baby.

Can I Take Care of My Baby?

> *In retrospect, the newborn seems to have been so safe, so protected in the uterus. . . . How can I make sure that the baby will survive?* (Galinsky, 1987, p. 64)

New parents are often very concerned about their ability to take care of their baby. This concern and worry helps parents focus and pay attention to the baby's well-being, and educators should notice and affirm parents' attentiveness. Within any *Pathways* session, this universal concern should always be discussed. Parents in the group will likely share similar concerns. One way to facilitate this discussion is to ask the group, "What are your biggest concerns about taking the baby home?" A mother once said, "Well, given all the things I still have to learn about taking care of my baby, I am amazed the nurses will let me go home with her at all!" This caused other parents in the group to laugh and some to say that they felt the same way. If the interactions take place with parents in their home, the educator might ask, "What have been your biggest challenges (or joys) so far?" This type of question allows the parent to share her experiences with the educator, which in turn provides insights and directions for the educator. The educator can use such parent comments to illustrate the universal anxiety that many new parents experience. Parents should be assured that in the days to follow they will continue to learn as they care for their baby, and their confidence will grow (Eagan, 1985; Kunhaardt, Speigal, & Basile, 1996).

It is also important to remind parents of additional resources they can access once they have been discharged from the hospital. For example, reminding them they can call their pediatrician or the infant feeding center for assistance gives them reassurance. The *Pathways* educator should highlight all available resources (e.g., parenting groups, breastfeeding support) by sharing brochures and flyers about programs in their community as well as lists of evidence-based websites (these will be identified in each Pathway section).

Getting to Know the Baby

> *The match between a parent and baby is clearly enormously important.* (Galinsky, 1987, p. 67)

In each of the core components of the *Pathways* curriculum, educators point out for parents the many capabilities of newborns. There are many opportunities for the educator to highlight the ways a baby expresses her individuality.

The fact that babies are so individual might be a new thought for some parents. If the educator learns there are experienced parents in the group, having them reflect on ways their new baby is different from their first (or second, or third, etc.) can illustrate this point very well. The educator might also describe how one baby can be very different from another baby in the way he needs to be calmed or comforted. If the session takes place in the home in a one-to-one session, questions such as "How does he react to having his diaper changed? and "What is the best way to calm him?" can help parents think about their baby's responses, likes, and dislikes.

The Parent–Child Relationship Is Interactive

> *The relationship between the parent and child is interactive: What the child does affects what the parent does, which in turn affects what the child does.* (Galinsky, 1987, p. 68)

As the baby's patterns change, so will the parents' techniques of meeting their baby's needs. Both the baby and parent will adjust to the new patterns and needs, and this drives the developmental process for both. A key message embedded within *Pathways* is that the parent and infant are on a journey together, and both parent and infant are developing new skills and competencies. In the early weeks and months, parents are learning what their baby likes and dislikes, while at the same time learning more about their baby's rhythms and patterns. Each parent learns what she is able to do to adjust to the baby. The baby is learning what life is like in his new world.

In addition, mothers and fathers tend to interact with the baby in different ways. Mothers generally learn what keeps the baby happy and calm and use this information in their interactions. Fathers tend to enjoy a baby who is a bit more active and seem to tolerate fussing and crying more readily than mothers do (Pruett, 1997). Mothers and fathers bring rich variations in interaction to the baby, as do other caregivers. A baby with two caring parents is fortunate to have two adults invested in his life with two different styles of interaction from which to learn. Research has shown that variations in interactions benefit the child's development (Planalp & Braungart-Rieker, 2013).

New parents can benefit from a developmental understanding of their baby as well as a variety of ideas to try. The variety of approaches is key, because although babies can show similar behaviors, they are still very much individuals. *Pathways* highlights the infant's developmental needs. This information can help to demystify for parents why babies cry, need to be held so much, need to eat frequently, and sleep in short bursts. Along with developmental information, the *Pathways* curriculum provides suggestions for a variety of techniques to draw out the best in the baby, such as how to soothe a crying baby or help increase an infant's alertness.

Getting to Know One's Self

> *Parents' actions and reactions to the baby are self-revealing, for those who choose to try to understand. . . . Everybody has their weak spots. . . . When parents are in the midst of this kind of turmoil they can feel depressed or guilty.* (Galinsky, 1987, p. 70)

A parent with a brand new baby is just beginning to get to know herself as a parent. It is important to explore what the parent has noted thus far as being more difficult than she anticipated. Coping with a crying baby, feeling exhausted, and challenges in feeding the baby are the most common responses (Tedder, 2008).

Within each Pathway, anticipatory guidance suggestions are meant to give parents insights into the next stage of their infant's development and the possible issues they will need to consider. The Developmental Context and Caregiving Implications sections include anticipatory guidance information to share with parents.

Attachment

> *Eventually, parents come to feel attached to the baby, either with "a sudden first gush of love" or in a more gradual way.* (Galinsky, 1987, p. 74)

The deliberate inclusion of information about attachment and bonding in a *Pathways* discussion affirms it is not universal to have a "gush of love" for the baby right after birth. Some parents equate the gush of love with evidence of attachment. Some parents find they do feel an immediate bond to their babies; others do not. Parents need to know it is normal to have mixed feelings and that as they get to know their baby, and as the baby responds to them, attachment grows. Attachment is much more than immediate positive feelings toward the baby after birth; it is an ongoing process that takes place over time (Kohlhoff & Barnett, 2013).

The Developing Parent: A Changing Sense of Self

> *As parents become attached to a baby, they realize that this is a transforming experience. A shrinking of self. A loss of self. A postponement of self—indeed, changing self.* (Galinsky, 1987, p. 79)

A *Pathways* session should include conversation and information about what parents should expect during the first weeks and months of parenting a new baby. Parents usually comment on how they expected to be able to accomplish more than they actually can, in terms of household tasks. They worry about how they will ever be able to return to work. They need affirmation regarding the effort it takes to nurture their newborn (Barnard et al., 1993; Brazelton & Cramer, 1990; Eagan, 1985).

PPD

> *The postpartum time is a time of change. Many people, envisioning postpartum depression, think of it as a single bizarre time of sinking into depression, of losing contact with reality. And for some, particularly women, that can happen. . . . In many others, men and women, during the weeks after birth, moods are cyclical, contentment alternating with despair.* (Galinsky, 1987, p. 83)

The *Pathways* session should always include information on the common onset of the "baby blues" and differentiate this from symptoms of depression (Gurian, 2003). In addition, the *Pathways* educator should be knowledgeable about hospital or community referrals for mothers who display symptoms of PPD or who say they feel depressed. The *Pathways* educator should, with the parent's permission, make a referral as soon as possible if there is concern about PPD. The educator should follow up with both the parent and the person to whom the parent was referred.

What is written in this section is intended to stimulate the educator's thinking about the specific needs of parents after the birth of the baby. In the hours and days after giving birth, educators must keep in mind the tremendous sense of transition or disequilibrium, or both, that parents may be experiencing. Being an empathetic listener and tuning in to the parents' perceptions, comments, concerns, and questions will provide the parents with support. A combination of support, information, and practical tips will go a long way toward assisting parents in working through this period of tremendous change in their lives. This time of change is a necessary phase of attachment (Mercer, 1986; Shahmoon-Shanok, 1990).

In summarizing the period of disequilibrium that parents experience in labor, delivery, and postpartum, insights might be gained from Alice in her entry into Wonderland:

> *"Who are you? said the Caterpillar. "I-I hardly know, Sir, just at present," Alice replied rather shyly.*
>
> *"At least I know who I was when I got up this morning, but I think I must have changed several times since then."*

Caroll, L., (1953) *Alice in Wonderland*, p. 55

T. Berry Brazelton and Bertrand G. Cramer (1990), in their book titled *The Earliest Relationship: Parents, Infants, and the Drama of Early Attachment*, described five paradigm shifts that parents must make after the birth of their baby. The paradigm shifts are identified in italics and implications for *Pathways* are discussed below:

1. *An abrupt ending of the sense of fusion with the fetus, of the fantasies of completeness, and omnipotence fostered by pregnancy.* (Brazelton & Cramer, 1990, p. 30)

Giving birth involves losing the definition of "self as pregnant" and redefining of "self as parent" to this baby. The birth itself marks the end of the physical fusion between the mother and child. As the parent shares the birth story, the *Pathways* educator must listen intently to understand what happened during the birth and immediately afterward. Understanding the parent's frame of mind and thoughts about the baby is key to the success of a *Pathways* session. For example, the educator might learn the parent felt a sense of failure when the birth was a Cesarean, or the educator might hear how appreciative the mother was of the father's support. The mother may say how pleased she is to have had a baby boy, or that she is disappointed to have had a boy.

Women in my postpartum groups have shared that, although they were happy to have their baby delivered, they have feelings of loss at no longer being pregnant. They explain that, before birth, they had a measure of control and peacefulness and now this is missing. They explain feeling a loss of control over the baby. By listening to parents, educators gain insights that guide the educator in conversations with parents.

2. *Adapting to a new being who provokes feelings of strangeness.* (Brazelton & Cramer, 1990, p. 30)

After birth, the way the baby looks, sounds, and behaves may provoke new perceptions about the baby. Or the way the baby looks and behaves may validate perceptions from when the baby was developing prenatally. Parents will sometimes comment that their baby's activity level during the prenatal period is much like what they observe in their newborn. Parents become familiar with their fetal baby through perceptions of movements and their awareness of activity cycles, but the baby who appears at birth is now seen, heard, and experienced in new ways.

3. *Mourning for the imaginary (perfect) child and adapting to the characteristics of this specific baby.* (Brazelton & Cramer, 1990, p. 30)

An initial conversation or interaction with a parent will sometimes reveal the parent's initial feelings of disappointment or surprise surrounding the birthing process or the baby. For example, some parents believed throughout the pregnancy that they would have no need to use pain medications and birth naturally, but instead needed substantial pain relief. For other parents, a the baby might just look "different" than they thought he would. Parents are reconciling the difference between their dreams and images of the baby before birth and the actual baby they are getting to know after birth.

4. *Coping with fears of harming the helpless child.* (Brazelton & Cramer, 1990, p. 30)

As parents move from pregnancy to postpartum, there can be a sense of urgency or even panic as they try to figure out their new roles. Parents will sometimes express a fear of leaving the hospital with their baby. Parents should understand these feelings are typical. No new parent leaves the hospital feeling entirely confident. This lack of confidence is the very thing that makes the parents alert and concerned about their baby. The *Pathways* educator can normalize this concern and affirm that it is appropriate and normal to have some anxiety. These feelings of *lack* of confidence can also help make parents open to information and support in ways they may not have been before the baby was born. The *Pathways* curriculum provides rich sources for topics and information that will engage new parents of all ages and backgrounds.

5. *Learning to tolerate and enjoy the enormous demands made on her (the mother) by the total dependence of the baby; in particular, she has to withstand the baby's intense oral cravings and gratify them with her body.* (Brazelton & Cramer, 1990, p. 30).

A newborn needs intimate nurturing, which may at times feel overwhelming and even overstimulating to the parent who is trying to integrate so many new things. This is particularly true for the breastfeeding mother but is true for all parents who must learn to cuddle and hold their baby in ways that help calm and settle the baby. The baby has literally been rocked, held, and talked to in the womb for months—the baby has never been alone. A newborn seems to feel most comfortable when being rocked, held, and talked to continuously, which are sometimes hard for parents to manage as they strive to meet their own needs as well. For some parents, this adjustment of balancing their needs and the baby's needs takes time to work out. It is important for the educator to reassure parents that it may take time to feel more comfortable and even begin to enjoy this phase of parenting.

The *Pathways* approach is one in which the educator affirms what parents have already shared or observed, frames it in a developmental context, and offers additional insights and information. Examples of how to accomplish this will be found in the section of subsequent chapters under the headings Developmental Context, Caregiving Implications, and Anticipatory Guidance.

Part 3
Facilitation Considerations

In my own educational practice with parents, I have thought about the important creed that guides physicians with whom I have worked: "Do no harm." I believe this creed applies to any professional who works with human beings, especially the youngest and most vulnerable, such as newborns and their families. I believe this because:

- The period of time right after the birth of a baby is a time when parents are open to learning. Parents are in a vulnerable position as they seek out help and advice about the care of their new baby. They trust professionals to have the right information.
- Professionals' words, and parents' interactions with professionals, send parents powerful messages. What an educator shares or shows can either add to the parents' knowledge and understanding or create misunderstandings and challenges (Boukydis, 2012).
- Parents are sensitive during this time of transition to external influences, which they may perceive as judgments or as information to be objectively evaluated and suggestions which can be taken or left (Barnard et al., 1993; Blackburn & Kang, 1991).

Indeed, working with new parents is a job that should be undertaken with thoughtfulness.

If the educator does or says too much, new parents may feel that they are not competent to find solutions and gather the information they need to care for their new baby. If the educator does not offer enough information and support, a new parent may have a sense of being abandoned or may become overwhelmed.

Ill-timed interactions or advice may interrupt the natural and intuitive responses that a parent and baby may have with one another and could interfere with the attachment process. I recall a parent who had been advised to let her baby "cry it out" until at least 4 hours had elapsed between feedings. This mother was visibly distressed while "waiting" for the time to elapse and did not attempt to comfort her baby—even though she desired to do so. The baby became so exhausted that, by the appointed feeding time, she did not feed well. The parent was responding to advice given by an "expert." Instead of responding intuitively to her baby's cues, she was instead purposefully ignoring them. It was painful to watch. The first days and weeks of mother and baby getting to know one another were lost to following "advice." This mother eventually decided to ignore the advice she had been given and feed her baby when her baby was hungry. This also improved her milk supply. The situation demonstrates how parents can be misled by "experts." In an evaluation of the group, the mother thanked us for supporting her and noted that she regretted the time she lost with her baby while she was trying to ignore her crying.

Yet, not all aspects of parenting are intuitive, and appropriately timed information can go a long way toward building the parent's confidence and competence. Deciding what to offer parents in your interactions and conversations with them takes a thoughtful approach. An educator develops this thoughtfulness by listening to what the parents share verbally and by reading their cues—whether given in words, body language, or facial expressions—before deciding what to share or highlight. Or a conversation might be directed by a baby's cues and signals.

Educators should always be cognizant of how the way they interact with both the parent and baby, as well as the specific information they share, may influence the parent. Educators must stay up to date with best practices and be prepared to offer information that is endorsed by national initiatives such as Safe to Sleep or by organizations that promote evidence-based practices, such as the American Academy of Pediatrics (AAP).

In addition to accurate information, one of the most valuable gifts an educator can offer families of newborns is support. Galinsky wrote, "Support is an interesting concept because it connotes a middle ground: help without taking over, listening, and an understanding and acceptance of new parents' feelings" (p. 84). How does an educator determine the "middle ground" for each *Pathways* session? Learning to be supportive is a skill developed through experience, by the educator's conscious effort to learn from each encounter and to commit to reflective practice. By studying your own practice, or reflecting, you are thinking about your work in a way that can help enhance your work with parents and infants. Osterman and Kottkamp (1993, p. 2) wrote that "to achieve this perspective (reflective practice), individuals must come to an understanding of their own behavior; they must develop a conscious awareness of their own actions and effects and the ideas or theories-in-use that shape their action strategies."

Reflective practice can help educators understand the link between what they are currently doing in their practice and how they might improve their effectiveness in the future. Through reflective practice, educators gain new insights and develop new ways of doing their work by identifying the complexity of the work (e.g., parent development, infant development, parent–infant interaction, facilitating versus tradition teaching). Simply stated, *Pathways* aims to help you identify your strengths as well as areas in which you can improve. Completing the guide will support you in developing deeper awareness about your own practice; you will be encouraged to appreciate the areas in which you are doing well, identifying specific areas of your practice to improve, and identifying steps to enhance your practice. The guide in Appendix E will assist you in beginning reflective practice.

Listening: The Prelude

> *Real listening is the creation of a sacred space in which another's words are contained and transformed into hallowed speech. This form of listening is intentional. Such a listener recognizes the responsibility involved, understanding that performing the ritual with an attention to the minutest detail can create the conditions for the healing of the speaker.* (Stone, 1996 , p. 53)

Successful facilitation depends on the educator understanding a parent's frame of mind and perceptions of the baby. With an understanding of the parent's experiences, the educator is able to learn how, for example, an unexpected Cesarean birth affected the parents, or that the completion of natural childbirth had a particularly empowering effect. Perhaps the baby is the first live birth after a loss or several miscarriages; these parents may feel overjoyed as well as reexperience the grief of losing the other babies. The educator must listen carefully to each family and use the information as a guide to her work.

***Pathways* aims to give parents the opportunity to process their birth experience.** When educators invite parents to tell about their experience, they give parents the opportunity to share and reflect upon recent events. In doing so, parents process what they have just experienced and perhaps, as listeners respond to what they share, gain perspective. (In a group *Pathways* session, the educator must take care that one parent does not monopolize the time with her story.) The educator must set the course for parents to tell a bit about their labor and delivery. Asking questions such as "Was your labor what you expected?" gets a response of yes or no. Open-ended questions generally elicit more information; the educator might ask, "How was your labor and birth different from what you expected?" The educator can ask if a Cesarean birth was scheduled or unexpected. This gives the educator insights into the parents' perceptions, as well as information about the baby's experience.

The educator should prepare the room for a group session in advance, so that as families arrive, the educator can give them her full attention. Prior to a *Pathways* session in a one-on-one format in a home visit, the educator should be prepared with all necessary materials and ready to focus on the family, using skills in listening and observing to tune in to both the parent and baby.

Getting Acquainted

The opening conversations, in which parents may share their perceptions, feelings, and interpretations of their parenting experience or their baby, often provide the educator with critical information. In a home visit setting, the educator can further personalize the session by weaving in information from an opening conversation about how the week has gone and what the parent has been thinking about.

As an educator greets families, he should use proven methods of establishing rapport (Emde, 1980), such as engaging in eye contact, being relaxed, and assisting the parents in finding seats and positioning the babies in such a way that it is easy for parents to respond to their baby as needed.

When parents are in a state of disequilibrium, they may share poignant, unexpected information with the educator. The educator must be prepared to respond without judgment. Educators can help parents process their experience by allowing them to speak about their experiences and perceptions. The following are examples of the kinds of information a parent may share. Consider what appropriate responses might be:

- an unexpected emergency Cesarean birth
- grave concern about the baby throughout the pregnancy or delivery, with the family still looking for resolution
- the first live baby after three miscarriages

The following questions will help elicit information while allowing the parent to process his experience. (In cases where a variation on a question appears, the second question is designed for a *Pathways* session taking place days or a few weeks after the baby's birth.) Be sure to ask questions that parents can easily answer and are sure to have the answers for. Asking them to share their observations and perceptions can provide solid ground. They will have information to share, and there can be no right or wrong answer. Often in the process of answering these kinds of questions, parents realize they know quite a lot about their baby already, and the educator can affirm this.

- "How did the labor and birth go?"
- "What concerns did you have about you or your baby during the labor or birth process?"
- "How are you feeling right now?" Or "How have you been feeling since the baby was born?"
- "What happened this morning?" Or "How have the past few days been going?"
- If the session occurs soon after the birth, rather than ask the name of the baby, or if the parents have named the baby yet, "What names have you been thinking about for your baby?" Many parents do not select or agree upon a name ahead of time. In some instances, they may feel that the name they had chosen before the baby was born now doesn't seem quite right. There are many reasons why a baby may not immediately be named. Naming is very important and parents often express some discomfort with the lack of a name. The educator should be supportive of parents, wherever they are in the naming process, and be aware that cultural differences in naming processes may also be in play.

Parent's Perceptions of the Baby

- "Tell me about your baby."
- "What have you noticed about your baby so far?"
- "What is your baby's crying like?"

Telling the parent she is an expert about her own baby at this early stage can be precarious and even dangerous. Although parents do know their baby better than anyone else does, they might not yet realize it, or be able to put it into words. In postpartum, parents are in a new phase of getting to know their baby; the sound of the baby's cry, how the baby looks, or even the baby's gender could be different than expected. Being able to express their perceptions helps parents process their experiences.

The Educator's Perception of the Baby

If this work is done in the hospital, whether at bedside, one to one, or in a group setting, the educator should observe each baby carefully to determine if the baby is in a quiet, alert, drowsy, fussy, or sleeping state. The baby's state of consciousness should guide the order and flow of the *Pathways* session.

The educator should also check bassinet cards, which give additional helpful information such as the date of birth and the baby's weight and length at birth. A baby with a lower-than-average birth weight may not have been full-term. If there are any discrepancies, the educator should gently ask for more information.

Use Caution in Revealing Personal Experiences

An educator who has had a birth experience herself may find that the intense emotional experiences of the families may trigger a desire to share her own story; the educator might begin to share, and find her own emotions triggered. At this point, it is difficult for an educator to attend to the thoughts and emotions of the parent or be able to observe the baby. Erickson and Kurz-Riemer (1999, p. 26) wrote that there can be therapeutic value in the educator sharing her personal stories but "it must be done carefully, sensitively and on a limited basis." If the educator chooses to reveal something about her own birthing or parenting experience, she must clarify in her own mind why this would be helpful to the participants. In general, in facilitation of this curriculum, it is best to use personal experience as an internal reference point for relating to participants.

An attuned educator must stay focused on the parents to be able to assess how they will use the information the parents have shared and to think about ways to affirm what parents have already learned. *Pathways* educators do not just give parents information, they allow parents to guide them in their choice of information to share. This approach gives a voice to the baby by acknowledging the baby as a person who needs others to respond to his cues and signals and supports the important groundwork that is being laid for the relationship developing between the parent and infant.

The following excerpts from session notes demonstrate an educator sharing a personal experience in a less-than-helpful way. A group for parents of newborns was being held in the family lounge of a local hospital. One mother was sharing her dismay that breastfeeding was not going well for her.

"My nipples are so sore, I think I should give up and bottle-feed. I think about that, but then I feel guilty as everyone says it is best to breastfeed the baby," said the teary-eyed mother.

The educator's response was, "Oh, I know just what you mean. With my first baby I had the same trouble and I decided to bottle-feed. There is absolutely nothing wrong with bottle-feeding and you shouldn't feel guilty."

This ended the conversation between the educator and the parent. The educator made no further attempt to inform or support the parent, losing the opportunity to promote breastfeeding as a cultural norm (which is recommended in a position statement from the AAP, 2012).

- The educator might have responded by affirming that many mothers experience discomfort in the beginning days of breastfeeding. This would give a broader context to the mother's concern.
- The educator might have asked if the mother had met with a lactation consultant. This would have allowed for the exploration of potential solutions.
- The educator might have mentioned the hospital's lactation consultant, to foster harmonious working relationships with hospital personnel, and explored the process of referral.

Years later, personal birth experiences can provoke powerful emotions which may interfere with the educator's ability to fully attune themselves to the parents. When personal experiences are shared by the educator, it can discourage the parents' sharing. If an educator becomes engaged in sharing personal experience it can also be distracting to the educator's ability to stay focused on both the parents and the baby or find additional resources for the family.

Keep in mind that as an educator you are there to focus on parents and babies, in order to provide information and support.

Setting the Stage

Physical and psychological attending are critical facets of *Pathways* facilitation. In his course Group Methods in Family Education, at the University of Minnesota, Ted Bowman focused on the concept of the group leader being a "Whobody." This concept originated in a book by Charles Morse (1971) titled *Whobody There?*, a story from a child's perspective about the differences between "anybodies" and "whobodies."

Whobodies show genuine interest and give personal attention. Bowman urged students to think of how this concept can be important to facilitation. Bowman said, "The Whobody factor in group leadership is that extra dimension of being there. Educators (as facilitators) can pay attention to this dimension of group leadership with a passion similar to content preparation or presentation. Competence and warmth need not be opposites.

They can complement one another and make a powerful impression and impact." (T. Bowman, personal communication June 10, 2001)

Another facet of "Whobodiness" is physical attending behavior. *Attending* means being present to another person, focusing on and following the other person, and conveying readiness and receptivity to listen to them, to understand them, and to work with them (Emde, 1980). Physical attending has to do with eye contact, open posture, relaxed body, facing the parent, and staying with the parent (Braun, Coplon, & Sonnenschein, 1984; McClure, 1998; Pawl & St. John, 1998). In *Pathways*, you will find suggestions for how to prepare the environment and position yourself to be able to attend. Note that suggestions include specifics such as where to sit as well as general environmental considerations.

Psychological attending involves listening to group members' spoken and unspoken messages—the whole message. *Pathways* Listening: The Prelude (outlined in the previous section) describes how the information a parent shares with the educator is key to understanding the particular ways in which that parent needs to be attended. In writing about this Vimala McClure suggested, "Perceive each situation with your heart. Empathize" (McClure, 1998, p. 29). What parents share with the educator will direct the focus and pace of the session. Listening to parents share is critical to the process of establishing intentional rapport (Blackburn & Kang,1991; McClure, 1998; Pawl, 1995). The intention of the educator is to be a "Whobody" and to model "Whobodiness" in every way during the session, which conveys a powerful message to parents: "Be a 'Whobody' to your baby."

***Pathways* group facilitation practices include** being present in the room and having the room prepared when families arrive, leaving the educator free to focus on parents and infants. The educator greets each participant and makes introductions, which establishes the educator's role in leadership of the session. It is critical that the educator establish tone, focus, and pace. Through listening, the educator gathers important impressions of the parent and baby and learns about their birth experience and the events of their hospital stay as part of the prelude.

In greeting families, the educator can gather very important information about the infants. For example, the educator may learn if a baby experienced birth trauma, such as a vacuum extraction procedure, or the cord wrapping around the baby's neck, which causes concern about the baby. The educator can learn, for example, which baby has been circumcised, which baby is waiting to be circumcised, and has not been fed, which baby is not to be unwrapped due to concern about temperature, which baby has a bruised head. Knowing about the individual babies assists the educator in planning the *Pathways* session. For the *Pathways* educator at Welcome Baby Level 3, this information provides assessment as to which infant may be best able to demonstrate orientation, habituation, and so forth.

As parents join other parents in the room, the educator works to establish linkages between families. The educator may make statements like, "Your babies share the same birth date!" or "You have both experienced a Cesarean birth." The educator may wish to wait to introduce herself in a more formal way until all the families have gathered.

The session may occur in a postpartum hospital setting. In this case, once the families have gathered and are settled in and the educator has had some conversation with each family, the educator might begin by saying something such as, "I am privileged to be able to be with you this morning. I know that you have just experienced one of life's most exciting and intense experiences—giving birth. These past hours have been special as you see, hear, and hold your baby in your arms and become acquainted with this new little person!"

Because parents are typically pleased to hear their baby's name acknowledged, the educator may wish to begin class by introducing the babies by their first names. If a baby has not been named, this can be acknowledged as well. That is why it is important that the educator ask, "Have you given your baby a name yet?" and not "What is your baby's name?"

There are advantages to working with parents in a group setting (Braun et al., 1984). Parents are introduced to the camaraderie and special support found in groups. Parents from very diverse backgrounds have real "Whobody" experiences with one another during group sessions because of their common intense and very recent birth experiences.

Expectations for Parents and Infants During the Pathways *Session*

The educator explains to the parents that the group will be influenced by the babies in attendance. If their baby is hungry, parents should be encouraged to feed him. When a baby cries, it can actually be helpful in illustrating calming techniques.

Assure parents that they may ask for help if they are unsure of what to do for their baby. The educator may say, "There are many things to learn about sleeping and crying, as well as how much babies can see and hear when they are awake. We will be following the lead of the babies in class. If a baby cries, we will focus on that baby's crying. If the babies are all sleeping, we will discuss sleep. If a baby is in a quiet and alert state, we will talk about the baby's ability to see and hear. As parents, you will also be following the lead of your baby, just as I will be doing as I lead this group. Babies can teach us about their development and needs as we carefully observe and interact with them. During class, anything your baby does is fine and will help us see all of the ways in which babies communicate."

Welcome Baby educators at Levels 1 and 2 will primarily work with the Teaching Teddy on the low table in the center of the circle and utilize observations of the babies in class to illustrate points whenever possible.

During a Welcome Baby Level 3 session, the educator should state that, with the parents' permission, the educator will work with babies on the low table at the center of the circle. Welcome Baby Level 3 educators may wish to incorporate the *Pathways* Teaching Photographs and Teaching Teddy to enhance and supplement maneuvers from the NBAS.

The educator strives to identify the teachable moments in order to capitalize on them during the *Pathways* session. The information that the educator has learned in greeting the parents may be helpful in emphasizing a certain Pathway. How to proceed depends entirely on who is in attendance and what they choose to share about themselves and their babies.

In a group setting, all of the babies present should participate in some way. Each baby presents an opportunity for observation (states of consciousness) or interaction. This might take the form of having the parent describe something about the baby's behavior or an experience that has occurred with the baby.

The educator should continuously model supportive, positive ways to interact with a young baby. The Teaching Teddy can be very useful in demonstrations. Through narration of the infant's behavior and responses to educator's interactions, parents are guided in a process of discovering ways to be sensitive and responsive to their baby and learning why this is so important (Cardone & Gilkerson, 1989). For example, the educator might invite the parents to describe what their baby did upon being diapered or unwrapped. This keeps parents active in the process of discovery and helps the educator understand what they perceive about their baby. The educator then uses the parents' comments and observations of their babies to highlight the concepts and information found in the Developmental Context, Caregiving Implications, and Parent Care sections of the *Pathways* curriculum.

A suggested activity for opening a *Pathways* session in a group setting:

"As we start class, I will adjust the window blinds and turn off the overhead lights. Table lamps, which provide a softer, more subdued light, are left on for the class. They provide low lighting and a feeling of intimacy. Babies have been practicing opening their eyes even before birth. Right from the moment of birth, babies can see, but often they are greeted with bright lights, making it difficult for them to focus.

"As I turn off the overhead lights, watch your baby's face and see if you notice a change. You may find your baby will open his eyes or just look a little more relaxed as he sleeps. Let's watch and see."

Typically, once the overhead lights are turned off, babies relax their faces or even open their eyes in the semidarkened environment. At this point, the educator can give parents a minute to study their baby's face. Once the educator senses everyone has had an opportunity to do this, the educator continues by asking: "What did your baby do?"

Because it is important to acknowledge the baby's newly given name, the educator may ask, "How did Catherine respond?" The educator should pause and listen to what the parent explains or says. The parent may say, "Oh, she has opened her eyes now and is looking around!" The educator can then begin with Pathway 3—The Social Baby. The educator can use the example of that child's alertness and responsiveness as an opening.

If a baby is crying or fussing, the educator should begin with Pathway 4—The Crying Baby in order to explore the situation, teach, and support the baby who is crying. The *Pathways* educator follows the lead of both the infant and the parents in deciding with which Pathway to begin.

A session's progress varies with the parent's interests and the particular needs of the infants present. The educator's responsiveness and flexibility in the session model the very responsiveness and flexibility the parents will need to care for their baby. The baby or babies present become the focus of the session. As the educator highlights and narrates babies' responses and behaviors, as well as responds to them herself, she guides parents in discovering how to learn about their baby.

Educators frequently ask parents to share what they observe about their babies. As parents comment or ask questions during the session, it keeps them active in the learning process. The *Pathways* educator is able to understand what parents perceive about their baby. This dialogue with parents throughout the session often raises questions or creates opportunities to illustrate important points.

Educators conducting home visits or one-to-one sessions can implement similar strategies. In home visiting programs, educators often have an opportunity to build a relationship over a long period of time. Home visitors, using *Pathways* information and strategies, have reflected on their greater success in establishing relationships with parents and being alert to particular experiences and concerns parents have.

The Hospital Educational Environment: Special Considerations

When *Pathways* is offered as a class prior to discharge from the hospital, it is critical that the teaching space be located close to, if not within, the postpartum unit, for the following reasons:

Security. Parents who leave the unit to attend class are taking their babies off the unit. Postpartum units have established safety and security precautions that likely cannot be enacted in other areas of the hospital should there be an incident. In addition, should a parent faint or a baby begin to have respiratory problems, being in the unit itself ensures appropriate assistance is available within moments.

Parents and nurses have multiple tasks to complete before discharge. The class needs to be located where their nurse can find the parents should it be necessary to see a consultant or pediatrician, or if the mother has an IV that needs attention.

Communication with the nursing staff. Nursing staff are encouraged to sit in on classes in order to learn more about what is being offered and experience the benefit to families. When nursing staff have a firsthand understanding of the class, they are much more likely to promote participation to their parents and support the class to their administrators.

Arrangement of the space. An ideal space is a large, carpeted room with approximately eight to 14 comfortable chairs that can be arranged in a semi-circle. It is important to position the chairs so that parents can slip the baby's bassinet in beside them. Without that direction, most parents will put the baby in front of them, thus placing the baby between themselves and the center of the circle where the educator will be.

Another important consideration is ensuring the flow of families into the space so that late-comers can be easily accommodated. Families will often arrive after the session has begun. This is a reality of working in a hospital setting, and it means the educator must maintain a welcoming, flexible environment. As the first families enter, they should be seated at the far end of the semicircle, which leaves the seating nearest the door available for those who come after the session is under way.

Environmental considerations. Hospital rooms will likely have bright overhead lighting. For *Pathways*, it is important to have lamps available to create softer and indirect lighting. The ability to darken the room and use indirect lighting is critical. Overhead lighting is not baby friendly, and most infants will not demonstrate a prolonged quiet alert state when the room is too bright. A darkened room with soft lighting also creates a sense of slowing down and peacefulness, which helps the parents focus and relax as well.

A small, low table is also very important. The table should be low enough so that parents can see clearly what is taking place when the Teaching Teddy or baby is placed on it.

A sink for hand washing is helpful. If there is no sink, the educator should use a cleansing lotion to take the place of hand washing. Having clean hands is an important component of universal precaution. The educator should be sure to use the cleansing foam that may be available in the room or wash their hands thoroughly before and after the session.

Working in a patient room. The educator always asks permission to enter and wears an official name tag. In many hospitals, official identification is required for any person entering a patient's room.

The educator should be prepared to introduce herself and give his name, program affiliation, and the purpose of the visit.

The educator assures that the parent has welcomed them in before proceeding. The educator describes who he is and what he does. If it seems to be bad timing, inquire if the educator might return later and leave the parent information about other educational opportunities.

If the parent welcomes the educator to stay, the educator will seat herself in such a way that she can engage in good eye contact. This facilitates a situation in which the educator and the parent can operate at the same level and gives the message that the educator is there to join with the parent in dialogue, not merely to give information. The educator first asks about the well-being of the mother and father and about the birth experience before turning her attention to the baby. (See sample questions in Listening: The Prelude.)

The educator should be purposeful in creating the best environment possible for the baby's ability to respond. For example, the educator should explain why the room needs to be darkened. It is important to ask permission and show care in moving any of the family's personal belongings if it is necessary to do so. In this way, the educator demonstrates respect for an individual's space and desires.

In order to foster an environment conducive to conversation with the parents, the educator should ask permission to turn off the radio and television. (The educator should know how to do this so they can offer assistance if the parent is having difficulty finding the right button.)

The educator assures everyone is seated comfortably before beginning, to avoid participants moving around. Likewise, the educator should decide where to position herself and any materials so she does not move around too much. The educator should always ask permission to touch or remove the baby from the bassinet. If the mother is in bed or seated near the bed, placing the Teaching Teddy or baby on a receiving blanket on the bed works very well. In this way, everyone involved in the session can easily observe the baby.

Group Advantages

Parents from very diverse backgrounds can find common ground in their recent birth and early parenting experiences. Participation in a *Pathways*-based group session introduces parents to the camaraderie and support that can be generated in a parenting group (Gaziano & O'Leary, 1998). In the group setting, parents have opportunities to share with one another and gain perspective. For example, experienced parents in class can be asked to share what they will do similarly or differently from their first experience. First time parents can be asked to share what they have been observing about their baby. An opportunity to speak about what they have learned from their experience (past or very current) encourages parent participation and gives the educator an opportunity to validate the parent's observations and feelings.

The energy, spontaneity, and rich content that can be generated in group *Pathways* sessions are often beyond what professional presentation or one-to-one sessions can accomplish. *Pathways* capitalizes on engaging parents right after the birth of their baby, when parents have a heightened interest in topics related to themselves and their babies. The intense and very recent birth experiences of parents can be used to build common ground between families. The comments, thoughts, and questions brought forward by group participants serve to illuminate many facets of infant development and parenting in dynamic ways.

The difference in babies and in parents' observations provides an excellent basis for exciting discussions in a group setting. Parents are provided with the opportunity to learn about the individual differences of infants in both what they see and what they discuss in a *Pathways* group session. It is clear as you get to know the babies in class that each is an individual, and this calls for individual responses rather than any kind of standard approach.

Parents who might never seek out a parent education group on their own have found themselves attending a *Pathways*-based session, such as Welcome Baby, because of their nurses' strong encouragement and because it occurs in the hospital, before discharge.

A nurse manager who observed a class wrote, "This is the most effective method of exposing families to a facilitated learning opportunity with an educational focus. All who participate share their excitement about the uniqueness of the class and about their infant's capabilities."

Bringing this experience into the hospital setting not only alerts parents to the capabilities and individuality of their newborn but also invites them to participate in ongoing education and support as they grow with their child. The group setting is an excellent forum for inviting and enticing parents to engage in other parent education opportunities. Program leaders may use *Pathways* as outreach in hospital settings, to connect families with their programs and encourage families to enroll in additional parent classes. Many early childhood family education (ECFE; for children birth to 5) programs throughout Minnesota, for example, use *Pathways* as a way to reach parents of newborns and very young infants. Having our Minnesota ECFE educators trained in *Pathways* and using *Pathways* to create classes in hospitals has greatly increased the number of families of very young infants participating in ECFE, even second-time parents, who attend the class in the hospital because they discovered it was so helpful with their first baby.

At the close of the *Pathways* session, educators can share information about various learning and support opportunities for parents, such as community-based classes such as infant massage, breastfeeding support, car seat safety, and infant cardiopulmonary resuscitation courses. Educators can give parents brochures and Internet links for these programs during the *Pathways* session, and reinforce and renew them as part of discharge planning.

Part 4
The Pathways

Pathways Descriptions and Organization of Components

Pathway: References the specific topic; content areas are numbered 1–8.

Although the curriculum is numbered, educators do not necessarily begin with Pathway 1—The Transitioning Baby. The choice of beginning Pathway depends on the baby and parent you are working with. For example, if a baby is crying at the start of a session, the place to begin is Pathway 4—The Crying Baby. Each session will develop its own course and direction based on the parents' interests and the baby's state of consciousness. The *Pathways* curriculum encourages the educator to embrace the teachable moment by taking into account both the infant's state of consciousness and the parent's thoughts and questions.

Key Information: This section gives the user essential background information and a more in-depth understanding of the concepts taught in the particular Pathway. This section is also intended to surface topics related to the Pathway that the educator may wish to include in her parent teaching.

Recommended Resources and Educator Tools: These resources provide the educator with more in-depth information and may highlight resources for the parent as well.

Parent Education Activities

Purpose: This is a description of the important concepts taught in each Pathway.

Instructional Content/Strategies: These are specific points that can be illuminated through parents' comments, observations of the baby, demonstration with the Teaching Teddy or baby, use of the red rattle, Teaching Photographs, and discussion.

Levels of Facilitation: Welcome Baby Level 1 will always appear first; Levels 2 and 3 follow the complete outline of Welcome Baby Level 1. Both Welcome Baby Levels 2 and 3 refer to descriptions of components outlined in Welcome Baby Level 1.

Materials: Each section lists the specific items the educator will need to facilitate that particular component. The complete list of materials needed follows:

- ***Pathways* Teaching Photographs:** The photographs found at the end of the manual are numbered 1–7 and correspond with each Pathway. Each photograph is labeled Figure A or B so as to provide clarity for the educator and correspond to directions in the demonstration or discussion. These pages can be carefully removed and trimmed and placed in sheet protectors or a presentation book for use in parent teaching. (See Appendix G, Creating Teaching Points, for instructions.) There are no Teaching Photographs for Pathway 8—The Premature Baby, because this chapter provides information and resources rather than teaching strategies. At right is a photograph of a teaching photograph booklet created by an educator.

Teaching booklet

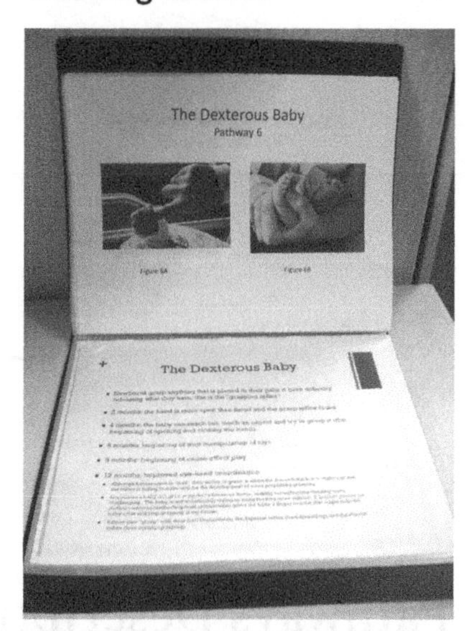

- **Teaching Teddy:** A Teaching Teddy (see photo) is a floppy-limbed teddy bear about 16–18 inches in length. A teddy bear is used instead of a baby doll because a teddy bear does not reflect a gender or race. A floppy-limbed teddy bear has the flexibility needed for modeling positioning and caregiving techniques that parents can use with their baby.

Teaching Teddy

- **Rattle:** The rattle can be created by emptying a 4-oz. plastic bottle (a small bottled-water container works well; see photo.) Remove the label, rinse and dry the bottle, and fill it halfway with unpopped popcorn kernels. Glue the cap on. Commercially available rattles may be used if they give a sharp sound when shaken. Welcome Baby Level 3 educators should use the red rattle from the NBAS kit.

Rattle

- **Cloth baby sling:** A sling that is suitable for use with a young infant to demonstrate baby wearing. Check consumer product safety recall information.

- **Infant undershirt:** The type used in the hospital that has long sleeves and mittens that can cover the baby's hands, or a pair of baby mittens.
- **Sleep sack:** Sleep sacks are currently recommended to keep infants warm while sleeping and take the place of quilts or blankets in the crib (see photo).
- **NBAS Kit**: For the NBAS-certified educator.

Teddy and sleep sack

Each Pathway relates to a particular state of infant consciousness, focusing on the significance of an infant behavior or caregiving implication. The Teaching Photographs can be used as a substitute when a baby is not in the preferred state for beginning a dialogue with the parent. For example, if a baby sleeps during an entire session, the educator can choose to use the Pathways Crying and Calming photographs to call up the image of a crying baby and shift to that topic. Examples and descriptions of infant states of consciousness can be found in Appendix A.

Ask: These are questions designed to focus parents on a particular aspect of infant behavior and to solicit information from parents that the educator can incorporate into teaching about the topic. These are sample questions that are tried and true. The educator will note that some of the sample questions are closed (answered yes or no by the parent) rather than open-ended. The purpose of this is to quickly identify which parents in a group setting can then be invited to "say more about that," helping the educator maintain group process. Open-ended questions follow, to encourage parents to share more. For example, the educator can inquire, "Who has noticed their baby suckling on his fist or fingers?" The educator may then ask the parent who has answered "Yes," to tell the group when it happened or "what you thought when you saw your baby doing that." Through selective use of open-ended or closed questions, the educator can facilitate the pace and direction of the session.

The parent generally describes the situation in some detail, surfacing the points the educator will want to highlight, either in the Developmental Context or Caregiving Implications sections. In this case, a parent might say, "It happened when I was changing her diaper. She began to cry, and then she jammed her fist into her mouth and started smacking away. She was so busy sucking, she didn't seem to notice the rest of the diaper change." The educator then has an opportunity to expand and note that this baby uses suckling to calm herself, pointing out that babies can comfort themselves by suckling: "This baby did a great job of finding her fist and was able to remain calm during a diaper change—which, for a newborn, is often an overwhelming experience." The educator should always use the parents' observations and comments and reference them as much as possible in the discussion and demonstration. This affirms the parents' ability to observe and describe important things. The educator's comments and information can provide the parents with additional insights and information.

Infant Observation/Activity: In this section are the guides for using Welcome Baby Level 1 or Level 2 facilitation, which incorporates the teaching and *Pathways* Teaching Photographs. For certain activities, it describes ways to incorporate babies' spontaneous behavior into the demonstration.

For example, in Pathway 4—The Crying Baby, the educator demonstrates graded intervention to soothe an upset baby, then uses the Teaching Teddy to demonstrate the Flex/Hold, an extremely effective way to calm a baby.

Overview: The approach is to focus attention on a particular baby while also commenting on the variability and ranges of responses that may be seen in other babies. Any helpful techniques for interacting with or helping the baby should be described and demonstrated. This becomes important information for parents who, for example, may be having difficulty getting their baby to become alert. Tips for the Level 3 educator include suggested modifications for administering the NBAS items and specific strategies to extend the learning concepts.

Developmental Context: Through discussion and demonstration, the educator frames the baby's behaviors within a larger developmental context. The Developmental Context sections are worded as the educator might speak to the parents, giving specific examples of the kind of information that may be shared, but this is not meant to limit the creativity or style of the educator. For example, the educator describes and demonstrates how to wrap babies so that their arms are flexed and their hands rest against their face, as they did in the womb. Or the educator discusses the fact that a fetus practices sucking and enjoys sucking, even though as a fetus he never sensed hunger (a fetus is nourished by the placenta and has a tummy full of amniotic fluid). After birth, the baby continues to use suckling as a way to comfort and calm himself. The educator could reference the parent's story and say, "just as you described your baby doing during the diaper change." The educator also adds information such as, "At times the baby's suckling will indicate the baby has become hungry, but hunger is not always the reason that a baby wishes to suckle." This informs parents about alternative interpretations of their infant's behavior.

Caregiving Implications: This section offers practical information that parents can use to meet their infant's developmental needs. The wording in these sections is that of an educator directly addressing a parent, for example, "Since babies enjoy suckling and it helps them feel calmer, be sure you position your baby in ways that allow him to suck on his hands and fingers."

Anticipatory Guidance: This section, as a stand-alone section, appears only in certain Pathways. It includes insights to share with parents regarding how their baby's behavior may change in the near future, to help parents anticipate how their baby or their own routine may change.

Parent Care: This section includes insights and encouragement for parents to monitor their own well-being. For example, a discussion of the sleep patterns of young babies is an ideal time to remind parents that they will likely become very tired (even sleep deprived) unless they find ways to rest during the day.

Facilitation Tips: This section will be found only in certain Pathways. Tips based on the author's experience guide the educator in taking advantage of spontaneous infant behaviors and situations, or both, that lend themselves to creating teachable moments.

PATHWAY 1

The Transitioning Baby

> *The power of first impressions is well known. None may be more significant than the first experiences of a newborn baby exiting the mother's womb. Our first impression of life outside the womb, the welcome reception we receive immediately after birth, may color our perceptions of life as difficult or easy, hostile or safe, painful or comforting, frightening or reassuring, cold and lonely or warm and welcoming. The events surrounding birth have the potential to set the stage for patterns of subconscious thought processes and behaviors that persist for a lifetime.* (Phillips, 2013, p. 1)

What You Will Learn in This Pathway:

- what the fetus experiences before birth
- adaptations a baby must make to life outside the womb
- how parents and caregivers can support the baby in the transition from the womb to the world
- typical feelings that parents may experience in the postpartum period
- symptoms of PPD

Why This Pathway Is Important:

- Newborns are experiencing many new sensations and need help from their parents and caregivers to adjust.
- Newborns tune in to voices they heard in the womb, which comforts and calms them. Parents may not realize how their newborn tunes into them.
- It is not possible to "spoil" a young baby, contrary to what many parents hear. Far from spoiling a baby, the initial love and attention parents give the newborn stimulate brain development and help build a child's social and emotional skills.
- Being held and soothed when he is fussing or crying builds the baby's trust, which leads to greater confidence and independence at later stages of development.
- PPD can impact the family—especially the mother-child relationship—and can have long-lasting negative effects.

Key Information

Life in the Womb

To fit the fetus's growing body inside the confined space of his mother's womb, it assumes a tucked and flexed position. This positions the fetus's hands near his face, making it easy for him to spend time suckling on his fist or fingers, to comfort and soothe himself (Boukydis, 2012). Taste buds in the tongue develop between 11 and 13 weeks gestation. When the fetus swallows amniotic fluid, it can taste basics such as sweet, sour, and bitter, based on the mother's diet. Suckling and swallowing before birth gives the fetal baby practice with the two skills needed to successfully obtain nutrition after birth.

The tactile sense develops in the fingertips from 7–8 weeks gestation (Vergara & Bigsby, 2004). The fetus begins to explore his environment through touch—touching its face and the boundaries of the womb, sometimes grasping the umbilical cord, and sensing gentle pressure (Tajani & Ianniruberto 1990). The vestibular system is active from 14 weeks gestation, allowing him to sense movement—its own and the movement of its mother. The fetus feels a rocking motion when the mother moves (Smotherman & Robinson, 1995). When the mother walks, the sound of her footsteps coordinates with the tactile feedback and vestibular sensations from the varying intensity of her movements (Lickliter, 2011). The neural pathways for hearing begin to develop at 12–14 weeks of gestation. Around 20 weeks, the fetus's brain begins to process sound. Researchers believe that the fetus likely hears the mother's internal sounds first (digestion, heartbeat), and then begins to process the sound of her voice. Newborns less than 2 hours old show a preference for their mother's voice over that of a stranger. The fetus's vision also develops prenatally. By 24–26 weeks, the fetus responds to differences in light filtered through the mother's skin and muscles and the amniotic fluid. Toward the end of the pregnancy the fetus's eyes flutter, and it can see, even though there is not much to look at (Birnholz, 1981). The fetus reacts to a bright light shined on his mother's abdomen by either turning away from or toward it, depending on the light's intensity. Within the confines and protection of the womb, the fetus practices many skills and has many rich sensory experiences in preparation for birth (deVries, Visser, & Prechtl, 1985; Smotherman & Robinson, 1995). Phillips (2013, p. 68.) wrote,

> *If a fetus has been fortunate enough to spend his fully allotted 266 days in the womb since conception, he has had the luxury of having all his emerging developmental needs met. The uterus and the placenta have provided warmth, protection, nutrition and oxygen, as well as close and continual proximity to the mother's heart and voice. Being in the womb is the "natural habitat" for the unborn fetus.*

Being Born

Milder contractions that occur earlier in the pregnancy prepare the baby for birth by getting him into position and easing his head into his mother's pelvis. During the birthing process, strong contractions help ease the baby down the birth canal. Because the baby's head has flexible skull plates, it changes shape to protect the brain. The experience becomes more intense for the mother when the amniotic sac ruptures. Without the amniotic sac acting as a cushion, the baby also feels the contractions. While the actual distance the baby traverses to birth is very short, the process can take a good deal of time. Like his mother, the baby experiences spurts of intense activity and times of rest (Shelov & Hannemann, 2004). At the moment of birth, the baby moves from a protected environment to one in which he is bombarded by new stimuli (Brazelton & Nugent, 1995; Maurer & Maurer, 1988). The baby takes his first breath of air and begins to breathe, which triggers blood circulation. All of the baby's organs now begin to function on their own. Once his umbilical cord is cut, the newborn must adjust to an entirely new way of living. Piontelli described the baby's experience of birth as being catapulted into a "profoundly different physical and social environment" (Piontelli, 2015).

The Newborn Baby

The newborn baby experiences major changes—bright lights, a multitude of new stimulating visual images, cool air instead of constant warmth, the loss of the confining walls of the womb, and the first feelings of hunger (Klaus & Klaus, 1999; Maurer & Maurer, 1988). This transition takes place in a very short time. Mothers who provide skin-to-skin contact and breastfeed immediately following the birth maintain the infant's close and continual proximity to her mother, easing the difficult transition. Studies (Moore, Anderson, & Bergman, 2007) have proven the benefits of skin-to-skin contact, for example, it "reduces crying, and helps the mother to breastfeed successfully" (Moore et al., 2007). Phillips wrote, "Being skin to skin with the mother is the newborn infant's 'natural habitat'— the one place where all his needs are met." The infant hears the mother's voice and senses her heartbeat. Many hospitals now routinely ensure new mothers and babies engage in skin-to-skin contact at birth.

A parent can also help the baby in the transition from the womb to the world by observing her and responding to her signals (Blackburn & Kang, 1991). Sensitive, responsive parents will learn to care for their baby in ways that support their child's developmental needs, building a positive attachment between parents and child (Greenspan & Greenspan, 1985; Hotelling, 2004). The quality of the relationship that develops—the attachment—has long-term effects that can lead to either lower or higher risk for future physical and mental health disease (Gudsnuk & Champagne, 2011).

Dependence Is Developmentally Appropriate

Even though the baby is now a separate individual, he needs continued connection and closeness to his parents, and parents will discover that their baby seems more content and comfortable being held. Some parents question whether this "spoils the baby" (Smyke, 1998). Far from spoiling the baby, a parent's touch and presence give the baby reassurance about this new world into which he has come. Some child development experts propose that the first 4 months of life are really like the fourth trimester (Karp, 2002; Lally, 2014). The baby needs to make adjustments to being in the world. During this fourth trimester, parents should nurture their babies by feeding them frequently, providing close contact, and giving responsive care (Blackburn & Kang, 1991; Brazelton & Cramer, 1990; Lally, 2014). This care not only affects the baby's social and emotional development, but also impacts brain development. During the first weeks and months of an infant's life the brain undergoes rapid and intense structural development. The baby's early experiences alter the structure and pathways of connection in his developing brain. As the baby experiences the world, his brain adapts, preparing him for future experiences (Lally, 2014).

Responsive Care

Responsive care is care given based on the cues and signals the baby gives the parent. For example, when a baby begins to squirm, look around, and suckle on her hands and fingers, she may be saying "I am getting hungry." When a parent recognizes this signal and feeds the baby promptly, the baby and parent are in sync and the baby experiences responsive care. Responsive care depends on parents reading their baby's cues and signals, which are embedded in a larger framework called "states of consciousness." Babies come into the world with six identifiable states of consciousness and identifiable clues, called cues, indicating what the baby may be needing or wanting.

The Six States of Consciousness of a Full-Term Baby

A *state of consciousness* is an observable group of characteristics that occur together, indicating the level of alertness (Brazelton & Nugent, 1995; Wolff, 1959). A baby's state of consciousness greatly influences how he responds to stimulation or to a caregiving attempt, such as feeding (Brazelton & Nugent, 1995). Information about their baby's states of consciousness can help parents make good decisions about effective times to try to interact with their baby. An understanding of the baby's state of consciousness can help a parent feel more confident; and with an understanding of state-related behaviors, parents are more likely to get the response from their baby that they expect (Blackburn & Kang, 1991). The six states of consciousness can readily be observed in the healthy full-term newborn. (See Appendix A for photographs of infants in these six states of consciousness.) Prematurely born babies will not exhibit such defined states, and their cues are more difficult to decipher (Als, 1982; see Pathway 8—The Premature Baby for more information about premature babies.)

1. Deep sleep

In deep sleep a baby is very still and his breathing is very regular. In fact, respiration can be so hard to detect that many parents double-check to be sure the baby is actually breathing. The baby's face will also be still, and there will be no eye movements under her closed eyelids. A loud noise nearby may cause the baby to startle but not awaken; it is hard to waken a baby from deep sleep. If the parent does awaken a baby in deep sleep for a feeding, for example, the baby may continue to fall asleep, frustrating the parent's efforts. Some babies use deep sleep as a way to tune out when things are overly stimulating (Brazelton & Nugent, 1995; Greenspan & Greenspan, 1985). In deep sleep, the baby is resting and growing, and it is best to not disturb her.

2. Light sleep

In light sleep a baby's body shows some movement. The baby's eyes flutter underneath his closed lids. He may smile, grimace, or make little sounds. His breathing pattern is very noticeable and irregular—which can be worrisome to parents but is a natural part of this state. The baby will be more responsive to loud noises. After an initial startle to a sound, the baby may begin to rouse; at other times he may also go into a deeper sleep in order to block out stimulation he finds irritating (Brazelton & Nugent, 1995). However, pleasant stimuli like a parent's voice may call him out of his slumber and cause him to become more alert and responsive. Babies spend the highest proportion of their sleep in the light sleep state (Anders, Goodlin-Jones, & Zelenko, 1998). When parents hear sounds and see a bit of movement during light sleep, they may assume the baby is waking up or is ready to feed; however, this is not an ideal time to try to play with or feed the baby.

3. Drowsy

In a drowsy state the baby's body is much more active, and she may open her eyes and then close them. She may have facial movements such as smiling or grimacing. In a drowsy state an infant who is left alone may fall back to sleep, but if some interaction or stimulation is provided—if someone picks up and talks to the baby—she may continue to rouse and become more alert (Blackburn & Kang, 1991; Brazelton & Nugent, 1995; Nugent, 1995). If it is about time for a feeding, picking up a baby in a drowsy state and getting her into an upright position while talking to her will usually bring her into the more alert state in which she is ready to eat and interact.

4. Quiet alert

In quiet alert state the baby's eyes are wide open, he displays focused attention, and his face is animated. He will be especially attentive to the parent's face and voice. This is an ideal time for parents to see their baby's ability to be social with them. This quiet alert state is often seen immediately following the birth (Brazelton & Nugent, 1995; Klaus & Klaus, 1999; Maurer & Maurer, 1988). It is both endearing and reassuring for parents to see their baby in this state. In her book Guiney (2013, p. 9) imagined the baby might be saying, "All of my energy goes to you. This is the best time for us to talk and play."

5. Active/fussy

In an active/fussy state the baby's eyes are open but her eyes are not particularly focused on any specific person or object. Her body is quite active. Although she may have a lot of facial movements, they are not bright and attuned as they are in the quiet alert state. She is very reactive to hunger, fatigue, stimulation, and excessive noise (Brazelton & Nugent, 1995). If a parent intervenes at this time the infant may return to the quiet alert state. Sometimes a baby enters into an active/alert state because she is beginning to feel hungry or is seeking attention. The baby may be said to be "fussing."

6. Crying

Crying is one of the newborn's clearest communication cues. His increased motor activity, his grimacing, and his loud wails clearly signal that he is distressed. He is not socially interactive at this time even though his eyes may be opened. When a baby is in a crying state, his limits for coping have been exceeded. A crying baby may try to find his fist or fingers to suckle and, if successful, may be able to calm himself down (Brazelton & Nugent, 1995). If a parent speaks to the baby, the baby may focus on the sound of the parent's voice and calm down. At other times, the baby will need to be picked up and comforted.

The Newborn's Preference for Being Flexed

Full-term babies are born preferring a flexed position, because of the way they were curled and flexed as they grew in the womb (Allen & Capute, 1990); newborns will instinctually try to maintain this familiar, comfortable position. The newborn is most comfortable when her parent is holding her securely, mimicking the confines of the womb. The effects of this physiological flexion can be seen when caring for a newborn. When she is diapered, her limbs are difficult to straighten and they snap back into place (Liddle & Yorke, 2004). This snap-back reaction will fade as the baby's body adjusts to life outside the womb. When the newborn is placed on her back, she typically begins to move and flail, looking rather uncomfortable—this is an entirely new way of being positioned. However, newborns should always be positioned on their backs to sleep. In Pathway 2—The Sleeping Baby, you will find tips for helping the baby adjust to this position.

While the fetus is in the flexed position, her hands and arms are positioned near her face. Once born, the baby will make attempts, some successful and some unsuccessful, to bring her hands to her mouth to suckle (Tajani & Ianniruberto, 1990). Parents may become concerned that the newborn will scratch her face; advise them to file the baby's fingernails when she is in a deep sleep. The self-soothing a newborn can do by sucking on her fist and fingers should be encouraged.

The flexed position also helps a baby conserve and use energy more efficiently by decreasing irritability and flailing, as well as helping the baby use energy more effectively (Als, 1993). Being flexed, maintaining connection to her parents, and limiting her movement will all support a baby as she transitions from the womb to the outside world.

Because the fetus can hear her mother's voice and those of others in the family, these familiar voices may be calming, and new parents should hold their baby and talk to her. The baby will even visually search for the sound of the familiar voice. By a few days old babies can recognize a familiar face. The newborn is coming to know the people in her life and the world she has been born into. Responsive, sensitive care provides her with the support she needs to make a smooth transition from the womb to the world. Responsive and sensitive care builds the brain connections and human capacities (Gudsnuk & Champagne, 2011).

A newborn baby is generally clothed and wrapped after birth to conserve her body heat. The blanket or sleep sack provides a boundary that mimics the tactile pressure of the uterine wall, which most babies find comforting. However, parents or caregivers have to unwrap the baby for a diaper change, bath, or feeding. The baby usually responds by fussing or crying, arms and legs flailing. The parents' observations of this behavior can lead to a discussion about adjustments for both themselves and their baby as they move from pregnancy to postpartum.

Babywearing

Babywearing is a way to attach a baby to the parent's body. There are many types of babywearing carriers, often called infant "slings." Some have been found to be unsafe, and parents should be advised to research potential babywearing carriers through the Consumer Product Safety Commission. In other cultures, babywearing is quite common; in the United States, it is more of a recent trend. In 1986, Hunziker and Barr found that babies who were "worn" 2 hours or more per day cried 43% less than the control group. In a later study in 1991, new mothers were given either a plastic infant seat or a soft infant carrier to wear for a year to determine whether there were differences in attachment. Indeed there were: Eighty-three percent of the infants carried in the soft cloth carriers showed secure attachment, whereas only 38% of the infants cared for in plastic carriers were securely attached. Other benefits of babywearing include:

- reminds the baby of the womb experience (and is therefore comforting and calming)
- organizes the baby's unregulated systems
- proximity to the parent is more conducive to interaction
- motion has a calming effect; the baby cries less
- convenient for many parents
- provides a safe, protected environment for the baby when going out

Safety Tips

Parents today have a wide selection of soft infant carriers from which to choose, and parents should be educated on safety concerns. "This may sound obvious, but babies need to breathe," says David Kaufman, a pediatrician with Children's Physicians of Omaha, NE (McMann, 2008, p. 32). "Make sure your infant is able to breathe through their nose when babywearing," and follow these additional guidelines:

- Never cook or handle hot liquids or sharp objects while wearing your baby.

- Adjust your carrier correctly, making sure your posture isn't compromised.
- Do not bend at the waist. Instead, squat using your legs. This will save your back and keep your baby from falling out of the carrier.

Kaufman believes that babywearing eases the newborn's transition to life outside the womb. "The majority of infants have just spent the past nine months in an environment that is in constant motion with a constant level of varying noises from the beat of mom's heart to the churning of her stomach; it is a noisy place to be! It is, therefore, very logical that infants will be calmer when in immediate contact with their care provider and in relatively constant motion."

Because these types of carriers are designed to be worn by all caregivers, fathers and partners can share in the baby's care. Babies carried in this way also have less chance of developing positional plagiocephaly (flat head), which can develop when a baby spends too much time on his back on a hard surface (McMann, 2008).

Although babywearing benefits both infants and parents in many ways, parents must be advised to check the safety of various designs. For example, the sling that holds a baby in a pouch, using generous folds of fabric, makes it hard to see the baby. A baby can slump into a position in which his chin curls toward his chest, which can restrict breathing and put a baby at risk of positional asphyxia—that is, suffocation caused by the position of the baby's especially vulnerable body. Remember that newborns and small infants can't yet hold up their heads (Gross-loh, 2010). The Consumer Product Safety Commission offers additional information and recommendations for the safe use of infant slings: www.cpsc.gov/newsroom/noticias/2010/muertes-de-bebes-impulsan-a-la-cpsc-a-emitir-una-advertencia-sobre-los-cargadores-de-tela-para-bebe

The Newborn Parent

Once the baby is born, parents face the new challenges of learning to feed, comfort, and protect their child, in addition to taking care of themselves. New parents are sometimes caught off-guard by challenges they hadn't considered would be a part of their postpartum experience (Kitizinger, 1995). In part this is because it is difficult for expectant parents to focus on postpartum issues while they are still pregnant. Before the birth of the baby, both the pregnant mother and father anticipate the labor and delivery and prepare for the baby by acquiring equipment and making space for the baby.

Women are especially preoccupied with the changes in their bodies. Many new parents expect to return to "normal" in 6 to 12 weeks, in part because many new mothers return to work within this time frame. The majority of men and women experience the postpartum period as one in which they are fatigued, anxious, and emotional and feel extraordinarily changed, both positively and negatively, by the birth experience and caring for their new baby. It can affect them in every realm of their lives (Kitzinger, 1995; Kunhaardt et al., 1996).

Unexpected Feelings and New Routines

New parents often describe feeling challenged trying to do tasks that were just routine before the baby was born. Everyday tasks with the baby can seem more like major undertakings. Some parents may find they are anxious about getting the baby into the car seat properly, about having the baby in the back seat where they cannot see him (even though this is the recommended placement for the car seat), and about safety on the roadway in ways they never experienced before the baby was in the car. Other challenges that arise during the postpartum period are initially feeling inadequate (or even fearful) about taking care of the baby (Bennet & Indman, 2003; Kitzinger, 1990). Feelings of inadequacy can surface just as the new parents are leaving the hospital (Placksin, 2000; Rosenberg, Greening, & Windell, 2003).

Many of the new mothers who attend our postpartum groups are surprised to find they become so wrapped up in their babies. Many thought they would still be committed to their careers but found that once their baby was born they no longer felt the sense of commitment to jobs they once loved. Instead, they found they felt fulfilled in caring for their babies and being mothers. Their former careers had taken a backseat. They were not looking forward to returning to work as they had planned. Other mothers describe feeling lonely being at home with their babies. They missed being in the workplace, both for social reasons and for the feelings of competence their work gave them (Eagan, 1985; Marshall & Tracy, 2009).

Loss of free time is more pronounced for mothers than for fathers, but both parents find their personal routines altered in unexpected ways. A couple's intimacy is typically put on hold during the immediate postpartum period to facilitate physical healing in new mothers (Ghasedi, 2004). Both parents may find they have increased emotional needs and must find new ways to communicate and adjust within their relationship if they want to protect their marriage or partnership (Nordin, 2000; Placksin, 2000).

Finding a New Normal

Rather than "returning to normal," both parents will find their lives have been changed. Instead of trying to make their new lives with their baby fit into the old routines and schedules, they will need to be flexible and find new approaches. Challenges like these can be very disruptive for some individuals or couples, and for other individuals or couples it can provide the impetus for growth and personal development. The challenges can enhance the couple's relationship or drive them apart (Nordin, 2000). Relatives or friends can be very effective in helping an individual or couple through these challenges by being supportive and understanding. Professional help should be suggested or considered when one, or both, of the partners continues to feel distressed and unhappy. Despite all of these intense adjustments, joy and excitement mingled with fear and anxiety, parents can emerge from the experience having grown in personal ways they never imagined possible (Kitzinger, 1995).

Expectations Fulfilled and Unfulfilled

Parents may have had a strong feeling (or may have been told during an ultrasound procedure) that they were having a girl but on the day of birth discover their newborn is in fact a boy, or vice versa. The color of the baby's hair, shape of the eyes, or whom the baby looks like may also differ from their expectations. In developing an attachment with the child, parents must undertake the difficult psychological task of reconciling the image of the child from pregnancy with the actual child (Brazelton, 1992; Galinsky, 1987).

When a parent's expectations, hopes, and dreams fit with the birth experience and the baby, parents experience a sense of fulfillment and well-being. When the parent's images are very different from reality, there can be a period of disappointment and even grief. Such unhappiness and grief can interfere with attachment if the feelings continue for a long period of time or if the parent's expectations do not change. The desire to do well by the baby is so strong that most parents do make the necessary psychological adjustments and come to love their baby even if he differs significantly from their prenatal images. This process is seen dramatically in parents who give birth prematurely (Barsuhn, 2008; Linden, Paroli, & Doron, 2013). A premature birth can dash their images and hopes. They may even experience profound grief about both the birth and their fragile baby and must work through a period of grief and loss. Yet, some parents of prematurely born infants can find meaning in their challenging experiences and often report experiencing personal growth, as well developing enduring relationships with their babies despite the initial challenges (Barsuhn, 2008).

New Parents Need Support Too

The point at which they take on a parental role is an important and sensitive period of adults' lives, and the comments they hear in the hours just preceding and after the birth of the baby can have a long-lasting impact. Galinsky (1987, p. 54) wrote, "If a doctor, mid-wife or nurse makes a disparaging remark or acts in negative ways it will probably penetrate deeply and be long remembered." It is for that very reason educators working with new parents should be extremely thoughtful in their comments, responses, and interactions with both new parents and their babies.

Addressing the Emotional Experiences of New Parents

"In any given one year period, 9.5% of the population (or about 18.8 million American adults) suffer from a depressive illness" (National Institute of Mental Health, 2004). Less than half of those suffering will pursue treatment. The increased demands of new parenthood, forced lifestyle changes, disruption of routines, and sleep deprivation experienced with the birth of a baby increase the risk for experiencing depression. There are three categories of depression related to postpartum disorders: baby blues, postpartum depression, and postpartum psychosis.

Baby Blues

Eighty-five percent of new mothers experience the "baby blues" (Ghasedi, 2004). The symptoms of baby blues can include mood swings, sadness, irritability, crying, sleep disturbances, anxiety, fatigue, sensitivity, and decreased concentration. These symptoms go away within a few weeks after giving birth. Treatment of this condition can include offering encouragement, reassurance that these feelings are normal, and practical assistance with household chores or the care of baby so the new mother can rest.

PPD

PPD, which generally affects up to 15% of mothers (Pearlstein, Howard, Salisbury, & Zlotnick, 2009), is more intense and serious. In populations where other stress factors, such as poverty, exist, the percentage of parents experiencing PPD is much higher. The signs and symptoms may appear very similar to the baby blues, but they last longer and are much more intense. These symptoms can interfere with the mother's (or father's) ability to care for herself and the baby. The Mayo Clinic (n.d.) listed the following symptoms of PPD:

- loss of appetite
- insomnia
- intense irritability and anger
- overwhelming fatigue
- loss of interest in sex
- lack of joy in life
- feelings of shame, guilt, or inadequacy
- severe mood swings
- difficulty bonding with your baby
- withdrawal from family and friends
- thoughts of harming yourself or your baby

Untreated, PPD may last for many months or longer. Not only does PPD affect the parent's well-being, it will impact the child too if left untreated. Maternal depression interferes with the ability to develop a healthy relationship and for the parent to meet the child's needs in functional ways. Research indicates that children of parents with depression are more likely to develop behavioral problems and have lower functioning in cognitive, social-emotional, and behavioral development. Parental depression in infancy can have a profoundly negative impact on the child's developing social interaction skills (Knitzer, Theberge, & Johnson, 2008).

If a woman experiences five or more of the above-listed symptoms, including depressed mood or significantly diminished interest for a period of 2 weeks or more, a diagnosis of PPD is made by a doctor or other qualified mental health practitioner. Opinions differ about the time frame of a PPD diagnosis; according to the *Diagnostic and Statistical*

Manual of Mental Disorders (American Psychiatric Association, 2013), PPD can occur within 4 weeks, 6 weeks, or 12 weeks, and some say up to 1 year (Ghasedi, 2004). Women especially may experience wide swings in emotions that are not typical for the individual. PPD can be treated; untreated PPD in both mothers and fathers has been linked to cases of infant homicide (Friedman, Horwitz, & Resnick, 2005).

New fathers can also experience PPD. Fathers with PPD can experience similar symptoms to mothers, but men have unique risk factors: step-parenting, ending a relationship with the mother, being under severe stress (e.g., experiencing unemployment), isolation, being poorly educated, being in a physically aggressive relationship, or being with a partner who is depressed (Ghasedi, 2004).

If you suspect a new mother or father is experiencing PPD, it is best to express your concern and offer to help that parent seek treatment. Professionals working with postpartum families must investigate further when parents seem to be expressing distress or feelings of depression.

Postpartum Psychosis

Postpartum psychosis usually develops very soon after the birth of the baby, and signs may be evident even the first day after giving birth. Postpartum psychosis occurs only once or twice in 1,000 births (Beck, 2006) and is a very serious disorder that warrants immediate intervention. The mother herself may say she feels "strange" and appear disoriented and confused. Symptoms include confusion, insomnia, disorganized speech, disorganized behavior, altered consciousness, hallucinations that are focused on hurting the baby or herself, paranoia, agitation, and delusion. A new mother exhibiting symptoms of postpartum psychosis should be considered a medical emergency and addressed by a qualified psychiatrist immediately.

The Effects of PPD and Psychosis on Infants

PPD is still a condition that often goes unrecognized and untreated. Not only does it have serious negative effects on new mothers, it can also have devastating effects on the family by causing distress and affecting the child's development by disrupting the attachment process.

Mothers experiencing PPD have a very difficult time being responsive to their infant and do not initiate or respond at "adequate levels to foster their infant's development" (Gurian, 2003). A young infant who is not receiving spontaneous and reciprocal responses tends to shut down and disconnect emotionally, which can set the infant on a negative developmental course. Infants affected by their mother's depressed mood may exhibit these signs: not looking at the mother, vocalizing less, little expression or a depressed look, fussiness and irritability, lack of interest in play and interaction, averting behaviors such as looking away or turning away, sleep problems, and in extreme cases, failure to thrive, as evidenced by lack of weight gain.

Getting Help

Many mothers go undiagnosed. Recognizing and treating PPD is critical because of the serious risks the child, the mother, and the family's ability to function (Pearlstein et al., 2009).

Depending on their role, parent educators have the advantage of seeing parents on a more regular basis than doctors do; some perform home visits and observe the parent–child interactions in a more natural environment.

The *Pathways* curriculum includes a suggested protocol (see Appendix C) to use when working with a depressed or distressed parent. The educators who developed the protocol discovered it was necessary to address the situation of the depressed parent and child in a number of ways to ensure adequate support was offered and that both parent and child were safe. The protocol is intended to be a guide and support for other educators and may not include all steps in a specific situation an educator can encounter.

Recommended Reading

Educator Tools:

ZERO TO THREE: www.zerotothree.org

Early Childhood Mental Health Resources

- Connecting With Babies: The Power of Parent/Child Interaction (video)
  www.zerotothree.org/child-development/early-childhood-mental-health
- Podcast: Early Experiences Count: How Emotional Development Unfolds Starting at Birth Featuring Ross Thompson, PhD
  www.zerotothree.org/about-us/funded-projects/parenting-resources/podcast

Postpartum: Baby Blues, Postpartum Depression and Postpartum Psychosis

- Postpartum Support International
  www.postpartum.net/
- Mayo Clinic: Diseases and Conditions Postpartum Depression
  www.mayoclinic.org/diseases-conditions/postpartum-depression/basics/symptoms/con-20029130
- HelpGuide.org Postpartum Depression and Baby Blues
  www.helpguide.org/articles/depression/postpartum-depression-and-the-baby-blues.htm

Babywearing

Explore these websites for more information on safe practices.

- Mayo Clinic: Is It Safe to Hold a Baby in a Baby Sling?
  www.mayoclinic.org/healthy-lifestyle/infant-and-toddler-health/expert-answers/baby-sling/faq-20058208

- Babywearing International
  http://babywearinginternational.org/what-is-babywearing/safety/
  http://babywearinginternational.org/

Parent Education Activities
Welcome Baby Level 1

Purpose:

To provide parents insights into how both they and their baby make adjustments in the first days and weeks after birth.

Instructional Content/Strategies:

- Discuss and/or observe the newborn's responses to new stimuli.
- Recognize the baby's need to be close to the parent (skin-to-skin or babywearing).
- Discuss the range of responses a parent may feel after the baby's birth.
- Encourage parents to seek support and engage in self-care.
- Alert parents to the potential of baby blues and symptoms of PPD.

Materials:

- Teaching Teddy lightly swaddled in a blanket
- Infant sling carrier for demonstration (optional, but research and choose one that has been deemed safe)
- *Pathways* Teaching Photographs: The Transitioning Baby
  Figure 1A: Baby lying on his back, unwrapped and crying
  Figure 1B: Baby being held close on a parent's chest

Ask:

"When you changed your baby's diaper, how did he respond?"

The typical answer is that the baby seemed unhappy and didn't like it or that the baby fussed or cried and may have kicked or pulled his legs up, making it difficult to get the diaper changed. "When the pediatrician examined your baby, how did the baby respond?"

The typical response is that he cried or fussed or that the baby seemed upset at being unwrapped, stretched, and moved about.

Infant Observation/Activity:

The educator begins with the Teaching Teddy swaddled and held in her arms. Then the educator gently lays the teddy down on his back and unwraps it. The educator may then begin describing a typical infant response. The baby might startle, begin to flail, bring his hand to his mouth, or attempt to curl his body up rather than be open and vulnerable. Use Teaching Photograph Figure 1A: A baby on his back, unwrapped and crying, to further illustrate the point that most newborns are unhappy when laid on their backs and unwrapped or undressed.

To illustrate how a baby feels more comfortable being held and close, bring the Teaching Teddy up to your chest and hold him close while flexing up his feet a little. Teaching Photograph Figure 1B shows a baby being held close to his mother.

Demonstration of Babywearing:

In many cultures, babies are carried in cloth slings. This method of "babywearing" has been found to provide a gentle way to transition a baby from the calm environment of the womb to the stimulation of the outside world. Because a parent wears the sling, the parent's body movements rock the baby in the same pattern he experienced in the womb (Liddle & Yorke, 2004). This often has a calming effect on even the most irritable babies. Studies have shown that babies who are carried in this fashion cry less and are more alert (Sears & Sears, 1996, 2001).

Developmental Context:

"All babies are typically a bit unhappy being unwrapped and laid on their backs. An example of this is when a baby's diaper is changed. Think of how your baby was tucked and flexed in the womb, with the boundary of the womb cushioning and limiting your baby's every move. Her hands and fingers were often positioned near her face and mouth—another way of feeling comforted and secure. She also could hear your heartbeat and sense your movements as gentle rocking. A baby will continue to want to maintain a flexed position in which it feels safer and more secure.

"You may see this during the diaper change when your baby curls forward and pulls his legs up. Watch as you unwrap your baby to see if he attempts to put his hands to his face or even begins to suckle on his fingers. These were ways the baby comforted and soothed himself in the womb. Your baby seeks to find comfort in the same ways after birth. Because your baby was rocked and held in the womb, you may find your baby likes to be rocked and held now. Most babies enjoy being close to their parents after they are born. Holding your baby close and providing comfort is helping your baby develop a positive relationship with you.

"Babies will vary greatly in how they express discomfort as they are unwrapped or undressed. Some will not fuss much but will work hard to regain a comfortable position. Other babies will become stressed, cry loudly, and flail the moment their blanket is loosened. Over time and with experience, your baby will become more comfortable in the back lying position.

"These differences in response are a result of the unique way each baby's nervous system responds. There is no right or wrong response, nor good nor bad. Because of this each baby needs to be treated individually. All parents need to find the pace and style that works best for them and their baby."

Caregiving Implications:

"In the womb, your baby had a definite boundary and rather cramped living quarters. After being born, your newborn is experiencing complete freedom of movement, which can sometimes be overwhelming or even frightening to the baby.

"Your baby will be comforted by suckling on his fist or fingers or simply by resting his hands on his face like he did so often before birth. He may feel most comfortable if you pick him up and hold him upright close to your chest so he can hear your voice and sense your heartbeat. (Figure 1B).

"An alternative is to use a soft infant carrier—often referred to as a "baby sling"—to allow your baby to stay close to you. When your baby is close to you it helps him feel calmer and more secure. This builds a positive attachment relationship. Most babies enjoy being held and carried, sometimes so much so that parents feel exhausted and their arms ache. This can be difficult for the parents when they need to have their hands free to accomplish tasks around the home.

"In other cultures, young babies are carried much more than in our own culture. Many parents simply 'wear' their babies by using a sling to attach the baby to themselves. You may find this method helpful in those early months when the baby needs to remain close to you. By using a sling, you regain the use of your hands, your baby can maintain being close, and at the same time it gives you more mobility. An additional benefit is that research indicates that babies who are carried more cry less!

"Some slings are designed to be used with newborns. Be sure to read all of the directions that come with the baby sling if you decide to use one. Look for and seek out information on recalls for particular slings.

"Note that parents whose infant was born prematurely should always discuss use of the sling with their doctor before using. For some prematurely born infants, the sling can present a life-threatening danger, because these babies do not maintain an airway when they flex their neck forward."

Parent Care:

"The birth of your baby was probably one of the most intense things you have ever experienced. It may have gone just as you hoped and imagined, or there may have been unexpected low points or frightening events you didn't expect. Just as your baby emerges from the womb into a whole new world through the birthing process, so do you as a parent.

"You are now able to touch and hold your baby, you see how he looks and what he sounds like when he cries. You are learning to care for your baby and getting to know your baby differently than how you knew your baby during the pregnancy. Your role as a parent changes now as well.

"Give yourself time to adjust. It is normal to experience intense emotions, both positive and negative. The birth of your baby can bring on many new feelings that can be surprising and at times overwhelming. The move from your role as a parent during the pregnancy to your role as parent to a newborn can cause you to feel many emotions. This is normal, in part due to the physiological changes your body goes through giving birth and adjusting afterward. It is not unlike the changes the baby feels in moving from the womb to the world.

"Talking to other parents or joining parenting groups can help you find both information and support. Accept offers of help or ask for help. Chores that you normally could do easily, such as groceries and laundry, may seem like challenges for the first few weeks. Try to keep your life as simple as possible, and rest when your baby sleeps. At first, a newborn baby will need to eat around the clock. Your baby will most likely sleep in short stretches, so if you don't rest when your baby sleeps it is easy to become very exhausted.

"Many new parents experience the baby blues. Baby blues means feeling sad, being teary eyed, sensitive, or feeling irritable for no reason. The baby blues usually lasts about 2 weeks. If you experience symptoms of feeling depressed, have problems sleeping, or experience feeling worthless or guilty, be sure to contact your doctor as soon as possible. You may be experiencing postpartum depression, and help is available."

Facilitation Tip:

If a baby needs a diaper change during a parent group or home visit, this can be an ideal time for the educator to make observations of how and why the baby is responding as he does during the diaper change. Ask the parents if they would be comfortable with the group focusing on their baby's diaper change and offer to change the diaper.

If you are doing this during a parent group, changing the baby on a low table will ensure parents can observe the baby's responses. Be sure the table is adequately covered with blankets and that these blankets are removed before any other baby or the Teaching Teddy is placed on that surface, in order to maintain sanitary conditions.

Welcome Baby Level 2

Materials:

- Low table
- Two extra blankets to create a soft, smooth, yet firm surface for the baby

Baby:

Ideally in light sleep, drowsy, or active alert state. (A baby in a deep sleep state may not be responsive enough, and therefore this activity is inappropriate for that baby.)

Ask:

See Welcome Baby Level 1.

Infant Observation/Activity:

See Welcome Baby Level 1. If the baby transitions to full crying despite using your hands as a boundary, or helping the baby suck, calm the baby using the Flex/Hold described in Pathway 4—The Crying Baby.

Developmental Context:

See Welcome Baby Level 1.

Caregiving Implications:

See Welcome Baby Level 1.

Welcome Baby Level 3

Materials:

See Welcome Baby Level 2.

Baby:

Ideally in a light sleep, drowsy, or an active alert state.

Ask:

See Welcome Baby Level 1.

Observation/Activity:

Follow the same directions as for use of the Teaching Teddy found in Welcome Baby Level 1.

Using the baby, add NBAS passive-tone-in-the-legs item to further illustrate the point of flexion at birth.

Incorporate the NBAS concept of rapidity of build-up to enhance discussion of individuality (Brazelton & Nugent, 1995). Narrate additional observations about the baby's state changes, color changes, and changes in breathing patterns. Note startles or tremors, or both, as indicators of the baby's stress. Observe and narrate all ways in which the baby attempts to self-calm.

Developmental Context:

See Welcome Baby Level 1.

Caregiving Implications:

See Welcome Baby Level 1.

Parent Care:

See Welcome Baby Level 1.

PATHWAY 2

The Sleeping Baby

> *In the first months, sleeping joins crying as a major issue for parents. Parents swap sleep stories with other parents, inquiring how much each other's babies nap, how much sleep the parents get, and especially how long babies sleep at night. Many have the mistaken notion theirs is not a sleepy child.* (Gerber & Johnson, 1998, p. 77)

What You Will Learn in This Pathway:

- how a baby's sleep patterns begin to develop even before birth
- distinguishing deep from light sleep and caregiving implications
- how a young infant uses a skill called habituation to tune out stimuli
- how parents can encourage good sleep habits
- details that are part of the Safe to Sleep campaign

Why This Pathway Is Important:

- New parents are often quite tired during the first months of their baby's life, and sleep is a key issue.
- When parents learn about how sleep patterns develop they can make thoughtful plans and decisions.
- The Safe to Sleep campaign has important specific guidelines to promote safe sleep practices that are not known or fully understood by new parents.
- Parents should be encouraged to consider their own sleep needs as well as their partner's needs.

Key Information

Sleep, and the lack of it, are often key topics on the mind of a new parent within a few days after the birth. A newborn will need six to 12 feedings throughout a 24-hour period (Martin, 2000; Shelov & Hannemann, 2004). This means that new parents will not get nearly as much sleep as they are accustomed to or desire. Assisting parents in adjusting their expectations as well as learning what they can do to shape their infant's sleep patterns can be very helpful. In addition, ensuring parents have accurate information about safe sleep practices is critical. This Pathway provides information about infant sleep patterns, the importance of sleep, and ways to offer accurate safe-sleep information.

Why Is Sleep Important?

Sleep is essential for healthy development. In infants, brain development and maturation rely on sleep (Allen, 2012). During the long stretches of newborn/infant sleep, important development is supported in the neurosensory system (Peirano & Uauy, 2003), in the structural development of the brain (Graven, 2010), and the physical growth of the infant (Tikotzky et al., 2010). Researchers have discovered that healthy infants deprived of 2 to 4 hours of sleep had short-term alterations of their cardiac functioning and some infants developed respiratory problems (Philbin & Klass, 2000; Trapanotto et al., 2004). Educating parents on both the importance of sleep and how to encourage quality sleep can help both baby and parent.

How Sleep Patterns Develop

Sleep patterns are established early in prenatal development and are independent of the mother's daily and nightly schedule (Karmiloff & Karmiloff-Smith, 2004). During the day when a mother is typically moving around, a fetus might be more restful as the mother's movement limits the baby's movement. This is the reason that mothers may notice the fetus becoming more active after they have become more inactive themselves. During the prenatal period, the fetus will have two types of sleep: active and quiet (deVries et al., 1985; Prechtl, 1977). In the third trimester, the fetus has very distinct movement patterns that include regular periods of sleep. A full-term fetus will have well-established patterns of sleep and alert times not necessarily linked to his mother's day and night routines. By the time a baby is born, he has established a routine that is independent of his mother's sleep pattern and is not yet cued by day/night cycles (deVries et al., 1985; Smotherman & Robinson, 1995; Tajani & Ianniruberto 1990).

After birth, a baby begins to develop a circadian rhythm that is influenced by a light–dark cycle that promotes alternating restful and wakeful activities (Tikotzky et al., 2010). Tikotzky and colleagues found that a healthy newborn infant spends approximately 16 hours sleeping per day during the first week of life, and by the 16th week of life this has decreased to 15 hours per day. They also found that the average duration of a sleep cycle was 47 minutes for a healthy term infant and consisted of stints of both deep and active sleep. Each sleep state has distinguishable features, described as follows, that can guide a parent in caring for their infant.

Newborn Sleep Patterns

Sleep during the newborn period is different from sleep during childhood and adulthood (Davis, Parker, & Montgomery, 2004a). When a baby is born, she must learn to eat when she feels hungry and digest what she eats, take in a variety of new visual and auditory stimuli, and adapt to unexpected changes. It is no wonder that a newborn needs a great deal of sleep for growth and development. This is a time of tremendous change and growth in the brain (National Scientific Council on the Developing Child, 2004) and growth of the baby's physical body (Leach, 2013). However, newborn parents may not feel that the baby sleeps a great deal: A newborn relies on frequent, small feedings for survival, so she needs to eat at regular intervals around the clock. Parents need to match their routines to the baby's needs and will be up during the night at least two or three times until the baby is older (Leach, 2013). After caring for the baby in the middle of the night, parents may find they are unable to immediately fall back to sleep, thus adding to the feeling of exhaustion. Having a new baby represents a big change in routines for new parents.

Reported ranges for how long young babies sleep per day are so broad that they are of almost no use in describing a "typical" newborn sleep schedule or in trying to determine what might be "normal." Parents will need to cope with their baby's unique patterns. By 2 to 3 months old, most babies will have developed a predictable pattern of sleep that is similar to the regular sleep patterns of the parents. (This is welcome news to parents!) In the first 6 weeks a baby will have approximately 2- to 4-hour stretches of sleep, a shorter time of being awake, and after feeding have another period of sleep. The need for frequent nourishment drives this pattern. While sleeping, a baby will alternate between two distinct types of sleep: light sleep and deep sleep (Brazelton & Nugent, 1995; Kopp, 2003). Parents will find it useful to be able to distinguish between these patterns of sleep.

Light Sleep Versus Deep Sleep

Light sleep is often referred to as rapid eye movement (REM) sleep, because rapid eye movements can be observed under the baby's closed eyelid. The baby's respiration is somewhat irregular and easily observed, and the baby exhibits facial grimacing, eye fluttering, sucking movements, and body movements. During light sleep the nervous system is processing experiences. The brain is replenishing itself neurochemically and mentally storing all of the events of the day (Ferber, 1985). If adults are deprived of REM sleep, they are unable to learn, perform usual tasks, and recognize familiar people (Placksin, 2000). Infants have many new experiences to process, and they spend about half their sleep time in REM sleep (Anders et al., 1988).

The most striking feature of *deep sleep* is that one can hardly detect baby's respiration, and the baby's entire body is very still. In fact, some parents have shared that they checked to see if the baby was breathing. Interestingly, in deep sleep a baby will sometimes startle but remain asleep (Brazelton & Cramer, 1990; Wolff, 1959). Watching the baby sleep and/or checking to see if he is still breathing are common preoccupations of many parents. A baby in a deep sleep can remain asleep even though there may be loud music or people talking loudly nearby. However, the sleep environment should be quiet and dark to promote quality, restful sleep (Gerber & Johnson, 1998; Goines, 2008). The newborn's sleep period is comprised of an alternating pattern between light and deep sleep.

The Developmental Course of Sleep

Before the newborn reaches 3 months, sleep is divided between active and quiet sleep. A baby under 6 months enters slumber through REM sleep. This will be followed by a cycle of deep sleep, another cycle of REM sleep, and so on until the baby begins awakening for a feeding. By 6 months, babies enter sleep through non-REM or deep sleep (Davis, Parker, & Montgomery, 2004b). As a baby cycles between the two types of sleep, she may experience partial awakening (Kopp, 2003). She may let out a brief cry, whimper, or move her arms and legs, making a parent think the baby is awake. If the baby is picked up, she may come to a more alert state and have difficulty returning to sleep. If she is left alone, she may find a way to comfort and calm herself and return to sleeping.

Misunderstanding the normal newborn sleep cycle is common and can lead to ongoing sleep problems for babies and their parents (White, Simon, & Bryan, 2002). Based on her work with parents, Tedder (2008, p.18) wrote, "One typical misunderstanding is for the parent to think that a newborn is waking up when, in fact, the baby is only transitioning from deep/still sleep to a light/active sleep cycle." She goes on to point out that sleep problems have been linked to maternal depression. Clearly, getting adequate and quality sleep is important for both the infant and the parents.

Understanding and Responding to Infant Sleep Behaviors

Promoting Self-Regulation

One of the skills a baby needs to master is that of falling back to sleep if she awakens briefly between sleep cycles and it is not a feeding time. At a feeding time, picking up a baby who is in REM sleep (or transitioning into REM) brings the baby into a more alert state—however, this is sometimes *not* what the parent wants in the middle of the night and not really at a feeding time. If parents can learn to watch and listen for a few minutes, they might find their baby falls back to sleep without feeding or needing a pacifier, rocking, or pacing. On the other hand, a parent may be hoping the baby will awaken for a feeding (K. Davis et al., 2004a; Ferber, 1985). If a parent tries to awaken a baby in a deep sleep, the baby may tune out and remain asleep despite the best efforts of the parent to wake the baby. Or the baby will feed for just a few minutes and fall back into a deep sleep. Parents may be told to flick the feet of the infant or place a cool wet rag on the baby's forehead, but these provide irritating stimuli that can become associated with feeding if done frequently. If a feeding time is approaching or has been missed, parents should be advised to observe the baby and attempt to wake the baby when the baby is in a light sleep state versus a deep sleep state. By picking up the baby in light sleep, bringing the baby to a more upright position, and gently rocking while calling baby's name, the baby will generally come to a quiet alert state and be ready for feeding and interaction (Blackburn et al., 2001; Brazelton & Nugent, 1995). Continual interruptions during nighttime sleep interfere with a baby's ability to be alert and pleasant during the day. This holds true for parents, too.

Habituation—Tuning Out the World

Habituation is the ability to tune out overwhelming or annoying stimulation by sleeping or shutting down responses to stimuli (Brazelton & Nugent, 1995). A baby who is habituating may look as though she is sleeping. However, habituation does not replenish energy as restful deep sleep does; instead, habituation consumes energy. The baby who looks like she is sleeping may in fact be working to tune out stimuli and remain asleep. Brazelton and Cramer (1990) explained it in this way, "Although habituation produces a state similar to sleep, there are differences. These infants have tightened, flexed extremities with little movement except jerky startles, and no eye blinks. The babies seem to be actively maintaining control over their environment, rather than relaxing into sleep" (p. 67). Bill Sammons (1999), a pediatrician, said, "Habituation is less stressful than being awake but is still draining" (p. 80). Unless parents recognize this and decrease the stimulation load, the infant becomes more and more fatigued. A good example of a baby habituating is a baby who "slept" through being handled by many visitors during his first weeks of life. Another example is the older infant who "slept" through a shopping spree in a grocery store with bright overhead lighting and talking all around him. Infants who "sleep" through these kinds of events are more likely habituating to the over-stimulation in their environments rather than truly resting. Babies who have been spending their energy habituating are likely to awaken and be fussy rather than refreshed and alert (Sammons, 1999). Parents should be informed about the difference between restful sleep and habituation and be advised to give their infants a comfortable place to rest and sleep. In real life, however, parents cannot always ensure an entirely restful sleep environment. Habituation helps an infant cope when necessary (Brazelton & Sparrow, 2003); it is truly an amazing skill that allows a baby to regulate his responses to adverse or overwhelming stimuli.

Circadian Rhythms

Patterns of sleeping and waking are controlled by a clock in the center of the brain near the vision processing center. Cues from daylight help reset our internal clocks—this is called a circadian rhythm. An external clock does not guide a newborn, as parents quickly learn! In these first weeks of life, short periods of sleep alternated with feeding around the clock are necessary for the baby's survival (Anders et al., 1998). Toward the end of the first month of life the baby begins to experience organized sleep periods, when sleep during the night becomes a little longer than sleep during the day. Parents may not even notice their babies are having more organized sleep, because the change occurs gradually and parents are so tired themselves by the end of the first month (K. Davis et al., 2004b). As the baby approaches the third month of life, a combination of daylight and feeding schedules helps her begin to regulate sleep and alert times, and her schedule begins to more closely resemble that of her parents (D. Davis & Stein, 2004). Parents can support the baby's self-regulation by keeping the baby's daytime sleep environment calm and quiet and darkening the room so that the baby does not have to habituate to get rest. During the day, watching the clock and offering feedings to the baby at regular 2- to 3-hour intervals will provide adequate daytime feeding (Shelov & Hannemann, 2004). If the baby must be awakened, gently help her become alert from a light sleep rather than try to awaken her from a deep sleep.

Considerations for Encouraging Quality Sleep

What is a quality sleep environment? First, it must be a quiet environment. The AAP Committee on Environmental Health (2003) warned that noise is a hazard for the fetus and newborn. The neonate has no way of escaping or filtering out noise (Philbin & Gray, 2002). In "The Importance of Quiet in the Home," Goines (2008) reported from a study in which she found that noise louder than 80 dB elicits a stress response, including changes in respiratory, vascular, visceral, and motor systems. Goines (2008) gave examples: Quiet living room conversation creates a background noise level of about 50 dB, whereas professional sporting events can exceed 125 dB. Noise in loud restaurants ranges from 85–112 dB. Goines recommends noisy toys be removed from the baby's environment. When noise becomes excessive, the neonate becomes overwhelmed and may use habituation as a coping strategy—using energy to habituate does not constitute quality sleep that refreshes the baby. In addition to compromising quality sleep (for the infant and parents), loud noise can also damage the infant's developing auditory system. Repeated exposure to noise may produce significant, unwanted, unremitting effects. Goines concluded, "A quiet home environment benefits not only the infant, but all family members. They may feel better, sleep better, and communicate better, not only with the infant, but also with each other. The simple 'shhh, baby sleeping' caution should be expanded to 'shhh, baby sleeping, resting, growing, learning, and developing'" (p. 175).

Darkening the baby's sleep environment, even during daytime sleep, helps the baby develop circadian rhythms based on darkness and light. In the beginning, a newborn's sleep/wake cycles are driven by the need to feed. Over time, day/light becomes a strong force in shaping the baby's day/night sleep patterns. Encourage parents to be mindful of their own energy levels, their need for good nutrition and rest, and their need for emotional support (Kitzinger, 1995; Leach, 2013).

Special Considerations for Nighttime

To help the baby feed well, it is important to be sure the baby is awake when a feeding has begun. With a very young baby there may be little alert time after the feeding begins, because the baby rapidly returns to sleep. When feeding at night, keeping the feeding experience uninteresting helps the baby come to know night is not a time to expect to be social, and parents should use a night light instead of a bright light (Leach, 1997). Parents should always be pleasant during nighttime feedings, but not animated (no singing or playing as this may bring the infant into an alert state from which it will be more difficult for the infant to return to sleep). Once the feeding is complete (the baby has been burped and changed), laying the baby back down to sleep in a darkened room, even if the baby is awake, signals to the baby it is time to go back to sleep.

Infants have to learn how to fall asleep when they are tired. A baby who is always laid down after falling asleep in the parent's arms will not be able put himself back to sleep when he awakens intermittently through the night (Sammons, 1999). If the baby cries when laid down, parents should not try to immediately pick the baby up. While the baby is lying in the crib, placing hands over the baby's body and helping him place his fingers near his mouth may provide comfort and may help the baby relax. A baby needs to be allowed to engage in self-soothing, as a part of learning self-regulation strategies (Brazelton & Sparrow, 2003). If he becomes very upset, picking the baby up and placing him in the Flex/Hold position can help resettle the baby (do this only with a healthy full-term baby, never a premature or ill newborn; see Figure 4B—The Crying Baby). Once the baby is calmed, parents can try laying the baby down to sleep again.

The Safe to Sleep Campaign

Sleep recommendations from the AAP (R. Y. Moon, 2011) and the National Institutes of Health give this strongly worded recommendation: The National Department of Health and Human Services emphasizes that anyone who cares for a baby—babysitters, grand-parents and childcare providers—understand the importance of placing babies on their backs to sleep. Every sleep time counts (Eunice Kennedy Shriver National Institute of Child Health and Human Development, 2013).

Brief History of Current Recommendations

In 1992, the AAP first published a recommendation that infants be placed on their backs to sleep in order to reduce the risk of sudden infant death syndrome (SIDS): Researchers had found that babies placed on their stomachs to sleep were at much greater risk of dying from SIDS. The AAP confirmed this recommendation in 1994 in an AAP Policy Statement, and updated the statement in 2005 and again in 2011. Because of the rise in infant deaths by other causes, including suffocation, asphyxia, and entrap-ment, since the 2005 AAP/SIDS updates, new recommendations were issued in an effort to reduce all sleep-related deaths (R. Y. Moon, 2011). An additional term, *sudden unex-plained infant death* (SUIDs) describes any unexplained infant death. Half of SUIDs are eventually classified as sudden infant death syndrome (SIDS). The classification of SIDS is used in the sudden death of an infant less than 1 year of age "that remains unex-plained after a thorough case investigation, autopsy, examination of the death scene, and review of clinical history" (Flook & Vinzce, 2012, p. 1). Other SUIDs deaths may be attributed to entrapment, suffocation, or asphyxia, often due to bed sharing. According to the Centers for Disease Control and Prevention (2013), more than 4,500 infants die annually in the United States of no apparent cause of death.

The Back to Sleep recommendation dramatically decreased the incidence of SIDS in the United States, by more than 50%. In *Pediatrics* March 2000 (Moon, Patel, & Shaefer, 2000), the task force identified that although the Safe Sleep campaign (a joint effort of the Public Health Service, AAP, and the SIDS Alliance) had been successful in decreasing SIDS deaths, additional, modifiable risk factors required more attention (R. Y. Moon, 2011). For example, African American communities and American Indian/Alaska Native communities continue to be at increased risk for SIDS deaths. The 2014 Centers for Disease Control and Prevention report listed SIDS as the fourth leading cause of death of infants less than 1 year old. A 2013 breakdown of SUIDs cases found that 45% of cases were categorized as SIDS, followed by unknown cause (31%), and accidental suffocation and strangulation in bed (24%; Centers for Disease Control and Prevention, 2014). The Centers for Disease Control and Prevention and AAP call for continued efforts to educate all parents and caregivers about Back to Sleep and the modifiable factors associated with SIDS. The Task Force on Sudden Infant Death Syndrome (R. Y. Moon, 2011) has made the following recommendations:

- Infants should be placed on their back for every sleep. Preterm infants should be placed in the supine position as soon as the infant is medically stable and prior to infant's discharge.
- A firm sleep surface should be used. Use a crib, bassinet, or portable crib/play yard that conforms to the safety standards of the Consumer Product Safety Commission and ASTM International (formerly known as the American Society for Testing and Materials).
- Placing infants in the parent's bedroom (room sharing) but without bed sharing is recommended.
- Keep all soft objects such as pillow, quilts, and comforters out of the crib to reduce the risk of SIDS, suffocation, entrapment, and strangulation. Bumper pads are not recommended.
- The baby should use a sleep sack for warmth instead of blankets.
- Avoid exposure to smoke during pregnancy and after birth.
- Avoid use of alcohol and illicit drugs during pregnancy and after birth.
- Breastfeeding is recommended, and mothers should exclusively breastfeed or feed with expressed milk if possible.
- Offer a pacifier at nap time or bedtime, but do not reinsert once the infant has fallen asleep.
- Avoid overheating by dressing infant appropriately, and avoid overbundling.

- Infants should be immunized according to the recommendations of the AAP and Centers for Disease Control and Prevention.
- Infants should not be in an environment with tobacco smoke.
- Avoid commercial devices that are marketed to reduce the risk of SIDS such as wedges and positioners.
- Home cardiorespiratory monitors should not be used as a strategy to reduce the risk of SIDS.
- Recommend supervised, awake, tummy time to minimize development of positional plagiocephaly and to facilitate development.
- Health care professionals and newborn/child care providers should endorse the SIDS risk reduction recommendations from birth and implement safe sleep practices.

Prone sleeping (sleeping on the tummy) is a major risk factor for SIDS. The original 1994 sleeping position recommendation read that any non-prone (side or back) position was safe. Later studies indicated that side sleeping carried a higher risk than supine sleeping, because infants placed on their sides may roll to their stomachs. Devices to position infants on their sides have not been studied, but they are marketed to parents nonetheless. Another challenge is the continuing education about Back to Sleep aimed at parents and caregivers, such as day care providers. The task force reported that approximately 20% of U.S. infants are still placed in the prone position for sleep. Infants accustomed to sleeping in supine (back) position are at particularly higher risk of SIDS when they are subsequently placed in prone position (Mitchell, Thach, Thompson, & Williams, 1999). Infants used to being positioned in supine were less competent when placed in the unfamiliar prone position. All infants need awake prone experience to strengthen their bodies so that they are strong enough to be able to lift and turn their heads and avoid blocking their airways. Another concern is that infants placed in prone are more likely to trap exhaled carbon dioxide around their face and then re-breathe the exhaled carbon dioxide—which affects central nervous system protective mechanisms, so infants cannot arouse themselves (Patel, Harris, & Thach, 2001).

Soft sleep surfaces and loose bedding pose other modifiable hazards. Soft surfaces such as pillows, quilts, comforters, sheepskins, and porous mattresses should not be used under an infant, especially during sleep. A significant number of SIDS cases have been attributed to the heads of the infants being covered by loose bedding. This can happen even when the infant is placed supine. If blankets are to be used, they should be tucked into the crib mattress so that the infant's face is unlikely to be covered. Blankets should reach only up to the infant's chest level (and be tucked in). Infants should not be placed on soft sleep surfaces such as waterbeds, sofas, armchairs or soft mattresses. Infant cribs should conform to standards set by the Consumer Product Safety Commission.

Overheating due to the amount of clothing or blankets, room temperature, and seasonal conditions all factor into some SIDS cases. The AAP (R. Y. Moon, 2011) recommended that infants be dressed lightly for sleep and that overbundling be avoided. Infants may wear sleep garments such as blanket sleepers that provide adequate warmth so that use of blankets and loose bedding can be avoided. Many parents have been taught by health care professionals to swaddle their infant. However, tight swaddling has been found to be detrimental: It may reduce lung capacity as well as result in overheating. Tight swaddling decreases the protective arousal response; the baby sleeps more deeply and is harder to wake, which may present a hazard. In addition, swaddling blankets that loosen pose a risk for suffocation (Oden et al., 2012).

Cosleeping (the baby sleeps in the parents' bed) is a risk factor. Parents should consider placing the baby's crib near their bed as an alternative. Death by an adult overlaying an infant has occurred in several instances. Currently, the AAP strongly discourages cosleeping because of the dangers of infants being in adult beds and the possibility of adult overlay (R. Y. Moon, 2011; Shelov & Hannemann, 2004).

Pacifiers may reduce the risk of SIDS but how they accomplish this is not fully understood. However, the evidence is so compelling that the AAP issued a recommendation in October 2005 saying that evidence that pacifier use inhibits breastfeeding or causes later dental complications is not as compelling as the studies that showed pacifier use may reduce SIDS. The AAP recommended that a pacifier be used throughout the first year of life, with the following guidelines (Hauk, Omojokun, & Siadaty, 2005):

- For breastfeeding infants, pacifiers should not be introduced until breastfeeding is well established. It is reasonable to delay pacifier use until the infant is 1 month old because SIDS is less common during this time.
- The pacifier should not be used as a substitute for feeding.
- The pacifier should be used when placing the infant down to sleep (day or night). The pacifier should not be reinserted once the child falls asleep.
- If the baby refuses the pacifier, he should not be forced to take it.
- Pacifiers should not be coated with any sweet solution.
- Pacifiers should be cleaned and replaced regularly.
- Pacifier use should be discontinued at 1 year old because the risk of SIDS declines at this age and the risk of otitis media is higher.

Awake Tummy Time

The AAP recommends awake tummy time to help the infant avoid developing flat spots on the head (plagiocephaly) and to help the infant strengthen shoulder and neck muscles. Changing the direction the baby is looking when placed supine can help avoid tight neck muscles. (Pathway 7—The Strong Baby provides further information on tummy time.)

Implications for Parent Educators

Health care professionals and newborn/child care providers are urged to endorse the SIDS risk reduction recommendations from birth and implement safe sleep practices in the AAP–Expansion of Recommendations for Safe Sleep Policy Statement (R. Y. Moon, 2011).

In a study conducted by the Department of Pediatrics and Adolescent Medicine (Ottolini et al., 1999) at the Children's National Medical Center (George Washington University), 348 healthy newborns were studied to determine variation in sleep positioning over the first 6 months of life. Of the newborns completing the study, only 34% maintained a consistent sleep position. Prone sleeping increased from 12.2% at birth to 32.6% at 6 months. Only one third of the pediatricians discussed sleep position beyond the newborn period. The pediatricians conducting the study concluded that more emphasis and education are needed to urge parents to continue supine sleeping from 2–4 months, which was found to be the most likely period during which the parents switched from supine to prone sleeping. This time period coincides with the greatest risk of SIDS. The study also found that parents used prone sleeping as a way to comfort their infant; parents should be advised against comforting their infant in this way.

The Danger of Using Personal Versus Professional Judgment

A number of health care professionals did not personally agree with the AAP recommendations for Back to Sleep, or did not practice using the AAP sleep guidelines. Peek, Hershberger, Kuehn, and Levett (1999) and other investigators found that 97% of the 102 nurses from the two hospitals they surveyed were aware of the AAP sleep guidelines but that only 67% agreed with them.

Peek et al. (1999) also noted that 55% of the infants were observed to be in a side-lying position, 29% in the recommended supine position, and 16% in prone positioning. Because side sleeping was observed in a majority of the infants, and one third of the nurses disagreed with the AAP guidelines, the researchers concluded that education of nurses about the Safe Sleep campaign was still necessary.

During the first days postpartum, parents often learn and model practices from nurses and other health care professionals, deemed to be experts in baby care. Parents who see their infants placed in the side-lying position by nurses (or other health care professionals) prior to discharge (Grazel, Phalen, & Polomano, 2010; Peek et al., 1999) may believe this to be the correct way to place the baby for sleep. Grazel et al. (2010) found that 85% of nurses throughout 19 NICUs could identify the recommended safe sleep strategies, but inconsistencies existed in the implementation of these strategies and in SIDS risk education for parents. The AAP thus reemphasized that health care professionals should be vigilant about endorsing and modeling SIDS reduction recommendations before infants are discharged from the NICU (R. Y. Moon, 2011).

The parent educator must have a clear understanding of best practices reflected in the AAP (R. Y. Moon, 2011) recommendations. The rationale for and statistics behind the recommendations can help counter misinformation parents may have received verbally or by demonstration. Educators working with parents and young infants should stay abreast of new information regarding safe sleep. The following websites offer both educators and parents up-to-date information on this important topic. Check the Safe to Sleep website (see link below) regularly for updates

Recommended Reading

American Academy of Pediatrics, Task Force on Sudden Infant Death Syndrome. (2011). Policy statement: SIDS and other sleep-related infant deaths: Expansion of recommendations for a safe infant sleeping environment. *Pediatrics, 128*(5), 2011–2084.

Colson, E. R., Willinger, M., Rybin, D., Heeren, T., Smith, L. A., & Lister, G. (2013). Trends and factors associated with infant bed sharing, 1993–2010: The National Infant Sleep Position Study. *JAMA Pediatrics, 167*(11), 1032–1037.

Educator Tools

Explore these resources:

- *Safe to Sleep®* campaign:
  Phone: 1-800-505-CRIB (2742)
  Email: NICHDInformationResourceCenter@mail.nih.gov
  Website: http://safetosleep.nichd.nih.gov
  Recommended brochure for educators to download:
  Sudden Infant Death Syndrome (SIDS) and Other Sleep-Related Causes of Infant Death: Questions and Answers for Health Care Providers (2014)
- U.S. Department of Health and Human Services, National Institutes of Health *Eunice Kennedy Shriver* National Institute of Child Health and Human Development NIH Pub. No. 14-7202 August 2014
- ZERO TO THREE—Sleep Myths
  Download at: www.zerotothree.org/child-development/sleep/sleep-myth.html

Parent Education Activities

Deep Sleep

Welcome Baby Level 1

Purpose:

To provide information about the patterns of infant sleep and safe sleep for babies, and to alert parents about the impact infant sleep patterns can have on their own sleep and rest needs.

Instructional Content/Strategies:

- Discuss the Sleep Safety Guidelines: using the AAP recommendations (R. Y. Moon, 2011).
- Differentiate the patterns of deep versus light sleep.
- Discuss appropriate practices in deep versus light sleep.
- Provide anticipatory guidance regarding the developmental course of sleep.
- Discuss sleep adjustments for parents and strategies to get rest.

Deep Sleep

Materials:

- Teaching Teddy dressed in a sleep sack
- Rattle that is noisy and makes a sharp noise
- *Pathways* Teaching Photographs:
  Figure 2A: Baby in a deep sleep
  Figure 2A: Baby in light sleep

Ask:

"Have you had any trouble awakening your baby for feeding?"

"Did your baby continue to sleep even when you had visitors and there was a good deal of noise?"

"Was your baby sleeping so deeply that you became concerned—even wondering if the baby was still breathing?"

"Have you wondered how a baby can sleep in the newborn nursery when there is so much light and noise?"

Parents will typically answer yes to all of these types of questions.

Infant Observation/Activity:

Begin with the Teaching Teddy in his sleep sack lying on his back on the table. Ask if the parents have been told they must put their babies on their backs to sleep. Be prepared to answer "Safe to Sleep" questions and to expand on the points parents may mention. Affirm that it is normal for parents to worry about SIDS. Discuss that the AAP recommends that babies not have blankets placed over them or quilts in their cribs. To keep the baby warm enough, parents should use sleepers. Show the blanket sleeper that the Teaching Teddy is wearing as an example. Remind parents that babies should also not be overdressed, lest they become overheated. Talk about the dangers of tight swaddling and the way in which the AAP recommends a pacifier be used.

Show the *Pathways* Teaching Photograph Figure 2A: Baby in a deep sleep. Describe the indicators of deep sleep:

- The baby's body is very still.
- The baby's respiration is slow and even (sometimes almost undetectable).
- The baby's eyes are closed and the baby's face is relaxed.
- Every so often, for no apparent reason, the baby will startle but doesn't awaken.

Incorporate any observations or comments the parents share that indicate the characteristics of deep sleep. Then tell the parents you will have them imagine the sleeping baby is subject to a loud noise. Shake the rattle sharply over the Teaching Teddy, and ask the parents to imagine the reaction a baby might give. A startle! This indicates the baby's nervous system and hearing are working as they should. Shake the rattle again. Ask them to imagine that this time the baby doesn't startle but only moves slightly. Shake the rattle a third time. Ask them to imagine that this time the baby gives no response and has tuned out the sound/disturbance completely.

Developmental Context:

"Your baby needs to sleep deeply in order to grow and develop. Most newborns can protect themselves from having their deep sleep interrupted by tuning out, or habituating. Some babies are able to tolerate more noise in the home and remain asleep more easily than other babies. As you observe your baby when he is sleeping, note what happens when there is a loud noise. Does your baby startle? Does your baby then settle back into a deep sleep? If you observe a number of instances in which your baby is not able to settle back to sleep, you may need to put your baby in a quieter place for sleep. Again, each baby is very individual in this regard. Most newborns are able to habituate to sounds and remain asleep if they are in the deep sleep phase."

Caregiving Implications:

"If you try to rouse your baby from a deep sleep for a feeding, it is likely your baby will not be easy to waken and, once awake, will not be able to stay awake. It can be a frustrating experience for both you and your baby.

"The deep-sleep cycle is relatively short and is usually followed by light sleep. If you notice it is about time for a feeding, and the baby is in a deep sleep, let the baby sleep a little longer (10–20 minutes), and watch for the baby to begin a light sleep cycle. By waiting, you are respecting your baby's message, which is, 'I'm not ready to be awake just yet.' This will not interfere with the overall feeding schedule. (Note that there are some situations in which the health care provider might instruct the parent to have the baby on a very rigid schedule. Parents should heed the instruction of the health care provider, and the educator should reinforce any special instructions the parents have been given. The parents should also recheck these instructions if circumstances change with their infant.)

Feeding done when the baby is in a more alert state will be more successful. If it is nearing a feeding time and the baby appears to be in deep sleep, loosen the blanket and observe to see when your baby moves from this very deep sleep to a lighter sleep pattern.

"Most newborns can tune out noises around the home and maintain their deep sleep. Note your baby's response next time the phone is ringing and the baby is in a deep sleep. Does the baby startle but then tune it out and remain sleeping? Or does the baby become restless and unsettled, perhaps startling at each ring of the phone?

"A baby who continues to respond or wakes up from a deep sleep due to noise may have a more sensitive system and require a quieter, darker environment. By observing your baby's responses to noise during deep sleep you will learn if your baby is able to tune out and sleep peacefully. Either way it would be helpful for him to sleep in a quieter, darker room in order to get a good sleep. Even if your baby is good at tuning out, the quality of the sleep he is getting may not be as restful. A quiet, dark sleep space encourages quality sleep.

"Each baby has his own individual needs. By observing your baby, you will be able to learn more about what your baby needs.

"Just as your baby needs to have a quiet, dark sleep environment, so do you. Think about your own needs for both quantity and quality sleep. Many parents find they need to take extra steps to get enough quality sleep once the baby is born."

Welcome Baby Level 2

See Welcome Baby Level 1, except for direct observation of the baby as described below.

Deep Sleep

Materials:

- Teaching Teddy, dressed in a sleep sack
- *Pathways* Teaching Photographs: The Sleeping Baby
  Figure 2A: baby in a deep sleep
  Figure 2B: baby in light sleep

Baby:

In a deep sleep.

Ask:

See Welcome Baby Level 1.

Infant Observation/Activity:

Show Teaching Photograph Figure 2A. Describe the markers of deep sleep outlined in Welcome Baby Level 1. Ask the parents to observe and determine if their baby is *possibly* in a deep sleep. (Using the word *possibly* gives both you and the parent an out if they incorrectly identify their baby's state.) Explain to the parents that you are going to shake the rattle near the baby's ear and that they should watch the baby's response. Tell the parents the baby might startle, which will indicate that the baby's nervous system is responding as it should. If the baby is in the parent's arms, warn them that sometimes the startle is quite dramatic and they might startle too!

If the baby is in deep sleep, proceed positioning the red rattle about 10–12 inches from the baby's ear, and then give it a good sharp shake. Usually, the baby will startle as well as the parents. In a quiet voice, narrate the baby's responses. Try this up to five times to see if the baby tries to tune out or is wakened.

The baby may decrease his responsiveness or wake up. In general, the baby's response will be reduced in the second/third rounds with the rattle, which is sufficient to demonstrate the point that the baby tries to keep sleeping despite the attempt to interrupt his sleep.

If the baby is in a deep sleep, the baby will likely tune out stimuli, such as the sound of the rattle. If the baby has a continued response, it illustrates that the baby is either in a lighter sleep or is not tuning out as well. These observations should then be linked in discussion to the information in the Developmental Context and/or Caregiving Implications sections.

Developmental Context:

See Welcome Baby Level 1. In addition, utilize the baby's responses in your discussion.

Caregiving Implications:

See Welcome Baby Level 1.

Parent Care:

See Welcome Baby Level 1.

Welcome Baby Level 3

For educators with administration and reliability training in the NBAS.

Deep Sleep

Materials:

- Low table covered with two receiving blankets
- NBAS red rattle
- NBAS flashlight

Baby:

In a light or deep sleep.

Ask:

See Welcome Baby Level 1.

Infant Observation/Activity:

If you are conducting this activity in a parent group setting, describe the characteristics of deep sleep while observing each of the sleeping babies in class. Determine which babies are in a deep or light sleep. Choose a baby in a deep sleep and administer the NBAS habituation item using the rattle. Explain what you will do and why, and ask permission to demonstrate with a baby.

Proceed with the habituation package, using the flashlight (if the room is sufficiently darkened to begin with) or the rattle. The rattle is likely to produce the more observable response. Use up to three or four trials, stopping when the baby has sufficiently decreased in responsiveness to illustrate the baby's ability to remain asleep and tune out repeated sounds. This differs from the criteria in the NBAS manual for achieving a true response decrement, in which you proceed with one additional trial. If the baby doesn't exhibit a response decrement by the sixth trial, use the baby's response to illustrate that some infants have a more difficult time tuning out and might be helped by darkening and quieting the room for sleep. Narrate and discuss the behavioral responses of this particular baby. Give examples of the range of responses that might be observed.

The idea is to show a decrease in responsiveness that demonstrates a baby's ability to tune out, or inability to tune out. A particular baby may be disturbed by the sound of the rattle and this shows that some babies may be more sensitive. Whatever the baby does provides an opportunity to discuss both habituation and individuality.

Caregiving Implications:

See Welcome Baby Level 1.

Anticipatory Guidance:

See Welcome Baby Level 1.

Parent Care:

See Welcome Baby Level 1.

Light Sleep

Welcome Baby Level 1

Materials:

- Teaching Teddy
- Teaching Photograph Figure 2B: Baby in light sleep

Ask:

"Have you noticed your baby makes noises while he is sleeping?"

"Have you thought your baby was beginning to cry, only to look and realize the baby was still sleeping?"

"Have you noticed the way your baby breathes when he seems to be in a lighter sleep?"

"Have you noticed that sometimes the baby sucks, stretches, or even smiles while sleeping?"

Typically parents will comment on how noisy the baby is during sleep.

Infant Observation/Activity:

Show Teaching Photograph Figure 2B and describe markers of light sleep. In a light sleep:

- The baby moves a little but does not startle as when in deep sleep.
- The baby's breathing is irregular and can easily be detected.
- The baby's eyes are closed but may flutter open at times. There may be movement under the eyelids.
- The baby will respond to sound or movements by becoming more awake.

Contrast these observations to characteristics of deep sleep. Ask parents to observe their baby and note whether their baby could be in a light sleep. The educator should observe the baby and narrate what is observed.

Use the Teaching Teddy to demonstrate how you would pick up the baby, position the baby in the most upright position possible, and use gentle vertical movements to try to awaken the baby. Having the baby in an upright position works to alert the baby's nervous system, and the gentle vertical movements support the baby's ability to waken. Talk to the baby as an additional stimulus to help waken the baby.

Developmental Context:

"In a light sleep your baby is more responsive to stimuli such as being talked to, touched, or moved about. In a light sleep your baby may move about and sometimes begin fussing or briefly cry. As your baby comes into light sleep, your baby might continue toward waking up because she is hungry or uncomfortable, or because there is something interesting to tune into—such as your voice.

"If left alone, a baby may continue to sleep and even go into another stretch of deep sleep. A baby is almost always in a light sleep before waking up."

Caregiving Implications:

"If it is time to feed the baby and the baby is in a light sleep, you can gently pick up your baby and begin talking. The more upright the baby's position, the more easily the baby can be awakened.

"If you hear your baby fuss or cry out during sleep, do not immediately pick her up—this increases her alertness. Wait and observe, or pat the baby rhythmically without picking the baby up. It might be that your baby is moving between deep and light sleep, and is not really ready to wake up. If left alone, a baby might drift back to a deeper sleep. A quiet, darkened room will promote restfulness.

"Babies can be very noisy when they are in a light sleep. Some parents find they are only comfortable with their baby sleeping in their room for fear they might not hear when their baby cries. Other parents find they cannot sleep with the baby in their room and choose to have the baby sleep in another room. These are decisions you will need to discuss and plan as a family.

"You can encourage the development of good sleep habits by having a routine of winding down and relaxing before bedtime. Bathing, playing soft music, and darkening the sleep environment, for example, create a routine the baby can associate with relaxation and sleep; note that darkening the sleep environment appears to help the baby develop a day/night association with sleep.

"Some parents choose to put their baby in a crib or bassinet from the first night. It is tempting to want to put the baby in bed with you. However, it is important to know that the American Academy of Pediatrics strongly discourages parents from sleeping with their babies. When an infant is placed in bed with an adult there are several dangers. Adult pillows and blankets may cover the baby unintentionally. Babies have fallen out of the bed or become wedged between the wall and the bed, causing the death of the baby. Parents who use drugs or alcohol may have a lessened awareness of their infant and may roll over on her. For these reasons the American Academy of Pediatrics recommends a separate but nearby sleeping arrangement for babies and parents.

"You can help your baby with the transition between awake and sleep by noticing when your baby has become fatigued and then moving the baby to a quiet, darkened room with less stimulation. You may play some soft music. The purpose of doing this is to provide your baby an environment for calming and relaxing, and giving her an opportunity to fall asleep on her own.

"Babies will sometimes fuss (a complaint) or cry (a signal for help) as they work toward falling asleep. Learning to tolerate a bit of fussing and crying as the baby is trying to fall asleep is important. Picking up the baby each time she fusses or cries briefly will simply bring her to a more alert state, rather than help her to fall asleep."

Anticipatory Guidance:

"Newborns generally have about a 3- to 4-hour cycle during which they awaken, feed, and return to sleep, sometimes quickly. Your baby had a similar cycle even before birth.

"At about 3 weeks there is a big change. An infant awakens, feeds, and then remains awake for longer periods of time. When the baby is awake, she is curious about new sights and sounds and searches out stimulation. Moving from an alert time to sleep is a developmental task for a baby. Look for cues that your baby is becoming tired and then give your baby an opportunity to take a rest.

"A baby's sleep pattern will change along with her growth pattern. As your baby enters into a growth spurt she may eat more frequently, which is usually followed by longer sleeping time."

Parent Care:

"Many new parents find themselves very sleep deprived in the first months of their baby's life. This is quite common, but there are some steps you can take to avoid becoming exhausted. Resting or taking a nap while the baby is asleep, even during the day, will help you avoid becoming totally exhausted. Limiting the number of visitors in the first weeks of the baby's life can help parents rest and regain their strength.

"Your baby may not sleep through the night for several weeks or even months. A young infant needs to awaken to feed two to three times per night, which means you will awaken to do the feeding. Looking at your schedule in this realistic way can help you plan and adjust your expectations.

"This new 'routine' of sleep (or lack of sleep) can be very challenging to most parents. The best advice is to sleep, or at least rest, when the baby sleeps. It might be the first time in years you have taken a nap! Parents sometimes find that this new sleep pattern is disruptive to their relationship with their partner. Talk to your spouse/partner and discuss how to meet this new challenging sleep pattern."

Light Sleep
Welcome Baby Level 2

Materials:

- Teaching Teddy, dressed in a sleep sack.
- Teaching Photograph Figure 2B: Baby in light sleep

Baby:

In light sleep.

Ask:

See Welcome Baby Level 1.

Infant Observation/Activity:

Describe the characteristics of light sleep and show *Pathways* Teaching Photograph 2B. Ask the parents to observe their babies to determine if they are *possibly* in a light sleep—use the word *possibly* to give both you and the parent an out if one of you incorrectly identifies the baby's state. Observe along with the parents. Proceed when a baby is in light sleep. If there is no baby in light sleep, proceed with the Welcome Baby 1 protocol.

If the parent thought the baby was in a light sleep but is no longer, note what state the baby is actually in and use it as a teachable moment by further describing the baby's cues.

If there is a baby in a light sleep, ask permission to pick the baby up and demonstrate how a baby in a light sleep might be awakened. Hold the baby in an upright position facing outward and gently rock the baby up and down with a vertical motion. Do this while standing near the parent, and request that the parent call the baby's name over and over as you hold the baby in an upright position. The parent's voice is an added stimulus for the baby to become alert. Describe the baby's behavior. The educator may not be able to see the baby's expression as clearly as the parent if the baby is facing the parent; in that case, ask the parent to describe what his baby is doing.

A baby will often move from light sleep or a drowsy state to a quiet alert state. Explain that the upright position and gentle vertical movement is one of the most effective ways to help a baby move from a light sleep to a more alert state; it stimulates the nervous system to alert state, and the parent's voice attracts the baby's attention. Most babies will move from the light sleep or drowsy state to an alert state. Encourage parents to try this method, and when a baby moves to a quiet alert state, proceed to Pathway 3—The Social Baby.

Caregiving Implications:

See Welcome Baby Level 1.

Developmental Context:

See Welcome Baby Level 1.

Parent Care:

See Welcome Baby Level 1.

Light Sleep

Welcome Baby Level 3:

See Welcome Baby Level 2.

PATHWAY 3

The Social Baby

What happens to the human brain during the first few years of life sets the child on a trajectory of thinking and feeling that lasts a lifetime. The more nurturing and enriching those experiences and environments are, the more the growing brain is wired to feel secure and safe, curious and engaged. (Lally, 2014, p. 3)

What You Will Learn in This Pathway:

- sensory capabilities of a full-term newborn (developed in the womb) that allow him to interact with and respond to others
- the way in which these sensory capabilities help shape not only the child's social-emotional ties with his parents but also help develop the infant's brain capacities
- ways parents can promote their baby's positive social and emotional development
- cues that indicate an infant's preferences and dislikes

Why This Pathway Is Important:

- A parent's way of caring for a baby will influence the baby's experiences and expectations about interaction.
- Parents may bring their baby home and have no idea their baby can see or hear, much less interact with them. They may not know that the way they interact with the baby is very important.
- Parents need accurate, up-to-date information in order to give thoughtful care to and shape their interactions with their baby.

Key Information

More than any other factor, social-emotional development has been linked to a child's future success in life (Ainsworth, 1969; Ainsworth et al., 1978; Bowlby 1969/1982; Brazelton & Cramer, 1990; Gopnik & Meltzoff-Kuhl, 1999; Greenspan & Benderly, 1997; Greenspan & Greenspan, 1985). Infants need connections to their parents in order to thrive and flourish. Competence in the realm of social-emotional development is necessary for the development of positive relationships. A good foundation in social-emotional development prepares a child to develop positive relationships with others and helps him learn to cope with stress (National Scientific Council on the Developing Child, 2004). The foundation for the attachment between the parent and baby is established through the many repeated social interactions between them over the first months of life (Brazelton & Cramer, 1990; Erickson & Kurz-Riemer, 1999). If the parents respond with sensitivity and consistency, the baby comes to know them as a source of help and reassurance. He learns that he can make his needs known and expect they will be met (Lally, 2014). Trust and confidence are developed and set the stage for a positive attachment relationship to form (Beckwith, 1990; Brazelton & Nugent, 1995; Greenspan & Greenspan, 1985). Even before birth, the fetus is developing skills that help him connect with his parents.

What Can the Fetus Hear?

By 22 to 25 weeks the cochlea (the spiral-shaped portion of the inner ear) and nerve pathways of the cochlea are well developed. The fetus hears many sounds, such as his mother's pulse, her intestinal noises, her breathing, and, with astonishing clarity, her voice. Sound conducts well through amniotic fluid, and the fetus's hearing is acute and well developed early in the pregnancy (Blackburn & Vandenberg, 1993; Klaus & Klaus, 1999). The fetus not only hears in the uterus but also practices the mouth and breathing movements of speech and crying. Because of this early development, the fetus can hear and respond to sounds *outside* of his mother's body. Recent studies have concluded that the fetus hears the pitch and tone of the voices of his parents' voices. Fetuses (as early as 25 weeks gestation) will startle at loud sounds and respond differently to voices that are familiar versus unfamiliar (Birnholz, 1983; Klaus & Klaus, 1999). The fetus turns toward the source of the sounds he hears and responds differently to his mother's voice, father's voice, and even siblings' voices. It is the particular pitch, tone, and rhythm of the parent's voice the baby will selectively turn toward after birth because of the prior exposure to voices before birth (Vergara & Bigsby, 2004).

Taste and Smell

Both the taste buds and the olfactory bulb begin developing at 8 weeks gestation and are fully functional by 15 weeks gestation. The ability to taste and smell helps the full-term infant guide himself to the mother's breast after birth, because the mother's nipples secrete a substance that smells and tastes like amniotic fluid (Klaus & Klaus, 1999; Schaal, Orgeur, & Rognon, 1995). Research has found that a newborn can distinguish the smell of his mother's breastmilk from that of other mothers within days of birth (Blackburn & Kang, 1991; Brazelton & Cramer, 1990).

Touch

The ability to perceive touch is developed as early as 7–8 weeks after conception (Vergara & Bigsby, 2004) and is completely developed by 23 to 27 weeks gestation. Fredrick Wirth, a neonatologist, has found that abdominal rubbing can be used to console a fetus who is kicking in utero (Wirth, 2001). Indeed, the confines of the womb and the continuous gentle pressure brought to bear by the womb walls become comforting and familiar.

What Can the Fetus See?

Several months before the baby is born, the fetus develops sight. The fetus blinks when bright light penetrates the womb, as studied with ultrasound and other advanced imaging techniques (Birnholz, 1981). Much of what is known about the development of vision comes from studies of prematurely born infants (Als, 1982). Very premature infants are born with their eyelids fused, but they still blink when exposed to bright lights. Prematurely born babies who are 30–31 weeks gestation show visual preferences, preferring to look at thick striped patterns versus thin striped patterns. By 35 weeks gestation, premature babies will look longer at shapes and patterns (Fiedler, Moseley, & Ng, 1988; Torczynski, 1989). Newborns will gaze into the eyes of their parents. This eye contact has a powerful role in the attachment process.

Parent Education

During a class for parents held prior to discharge, a mother remarked that her newborn seemed to be "looking around" all the time. The educator observed that this newborn was in a quiet alert state and was indeed looking directly at her mother's face. As the mother spoke to the educator, the infant continued to respond to the sound of her mother's voice by widening her eyes and raising her brow and looking in the direction of the mother's face. During this particular session, which was attended by five parents, another baby visually followed a bright red object and then followed her mother's face as she moved slowly to one side then the other. When the mother of the baby who had been "looking around" witnessed this and also heard information about the visual capabilities of newborns, she remarked, "That's news to me!"

She looked down and began to speak directly to her baby. The newborn immediately began to widen her eyes even more and increased her attention to her mother's face and voice. She smiled fleetingly at her mother. In response to the smile, the mother began to speak again to her baby, this time looking into her daughter's eyes. This rich parent–baby dialogue went on for several minutes. This newborn had been in the quiet alert state for several minutes before the mother began to directly interact with her daughter.

What made the mother change her interaction? The mother explained that even though her daughter had been looking around many times in the past 2 days since her birth, she thought she was just "looking" and not really able to see or respond. She had also learned through the session that babies know their parent's voices from listening before birth. The important information this mother gained from the session changed the way she interacted with her daughter in significant ways. Why is this so important? These perceptions and expectations can alter the parents' behavior toward their child and influence their relationship and, consequently, the child's development (Boukydis, 2012; Brazelton & Sparrow, 2003).

Serve and Return Interactions Build the Child's Brain

Serve and return is a term used at the Harvard Center for the Developing Child to describe the way in which babies signal their parents and in return the parents respond. It can be visualized much like a game of tennis, in which the ball is volleyed back and forth with the intent to keep the ball in play. The "serve and return" interaction between parent and baby—in which young children naturally reach out for interaction through crying, babbling, facial expressions, and gestures and then have adults respond with the same kind of vocalizing and gesturing back at them—builds and strengthens brain architecture (National Scientific Council on the Developing Child, 2004). These interactions also create a relationship in which the baby's experiences are affirmed and new abilities are nurtured.

Children who have healthy relationships with their primary caregivers are more likely to develop insights into other people's feelings, needs, and thoughts, which form a foundation for cooperative interactions with others and an emerging conscience. A sensitive and responsive parent-child relationship (which Lally, 2014, called the "social womb") also is associated with stronger cognitive skills in young children and enhanced social competence and work skills later in school, which illustrates the connection between social-emotional development and intellectual growth (National Scientific Council on the Developing Child, 2004).

Social-Emotional Development Is Critical

When the baby responds to the parent by calming down, looking at the parent when she speaks, and gazing with intense interest into her eyes, the parent receives positive feedback from the infant. This type of positive feedback from baby helps develop confidence in the parent (Blackburn & Kang, 1991; Brazelton & Nugent, 1995). When the baby gets a positive response from the parent:

- It encourages the baby to try again, increasing the number of trials a baby will make.
- Increased trials amount to practice in mutual gazing and social interactions.
- A baby who is skilled in capturing an adult's positive attention will build confidence and competence in interacting with others.
- Confidence and social competence lead the baby to begin to explore and learn about the world.

Parents who are rewarded by their child's responses are more likely to spend time engaging and interacting with their baby. The baby then has more opportunities to learn from the parent and enjoy social interaction. The relationship develops and attachment grows in a positive direction (Brazelton & Cramer, 1990; Ramey & Ramey, 1999; Shapiro, 2003). John Bowlby (1969/1982) first described *attachment* as a unique relationship between an infant and his caregiver that is the foundation for healthy development. Mary Ainsworth (1969) expanded Bowlby's work and developed a way to categorize attachment types as secure, anxious, or ambivalent. The secure attachment provides a secure base from which the child can confidently explore the world and develops when the parent reads and responds appropriately to the infant's cues—and the infant's needs are met. Ainworth's work was taken up by Mary Main (Main, Kaplan, & Cassidy, 1985), whose studies found that how adults remember their own attachment representations may influence how these adults then parent their own children.

Gaps in Information for Parents

Even in the first moments after birth, interactions between the parent and baby are important (Brazelton & Cramer, 1990; Klaus & Kennell, 1995). Parents may not necessarily understand how able their baby is to see them and to respond to voices and other sounds. It wasn't that long ago that experts claimed a baby couldn't see at birth. In the late 1960s and early 1970s, there was a virtual explosion of research that confirmed a baby could see at birth, amongst many other new discoveries. While it was it acknowledged that babies could see, researchers believed it could be only patterned objects with high contrast (black and white). It is now known that a newborn's visual ability is far greater. Babies prefer to look at patterns that are more facelike, and above all prefer to gaze at human faces as opposed to patterns (Walton, Bower, & Bower, 1992). Research over the past 25 years has revealed many remarkable insights about the development and experience of both the fetus and the newborn. Yet much of this type of information is not common knowledge among parents.

Crying as an Example

Evidence clearly shows that a quick response to a crying baby lessens crying and reduces crying overall (Leach, 2013). A common misconception is that an infant can be spoiled by responding too quickly. Some information parents receive via family or friends is that it is "good for the baby to cry" or "letting him cry teaches him to be independent."(Kopp, 2003). A young baby "serves" by sending the signal he is uncomfortable or hungry by crying. In the "return," the parent responds by making the baby comfortable or feeding him. Through this interaction, the baby is learning that he can call for help and that someone (his parent) will respond and meet his needs.

Strict Scheduling Can Interfere

Child care practices that promote strict scheduling of the newborn are especially worrisome. They instruct the parent to ignore the baby's cues and set strict scheduling regimens. However, ignoring the baby's cues can result in physical problems such as dehydration and psychological problems such as depression (Beckwith, 1990). The more parents know about the capabilities of babies, the more they can make mindful choices about caring for their baby. How the parents view their baby impacts their behavior toward the baby (Hernández-Martínez, Canals Sans, & Fernández-Ballart, 2011). By understanding how parents view their baby, the educator will be better able to know what to affirm, what information to offer, and perhaps what misconceptions to try to correct.

Research is clear that experiences occurring in early development can have long-term effects on both physical and mental health (Hilt, 2015). When parents are stressed or unable to be sensitive to their infant's cues, the infant may be at risk for "a cascade of biological changes that compromise the functioning of infants, leading to effects that persist into adolescence and adulthood"(Gudsnuk & Champagne, 2011, p. 1). A baby who is not cared for in a sensitive, responsive way still develops a relationship with his parent and a self-image; however, instead of feeling trust in his parent and in himself, he may develop depression or anxiety around interacting with others (Erickson et al., 1985; Gerber & Johnson, 1998; Greenspan & Greenspan, 1985). Instead of developing confidence, a baby who asks for assistance may protest in extreme ways or give up and shut down (Brazelton & Nugent, 1995). If the baby repeatedly experiences a lack of response to his needs, he learns his needs are not important to his parent and eventually may come to feel he is not important (Greenspan & Greenspan, 1985). Parents who do not provide responsive care will likely find that their infant becomes less responsive (Kopp, 2003).

Living in the Real World

No parent is able to be sensitive and responsive all of the time. There are no perfect parents or perfect babies (Beckwith, 1990; Erickson & Kurz-Riemer, 1999). In fact, Beeghly and Tronick (2011) described periods of miscoordination as normal—manageable challenges to the infant's self-regulatory system help develop resilience. Parents' awareness of infant states of consciousness and cues of engagement, disengagement, and stress can help them provide the appropriate, sensitive care that helps promote a secure attachment. The baby's first relationship with the parent, becomes a model for future relationships (Brazelton & Cramer, 1990; Erickson & Kurz-Riemer, 1999: Greenspan & Greenspan, 1985). A review of the capabilities of the fetus sets the stage for exploring the capabilities of the newborn baby.

The Newborn's Sensory Capabilities

Newborn Hearing and Language Development

Newborns have different responses to speech and nonspeech sounds. They are attracted to the sounds of human speech. Babies have grown familiar with the sounds of their parents' voices before birth and will prefer a parent's voice over that of a stranger. Babies also prefer to listen to a type of speech called "motherese" (Birnholz, 1983; Karmiloff & Karmiloff-Smith, 2004), which is how many mothers naturally speak to an infant: She speaks in high-pitched tones, exaggerates and repeats sound, uses short sentences, and makes her voice rise and fall. The content of motherese is generally the use of baby's name, prompts, or questions.

Newborns are not passive listeners; they prefer to look at the source of the sound or speaker and study it. In face-to-face interaction, newborns will mimic things such as sticking the tongue out or rounding of the mouth (Klaus & Klaus, 1999). Babies develop language through interaction and hearing. One of the most important messages to convey to new parents is that by talking to the baby, they are stimulating the growth of the baby's brain and his ability to learn in profound ways that contribute to the attachment process. (C. Moon, 2011). Scientific data reveal that early interaction with babies increases their later communicative ability (Ramey & Ramey, 1999; Shapiro, 2003, Walton et al., 1992). Hearing is critical to the development of a child's speech and language development, learning, and interaction with others.

Hearing Loss Is Common

Hearing loss is a common birth defect affecting 3 in 1,000 babies born each year (March of Dimes, 2015), occurring nearly 3 times more frequently than cleft lip or palate and Down syndrome, and 5 times more frequently than limb defects. Three to four infants out of 1,000 will have a permanent sensorial hearing loss. In the past, methods for detecting hearing loss were ineffective, and about 50% percent of newborn hearing loss went undetected. Until recently, the average age for identification was 2½ years or later for mild and moderate losses. Early identification can make a difference and lessen the impact of the hearing loss on the both the child and the family.

Universal Newborn Hearing Screening

Currently, most states have legislative mandates related to universal newborn hearing screening. Almost 90% of newborns are being screened prior to discharge from the hospital. However, many programs find there are few places to refer parents for follow-up because of the shortage of experienced pediatric audiologists. In addition, many parents do not follow through with care when a screening indicates the need for a further evaluation. Only 53% percent of infants with hearing loss are enrolled in early intervention before they are 6 months old. Currently, early intervention systems are designed to serve infants with severe/profound losses, but the majority of infants identified have mild, moderate, and unilateral hearing losses. The national goals for hearing screening are:

1. All newborns will be screened for hearing loss before 1 month old, and preferably before hospital discharge.
2. All infants who screen positive will have a diagnostic audiology evaluation before 3 months old.
3. Infants with an identified hearing loss will receive appropriate intervention before 6 months old.

Hearing Loss Can Occur at Any Time

Some of the red flags that indicate a child may not be hearing well are parent or caregiver concerns; a family history of hearing loss; presence of a syndrome known to include a hearing loss; malformation of the head, neck, or ears; head trauma; and recurrent or persistent otitis media with fluid present for at least 3 months. A child may exhibit behaviors such as not responding to the parent's voice or sounds in the environment. The child may need to watch the speaker in order to hear what is said. A child with a hearing loss may not develop speech and language skills as expected. If a parent expresses concern about their child's hearing, refer them immediately for a screening or evaluation. No child is too young for a hearing test, and children should receive intervention immediately when the hearing loss is detected.

Newborn Vision

Right from the moment of birth, the newborn opens his eyes and begins to learn about the world through sight. If the surroundings of the newborn are quiet, the lights are dimmed, and the newborn is allowed to remain with his parents, the newly born infant will typically become quiet and very alert. In the quiet alert state, the infant's eyes are wide open, and he is responsive to his parents' voices and faces. He will look intently and directly at his parents. When spoken to he may widen his eyes and focus even more intently. This is very rewarding and important feedback for parents to receive from the infant. These first endearing looks exchanged between the parents and infant help set the stage for attachment to grow. Above all else, babies love to look at their parents' faces (Brazelton & Cramer, 1990; Klaus & Klaus, 1999).

Enhancing the Baby's Ability to Respond

The bright lights found in most hospital settings can inhibit the baby's ability to gaze at his parents and the world around them. Because of this, many new parents have not had their infant give them direct eye contact or seen the full range of responsiveness of which their infant is capable. If the lights are dimmed, a baby may become alert. The newborn will study the faces of their parents and track their movements. The human face is the most exciting pattern for them to study—this has been borne out by many research studies. Even more remarkable is that an infant, as soon as 4 hours after birth, can recognize his own mother's face (Klaus & Klaus, 1999; Walton et al., 1992).

Even though a newborn's eyes are still functionally immature, newborns are able to use their visual abilities to make visual contact with the new world and learn about the people and things in it. Newborns have pupils that are responsive to the degree of brightness. If it is too bright for the newborn, he will simply close his eyes (Brazelton & Nugent, 1995). The bright lights found in hospital newborn nurseries are more likely to impede the visual responsiveness of a newborn than encourage it. In addition to preferring a darkened environment, newborns are best able to focus on a face or object that is not too close or too far away. If the parents put their own faces too close to the newborn, the newborn will shut his eyes or even turn away. This is not the type of response that encourages the parent to be social with the infant. If the parent tries to engage the baby visually and is too far away, the baby will not respond by looking interested or giving the parent a positive response. Again, a parent does not find this lack of feedback rewarding.

Look for Individual Preferences

So what is the right distance for early parent–infant interactions? The "ideal" focal distances found in professional and parent literature varies: 7–8 inches, 8–10 inches (Brazelton & Nugent, 1995; Klaus & Klaus, 1999), and, according to one source (Klaus & Klaus, 1999), 10–15 inches. What researchers discovered is that in order for the infant to not only see and engage in visual responsiveness, the person (or object) must be not too close and not too far. Parents should be encouraged to observe their baby's responses and establish the ideal zone in which their baby prefers to interact. Understanding how to read the baby's cues of engagement, disengagement, and overstimulation will be helpful to parents. For some parents, this will be intuitive; others will need help to identify how their infant is responding.

Visual Preferences of the Young Infant

Many toys marketed for newborn infants come in black and white or have contrasting colored patterns. Black and white provides the highest contrast, and the bold patterns catch a baby's attention. Babies will be attracted to and look at black and white patterns, but not with the intense interest they demonstrate when gazing at and studying a parent's face. No boldly patterned toy can provide the rich and varied stimulation of face-to-face interaction with parents. Newborns in fact *prolong* their attention when they are looking at their parents' faces (Blackburn & Kang, 1991; Brazelton & Cramer, 1990; Klaus & Kennell, 1995). In experiments, newborns imitated some of the parent's facial movements such as sticking their tongue out or opening their mouth wide (Klaus & Kennell, 1995).

Media is not recommended for very young children. The AAP (Brown, 2011) found that 90% of parents of children younger than 2 years old watch some type of digital media; the AAP discourages use of media by children under 2 because it minimizes their active and creative play. The policy statement had this to offer parents of very young children:

> *Unstructured playtime is more valuable for the developing brain than any electronic media exposure. If a parent is not able to actively play with a child, that child should have solo playtime with an adult nearby. Even for infants as young as 4 months of age, solo play allows a child to think creatively, problem solve, and accomplish tasks with minimal parent interaction.* (Brown, 2011, p. 4)

Judging Baby's Preferences and Dislikes

A baby's *cues of engagement* indicate whether the distance is correct or the interaction is enjoyable. Cues of engagement include a widening and brightening of the eyes and focused attention on the person or object. The newborn who is showing cues of engagement may also be able to follow his parents' faces or an object when moved slowly to one side by tracking with his eyes and even turning his head to keep the visual target in sight. The engaged baby responds to sounds by turning toward the sound itself (Blackburn & Kang, 1991). For optimal social interaction to occur, the infant should be in the quiet alert state.

Cues of disengagement include looking away, looking worried, dull-looking eyes, or closing of the eyes (Brazelton, 1992). When the newborn displays cues of disengagement, the adult should stop the interaction and alter it in a way that results in the infant shifting to cues of engagement.

Cues of overstimulation are more intense and can have serious consequences if ignored. Signs of overstimulation include fluctuations in the infant's body color, as evidenced by the infant becoming pale, very flushed, or mottled in appearance. The infant's respiratory system can be affected by overstimulation: The breathing pattern becomes irregular and hiccoughing or spitting up begins (Als, 1982; Brazelton & Nugent, 1995). However, not every occurrence of hiccoughing or spitting up is a sign of overstimulation.

Other signs that indicate an infant has become overstimulated are increased startles or tremors and changes in the baby's body tone, such as becoming very hypotonic (floppy)—or, at the other end of the spectrum, becoming hypertonic (stiff, rigid). Fragile infants may respond to overstimulation by having bradycardia (faster heart) responses or apnea (cessation of breathing), or both (Als, 1993). When a baby is exhibiting cues of overstimulation, it is important that the parents and caregivers intervene and eliminate or lessen the source of the overstimulating or disturbing stress.

Why This Is so Important

Parents feel rewarded when their baby engages in visual exchanges with them; parents who find a reward in capturing their infant's attention will repeat the process over and over (Barnard et al., 1993; Gopnik & Meltzoff-Kuhl, 1999; Greenspan & Greenspan, 1985). The repeated interactions in turn give the infant rich and positive feedback and encourage the baby to pay attention longer and more often. Focused attention is one of the foundations of all learning. For parents, the baby's visual attention and responsiveness to them show them they are important to their baby (Blackburn & Kang, 1991; Brazelton & Cramer, 1990).

The baby's responsiveness can also prove that he has emerged from the labor and birth process healthy and intact (Brazelton & Cramer, 1990). Parents who have not experienced their infant's abilities in the quiet alert state may underestimate their infant's abilities. Without this important information about their newborn's abilities to see and hear, they may not provide these enriching experiences for their baby.

Implications for Learning

Most parents want to provide learning experiences for their children. New parents are bombarded with offers and recommendations for music, videos, toys, and games for their very young children, with claims to unsubstantiated benefits. Videos teach children in a passive way but do not help develop social-emotional skills, nor do they help develop the child's communication skills (DeLoache et al., 2010). It is critical to alert parents to the social skills with which their baby comes into the world so that they may enjoy social interaction with the baby from day one, at the same time laying a foundation for future learning. Research (Barnard et al., 1993; Barnet & Barnet, 1998; Erickson et al., 1985; Greenspan & Greenspan, 1985; Leach, 1995; Pawl, 1995) has clearly shown that a relationship with a sensitive and responsive caregiver contributes to a child's ability to pay attention, respond, communicate, and interact—foundational skills for all later learning. Parents should be encouraged to understand that everyday interactions with their children not only build a positive social relationship between them but also promote their child's intellectual development (Ramey & Ramey, 1999). No video, toy, or game can make that claim!

Pathway 3—The Social Baby alerts parents to the opportunities to engage their newborn in social exchanges from the moment their baby is born. The instructional portion of this Pathway informs the parents about techniques that can enhance their infant's ability to respond visually, and the instruction demonstrates the effectiveness of the parent's voice in capturing the infant's attention and explains why talking to the baby is very important.

Recommended Reading

National Scientific Council on the Developing Child. (2007). *The timing and quality of early experiences combine to shape brain architecture* (Working Paper No. 5). Retrieved from http://developingchild.harvard.edu/index.php/resources/reports_and_working_papers/working_papers/wp5

National Scientific Council on the Developing Child. (2004). *Young children develop in an environment of relationships* (Working Paper No. 1). Retrieved from http://developingchild.harvard.edu/index.php/resources/reports_and_working_papers/working_papers/wp1

Educator Tools

Explore these websites:

- Harvard Center for the Developing Child
  This organization provides the public with up-to-date information regarding brain development, impacts of poverty, and adverse life experiences. They post many helpful short videos as well as evidence-based research.
  http://developingchild.harvard.edu/key_concepts/serve_and_return
  There is a short video on "Serve and Return", a Question and Answer section, and additional information on the science of neglect.

- ZERO TO THREE
  ZERO TO THREE is an organization dedicated to a child's first 3 years of life—providing parents and professionals with an array of resources including information handouts, videos, podcasts, and opportunities to sign up for programs to help parents track their child's development and learn about activities to promote development.
  Explore: www.zerotothree.org/child-development/play/tips-and-tools-play.html
  Download "The Power of Play," and read "Playing with Babies," and "Baby

Playtime Ideas." There are many resources that can be shared with parents and used in parent education groups.

Parent Education Activities

Welcome Baby Level 1

http://developingchild.harvard.edu/key_concepts/serve_and_return

Purpose:

To ensure parents realize the potential of their infant to engage in social interaction and the importance of this social interaction in building the baby's capacities to relate and learn.

Instructional Content/Strategies:

- Discuss the importance of early, enjoyable social experiences.
- Demonstrate the conditions that enhance the infant's responsiveness.
- Demonstrate interactions that can effectively engage the baby.
- Identify cues of engagement, disengagement, and overstimulation.

Visual Capacities

Materials:

- Teaching Teddy
- *Pathways* Teaching Photographs:
  Figure 3A: Baby gazing directly into the face of her mother
  Figure 3B: Baby turning to her father's voice

Setting:

Darkened room illuminated with indirect lighting.

Ask:

"Was your baby alert after being born?"
"Have you noticed your baby looking at you or focusing on something?"

Typically, babies are very alert after birth, and parents have an opportunity to confirm that their infant can see. Most parents will have witnessed their baby's alert period (unless an emergency or concern about the baby's well-being kept the parents from interacting with the baby). A baby typically enters a deep sleep after this initial period of alertness after birth. The bright lights found in most hospital settings inhibit a baby from continuing to look around, so darkening the room is essential.

Infant Observation/Activity, Part 1:

Darken the room, using table lamps to provide some lighting. Explain that babies can see even before they are born, but of course they cannot see or focus on objects; they can only sense light. If you choose to darken the room at this point, encourage parents to watch their baby's response as the room is dimmed. Often a baby will open his eyes, or a baby in a sleep state may relax his face.

Identify if the baby is in the quiet alert state. If so, point this out and describe the characteristics of the quiet alert state as well as the capabilities of a baby in a quiet alert state. Show Figure 3A: baby gazing directly into the face of her mother.

Infant Observation/Activity, Part 2:

Discuss *Pathways* Teaching Photograph 3A, the alert baby who is looking at the mother's face. It is important to emphasize that the baby in Figure 3A is not only alert (eyes open), but also calm and focused. *This is the quiet alert state.* Discuss how a baby in a quiet alert state enjoys watching and studying the face of his parent. Encourage parents to play with their baby when he is in this quiet alert state.

Use the Teaching Teddy to model the upright position and gentle vertical movements that can help increase a baby's alertness. Hold the Teaching Teddy about 10–12 inches out from your body and use a gentle vertical motion. Model how to use a higher pitched voice to attract a baby's attention. Once you have the "baby's" (Teddy's) attention, model moving slowly to one side and discuss how a baby in a quiet alert state who has focused on the parent's face and voice would follow the movement.

Explain to parents that somewhere within the range of 8–15 inches will be the distance their baby prefers for interaction. Encourage parents to observe their baby to find the specific distance at which their baby seems to focus best. Parents should be instructed to look for the cues of engagement—a widening of the eyes, lifting of the brow, and shiny eyes that can follow movement. Discuss cues of disengagement.

If a baby is in a quiet alert state, ask the parents to try to get their baby's attention by placing him in the position you modeled with the Teaching Teddy and to try similar ways to help their baby focus on their face and voice. If you note that the baby focuses on the parents' face, ask the parents to move slowly to one side and see if the baby will follow. Narrate what the baby does to further illustrate that, by helping the baby become alert and then focused, parents contribute to their baby's ability to learn about the world. Nothing could be more interesting to a new baby than his parent's face.

Developmental Context:

"Right after birth your baby's eyes are very sensitive to light, and dimming the lighting will often help a baby be able to open his eyes and look at his new surroundings. The newborn nursery and hospital have bright lighting for safety reasons. For example, hospital staff need to be able to see the babies to ensure they are breathing well and that their color is normal. This type of lighting is often too bright for the newborn's eyes, so the newborn rarely opens his eyes when in this bright light. If you desire to get your baby alert, dim the lights in your room. Bringing your baby to a more upright position will also help your baby become alert. You can also rock him gently using vertical motions while he is in a more upright position.

"A baby can see from the moment of birth. What can grab and hold a baby's attention are images or objects that have patterns with contrast. The human face, especially your face, is what your baby finds most interesting to look at. You can provide a wonderful experience for your baby by just looking at your baby, helping him focus on your face and then talking to him. He will find your voice familiar and your face the most interesting thing he has ever seen! Helping your baby pay attention is a first step toward helping your baby learn about the world."

Caregiving Implications:

"Many toys and digital media marketed for newborn infants come in black and white or have bright colored patterns. This is because black and white provides the highest contrast and the bold patterns catch a baby's attention. A baby will certainly want to look at these patterns, but not with the same intense interest as looking at your face. When your baby looks into your eyes you often begin to talk to the baby, adding even more for the baby to learn about. You are able to note your baby's cues and respond in a synchronous way—a very important way your baby learns about social relationships. Nothing will be as interesting to your baby as your face. Your face and voice can respond to your baby; for example, you can change your expression or make your voice softer or louder depending on what your baby seems to enjoy. Toys or videos do not have this ability. In fact, research shows that children who watch television and videos and have fewer social interactions are not able to learn as well or as quickly; in addition, very young children who are exposed to digital media do not develop creativity and do not get as much exercise.

"When you hold your newborn baby's face somewhere between 8–15 inches from your face, your baby can focus intensely. He will first look at your face in general, then your eyes and hair, and usually come back to looking right into your eyes. Your baby became familiar with your voice during pregnancy. Now when your baby hears your familiar voice he can connect it with your face. Nothing can hold a newborn's attention more than his parent's face and voice!

"When parents and babies play the 'looking game,' the baby learns to look longer and pay more attention. This is an important first step in learning—paying attention. The baby learns about the people around him and eventually learns to have this kind of interest in other people and objects. This is the best way a parent can begin to help the baby become a good learner.

"Be sure to look at and talk to your baby every day. Place interesting things in places where your baby can see them—but also check if your baby really seems to like these things or if these interesting things are perhaps overstimulating. For some babies, too many interesting things to look at will cause them to turn their eyes away, fuss, or cry. Sometimes this can even happen if your baby is too tired to look at you. Be sure to notice when your baby is not enjoying something and make a change. Give him a beak and try again later."

Anticipatory Guidance:

"Newborns will visually interact with people and objects within the range of about 8–15 inches. While they can see a greater distance than this, 8–15 inches is the distance within which they can see best and focus right after birth.

"By 2 months old, a baby's eyesight is more developed and the baby will begin looking at and focusing on people and objects about 3–4 feet away. By 2–3 months, a baby will want to play with you because he enjoys it so much. Sometimes he may fuss or coo as a way to call you over and get your attention. Babies quickly become very good at letting you know what they want and how important you are to them. If you pay attention to your baby when he is trying to get your attention, this is not going to spoil the baby. If you respond to his request to interact, he learns he can communicate.

"By 4 months old, a baby's vision is similar to an adult's vision, and the baby can focus on people and objects both near and far. The baby will have begun using his hand-eye coordination and toys should be within his reach to reward his efforts. Parents often report that at about 4 months the baby looks around so much while feeding they must find an uninteresting place to feed their baby."

Welcome Baby Level 2

See Welcome Baby Level 1.

Welcome Baby Level 3

Materials:

- Low table
- Red rubber ball, about 3 inches in diameter

Setting:

Darkened room using indirect lighting

Baby:

Spontaneously in, or helped into, a quiet alert state.

Ask:

See Welcome Baby Level 1.

Infant Observation/Activity:

Ask permission to use a baby to demonstrate the visual responsiveness of a newborn. Observe the baby carefully to determine that the baby is truly in a quiet alert state. If the baby is not in a quiet alert (State 4), use facilitation techniques which will bring him to a quiet alert state. Narrate the techniques used, as these can become helpful tips and insights for parents.

Explain specifically that bringing the baby to a more upright position and adding gentle vertical movements will often help the baby become more alert. The upright position and vertical motion are effective in eliciting an alert state. Parents often use a supine position and visual, auditory, or sensory stimulation to alert a baby, which are not nearly as effective. The upright position and gentle vertical movement are not as commonly known or modeled for parents, and this Pathway provides an excellent opportunity to demonstrate this strategy.

Talk to the baby to see how the baby responds to your voice, and determine the baby's level of responsiveness before attempting to administer the inanimate visual NBAS item. Explain to the parents that babies can open their eyes and see right from the moment they are born. Lower lighting can enhance the way they can focus and even follow a moving target such as a bright object or a person's face.

The baby should be placed on two blankets on the low table. If the class takes place in a parent group setting, the low table allows everyone to get a full view of the baby. The baby's lower body should rest on the table, while the baby's upper body is supported on one of your arms so that the baby is at approximately a 45-degree angle. Use your other hand to bring the red ball into the baby's view. This allows for all parents to observe the baby's dramatic response. We advise practicing this activity with several babies, explaining to parents that you are in the process of learning a technique.

Set up the situation so that any response the baby shows illustrates the continuum of visual responsiveness. Then again, the baby may only briefly follow the parent's face or the bright object. He may be very engaged and not only focus on the object for a prolonged period but also track with both his eyes and head.

At Welcome Baby Level 3, you should comment on the baby's performance only after the baby has tracked the ball, so the baby will not be distracted by the educator's voice. You should be fully attentive to presenting the ball at the appropriate pace for the baby.

Comment on any adjustments made either with the baby or in the distance of the red ball that elicited the baby's best performance. This information is useful to parents who will learn they may need to adjust their presentation to get their baby's attention.

Facilitation Tip:

The educator uses the red ball instead of her own face, because the ball is more visible to group participants, and so that she does not appear to be in any kind of competition with the parents for the baby's attention. This baby and his parents may not have yet had the wonderful experience of meeting visually. Having a baby show invested or focused attention on the educator, in front of the parents, is inappropriate. The point of the demonstration is to alert the parents to their baby's capacity to interact visually. Armed with both the demonstration and information, parents can then experiment with how to effectively engage in visual interchanges with their baby.

You should be quiet while the baby participates in following the ball. There should be no running commentary at this point, because you are focusing on the baby's performance.

Once the baby has successfully tracked, you can then mention that the ball is somewhere between 8 and 15 inches away, the light is low, and the baby is in the quiet alert state, and point out that the ball was moved slowly for the baby to track. Encourage parents to try this when their baby is alert by showing the baby their face and, once they have eye contact, moving slowly to the right or left.

In this way, you are giving the parents information along with a demonstration and interaction with the baby about how to have a successful visual experience. For some parents the notion that their baby can see at all is new information. Informed parents who knew that babies could see at birth are thrilled to see it confirmed in their baby.

The baby's ability to be alert and engage in social interactions right after birth is incredible. Newborns 4–8 hours old can be the best candidates for demonstrating visual competencies. Babies who are a bit older (3–4 days) may be over their "cortisol high" from the birth process and have entered a more sleepy period and are not as able to demonstrate social interaction or visual and auditory competencies as well.

Likewise, boys who have been circumcised are generally alert just after the procedure, but some time afterward seem to habituate and are very hard to waken. Being able to judge which infant might be a candidate for demonstration of a skill it takes time to learn.

Developmental Context:

See Welcome Baby Level 1.

Caregiving Implications:

See Welcome Baby Level 1.

Anticipatory Guidance:

See Welcome Baby Level 1.

Parent Care:

See Welcome Baby Level 1.

Auditory Capacities
Welcome Baby Level 1

Materials:

- Teaching Teddy
- Teaching Photograph Figure 3B: Baby turning to her father's voice

Ask:

"Have you noticed that your baby seems to know your voice?"

"Does your baby look or turn toward you when you speak?"

Typically, the answer is yes. Many parents report that they noticed this in the first minutes after the baby's birth—that the baby turned to their voice, or the baby calmed down when the parent spoke. For many parents, this is quite an emotional moment.

Infant Observation/Activity:

Position the Teaching Teddy like the baby is positioned in Figure 3B. Demonstrate speaking to the baby in a high-pitched voice from one side continually, then slowly turn Teaching Teddy's head using the hand that is supporting Teaching Teddy's head to the direction your voice is coming from.

Show the photograph Figure 3B of the baby turning toward her father's voice. Explain that, in the photograph, the educator and the father were competing for the baby's attention by speaking to the baby at the same time. Explain that the baby heard both voices and that the baby turned toward the voice that was familiar—that of her father.

Developmental Context:

"By 24 weeks gestation (4 months before birth), your baby could hear your voice. For many years researchers believed the fetus primarily heard sounds within the mother, such as the heartbeat. More recent studies have concluded that while the babies do hear the heartbeat, they also hear the particular pitch and tone of their parents' voices.

"Your baby heard the sound of the mother's voice, the father's voice, and even the siblings' voices. It is the pitch, tone, and rhythm of the parents' voices the baby will turn toward after birth. Your baby came into the world already being familiar with the voices of his family."

Caregiving Implications:

"The sound of your voice is familiar and comforting to your baby, as well as exciting. In the womb, your baby heard your and your partner's voice regularly. When you spoke, your baby listened. In listening, your baby is continuing to learn about the language you speak and about communication.

"As your newborn listens to your voice, his interest and understanding of communication builds and adds to the relationship between you and the baby. There are so many new sights and sounds surrounding your newborn. Your voice is familiar and comforting. Continue to speak to your baby as a way to keep the connection you shared before he was born. Speaking to your baby also teaches him to speak and helps him learn many things. Children who are spoken to have a much greater vocabulary by preschool age than children whose parents do not speak to them as much.

"When your baby is fussy or crying, try speaking to your baby in soothing tones. Often, the baby will be comforted just by hearing your voice. Talk to the baby about things you are doing. Tell him about everything.

"Talking to your baby is one of the best ways your baby learns to pay attention and to associate words with people and activities."

Anticipatory Guidance:

"By talking to your baby, you are providing your baby with a language-learning environment. It is one of the best ways to set the stage for your child to learn to speak and express himself using words.

"At about 2 months old, you will notice your baby beginning to have conversations with you! When you speak, your baby will begin to coo in response. Your baby is learning the give and take that occurs in communication, one of the foundations for later learning."

Parent Care:

"Being a new parent is a very intense experience, and meeting others who are going through the same experiences and challenges can be rewarding. You may have experienced this special kind of camaraderie in prenatal classes. In our community these are some groups for new parents." (Research what is available in your community and provide program brochures, or make a list of local programs with meetings times and contact information.)

Auditory Capacities

Welcome Baby Level 2

Materials:

- Teaching Teddy
- Teaching Photograph Figure 3B: Baby turning toward her father's voice

Baby:

In a quiet alert state.

Ask:

See Welcome Baby Level 1.

Infant Observation/Activity:

In a semi-darkened room, demonstrate the continuous high-pitched speech that gets the newborn's attention. Ask the parent to say something like, "Hello baby, Mommy (or Daddy) is over here, come over here, I am over here." Do this as an example, but do not actually attempt to engage the baby in searching for your voice at this point.

Ask permission to hold the baby. The baby *must be in a quiet alert state.*

With one hand supporting the baby's head and one hand supporting the baby's buttocks, hold the infant face up, parallel to the floor at your shoulder level. Be sure the baby is in a midline position (see Figure 3B). Midline position ensures the baby's head is in a neutral position.

Explain that babies have already heard their parents' voices in the womb and that babies will search out the voice of their parent.

To prepare the baby, ensure he has maintained a quiet alert state. Seat yourself opposite the parent. Hold the baby in a midline position out toward the parent until the baby is about 12 inches from the parent and is raised to be on the same plane as the parent's face.

Request that the parent call to the baby in the type of continuous high-pitched speech (motherese) that the educator demonstrated, reminding the parent to *continue* to call the baby over and over. The baby will likely brighten, shift his eyes to the direction of the parent's voice, begin to turn his head, and may even turn and locate the face and voice of the parent.

Sometimes the baby will turn and gaze intensely into the parent's eyes. This often creates an emotional response for the parent and the parent may reach out to hold the baby or give the baby a kiss. The parents may wish to hold the baby. Quietly narrate the baby's response, indicating all the ways in which the baby responded to the parent's voice.

Developmental Context:

See Welcome Baby Level 1.

Caregiving Implications:

See Welcome Baby Level 1.

Parent Care:

See Welcome Baby Level 1.

Welcome Baby Level 3

Materials:

- NBAS red rattle
- Teaching Photograph Figure 3B: Baby turning to her father's voice

Baby:

In a quiet alert state or drowsy state.

Infant Observation/Activity:

Ask permission to hold a baby and bring the baby to a quiet alert state. While holding the baby in midline, administer the NBAS inanimate auditory item, allowing for a successful trial on each side. This will help you assess the baby's potential responsiveness. Prepare as in Welcome Baby Level 2. In addition, explain that you, as the educator, will also call to the baby as a way to demonstrate the baby is more attuned to the parent's voice. If you choose to use this competition for the baby's attention, there are important procedures to note. Always explain and demonstrate to the parent how to call the baby and demonstrate the continuous high-pitched voice.

Kneel or sit near the parent's chair and place the baby between yourself and the parent. With one hand supporting the baby's head and the other hand supporting the baby's buttocks, hold the infant face up, parallel to the floor at shoulder level. Support the baby's head in such a way that the baby will have real freedom to turn. Check to be sure the baby is not rooting on his hands or the blanket and that the baby's head is in a midline position. If the baby is not in quiet alert state, bring the baby into a State 4 before beginning. If the baby is in an alert active, State 5, work with the baby to get him into a quiet alert state by wrapping him in a blanket to contain his movement. If the baby is drowsy (State 3 in the NBAS), note how successful he was with the rattle trial. If the baby is still observably responsive, proceed.

When the baby is in position, tell the parent, "Please call to your baby." Hesitate just a second or two to determine the pitch and volume the parent has chosen, and match it to call the baby. Some parents call their the baby in a very soft voice. If the educator's voice is noticeably louder, the baby may turn toward the educator simply because he didn't hear the parent's voice.

The baby's performance becomes the confirmation that babies can see and hear and put real effort into doing so if given the right conditions. This demonstration becomes the backdrop for talking about the importance of providing such interactive experiences for young babies.

Facilitation Tip:

I typically say, "Oh, come over this way and see me!" As the baby begins to turn toward the parent, I typically say, "Oh, you are listening to that special person!!" And as the baby looks at the parent, I say, "You've found Mom or Dad! Your baby knows your voice." If the baby doesn't turn and search for the parent's voice, note all the ways in which the baby does respond differently to the parent. I have discovered that even when the baby is in a drowsy state, a parent's voice is so potent that the baby will turn toward the parent and often move to a quiet alert state.

Developmental Context:

See Welcome Baby Level 1.

Caregiving Implications:

See Welcome Baby Level 1.

PATHWAY 4

The Crying Baby

> *The problem of infant crying is very real to every parent who presents with complaints of infant crying. Parents should not feel alone or helpless when handling infant crying. It is helpful to normalize but not minimize the situation.* (Evanoo, 2007, p. 333)

What You Will Learn in This Pathway:

- the possible reasons a baby cries
- effective ways to intervene with a crying baby
- ways to promote self-calming
- details about the Don't Shake campaign (preventing abuse of infants)
- information about the expansion of shaken baby syndrome (SBS) to include abusive head trauma (AHT)
- ways to alert parents to the unexpected stress they may experience when their baby engages in intense or prolonged crying episodes
- how to teach parents the Flex/Hold

Why This Pathway Is Important:

- Crying is a stressful situation for parents.
- Babies who are crying are signaling for help.
- When educated about the possible reasons their baby may be crying, parents can provide more thoughtful interventions.
- It is recommended that all new parents be educated about SBS, and educators need detailed and accurate information to share with parents.
- Parents need to be encouraged to practice self-care to reduce stress.
- Parents can be taught to both observe and help their baby learn self-calming skills.

Key Information

In the moments after being born, the baby's first cries serve important purposes. Crying initiates the process of opening the lungs and drawing air into them. It helps the baby begin the task of breathing on her own (Mays & Cohen, 2002; Shelov & Hannemann, 2004). For new parents, hearing the baby's first cry is often met with a sense of relief and assurance. The first cry signifies a sense of well-being in the transition from the womb to the world. After the baby has cried for the first time, crying takes on different meanings, depending on the baby's need and the context in which the baby is crying (Barr, 2012; McGlaughlin & Grayson, 2001).

Crying Is a Form of Communication

First and foremost, crying is a powerful way the baby communicates with her parents. Crying is very hard to ignore and usually brings an adult to the baby's side fairly quickly. Crying brings the parent closer to the baby for help or interaction. Crying is normal infant behavior and should not be seen as undesirable but rather typical and expected. In fact, crying promotes healthy social-emotional development and attachment (Brazelton & Sparrow, 2003). As a parent comes to baby's aid, the baby learns that the parent is a reliable caregiver. The parents in turn, learn what works to help comfort and calm the baby—thus developing competency in the role of parent.

Some parents have expressed the notion that a "good" baby is one who does not cry often. This can be deceiving. Some babies who don't cry very often, and don't signal hunger, can have slow weight gain. In severe cases, "good" babies develop failure-to-thrive (Baranowski, Schilmoeller, & Higgins, 1990). Babies who cry often signal to their parents that they need assistance, feeding, or interaction. Reframing crying as a way babies help parents learn what they need can help parents develop. Studies of infant crying behavior have found that both the amount of crying and the type of crying can vary considerably among newborns. In general, these studies have found that over the first 3 months of life there is a peak in crying around 6 to 8 weeks, with a subsequent significant decrease in crying at about 3 to 4 months (Barr et al., 2014; Runyan et al., 2009). There are a number of reasons why a baby cries, and understanding them helps parents determine the best course of action. Why does a baby cry? Here are some of the reasons.

Crying Due to Overstimulation

A very young baby is somewhat protected from overstimulation by having an immature nervous system. When overstimulated, one of the baby's protective responses may be to suddenly fall asleep. As discussed in Pathway 2—The Sleeping Baby, this shut-down sleeping is really habituation to adverse or overwhelming stimuli; it is not a restful type of sleep because the brain and body are working at the same level as if the baby was awake. A baby who has been habituating for a period of time may wake and immediately begin to cry, because the need to shut down has overlapped with feeding time. In other words there is a cost to having to habituate. This ability to shut down disappears by about 2 months old (Sammons, 1999). At around 2 months old a baby is much more aware of her surroundings and will begin to cry in response to being overstimulated. Parents will need to "put themselves in their baby's booties" and try to understand if there is too much visual stimulation, too much noise, too many people handling the baby, etc. (Hogg, 2001).

Babies are very individual in sensitivity and responsiveness. What fascinates and entertains one baby may cause another baby stress. Take a close look at the baby's waking environment. What is she seeing? Consider ways to shield the baby from overwhelming sights. What is she hearing? What might she smell? Some parents have found that their babies are overstimulated by strong smells in the kitchen. Be sure that the sleep environment is soothing and not stimulating. As the baby gets older, naps become even more important (Hogg, 2001; Leach, 1995). A well-rested baby has more endurance for dealing with daily stimulation. If the baby is able to self-soothe by suckling on her fingers or thumb, encourage it. That baby may also develop an attachment to a special toy or blanket that can be useful to help the baby reorganize and cope with stimulation. Holding the baby so that she has nearly full body contact with the parent and is swayed gently may also be helpful (Hill, 1999).

Crying Related to Feeding

The AAP (2012) advised parents that waiting until a baby is so hungry that she is crying to be fed is not in the best interest of establishing good eating patterns. (For more information about this, see Pathway 5—The Oral Baby). Instead, parents should learn their baby's early hunger cues and note the typical time interval between feedings, so that they feed the baby before the crying is from hunger. Brazelton and Sparrow (2003, p. 15) wrote, "A hungry newborn will cry in short, continuous bursts. This crying is insistent, medium in pitch." When a baby is hungry, she will suck with a series of forceful sucks and then settle into a pattern of suckling, pause, look around, and again suckle.

Crying that occurs during or after feeding may be due to a build-up of gas. Some babies may need to be burped a few times during a feeding (Shelov & Hannemann, 2004; Younger Meek & AAP, 2011), whereas others may not wish to be interrupted. A condition called *gastroesophageal reflux* plagues some infants. Reflux, as it is commonly referred to, is a result of a lax cardiac sphincter at the esophagus end of the stomach. A baby may regurgitate some of the feeding mixed with stomach fluids. Because babies have weak muscles, some of the milk, along with stomach acids, are brought up into the throat and esophagus and cause pain (Shelov & Hannemann, 2004). Many babies spit up a fair amount but do not suffer from reflux. They eat happily and spit up often, yet still gain weight and enjoy their feedings. If a baby is crying nearly all the time after feeding or not gaining weight, the pediatrician should be consulted. All babies benefit from being held in an upright position after feeding and avoiding excess movement; they may spit up less immediately after a feeding (Mays & Cohen, 2002).

Another tip to prevent crying related to feeding is to frequently burp the baby, because air buildup causes the baby discomfort; she will be unable to eat even though she may be hungry and wants to continue to suckle.

Crying Due to Physical Discomfort

Babies do not enjoy extremes in temperature and frequently cry when they are either too hot or too cold. A newborn's hands and feet will feel cool to the touch. Parents should be advised to feel the baby's chest or stomach area for a better sense of the baby's comfort level in terms of temperature. If a baby begins to develop a rash, it should be treated immediately in the manner the baby's doctor recommends. A baby's skin can burn very quickly; advise parents to avoid exposure to the sun, and check with the pediatrician before using any sunscreen product (some sunscreens can be used on infants, usually recommended only for babies over 6 months old). A baby's clothing should be soft and allow freedom of movement. Baby's garments should be washed in a mild detergent, rinsed well, without fabric softener, because additives can cause irritation to the baby's skin or trigger allergic reactions (Elbrit, 2000; Shelov & Hannemann, 2004).

Crying Due to Medical Situations

Parents calling the doctor's office or nurse line with a concern about their baby's health are always asked if the baby has a temperature, so parents must feel comfortable and competent when it comes to taking their baby's temperature. Other indicators of illness can be a change in the baby's color or having a distended stomach, or both. Any unusual behavior should be noted and described to the health care provider.

Ear infections, which many babies develop even at very young ages (Elbrit, 2000; Shelov & Hannemann, 2004), may cause a baby to cry—they are painful and will interrupt the baby's sleep and eating patterns. Poole and Magilner (2000) studied crying complaints that were seen in the emergency department of a major metropolitan hospital and found that of 56 children presenting with a complaint of unexplained excessive crying, 16 had some type of infectious disease and 9 suffered from some type of trauma. These traumas ranged from a scratch on the surface of the eye or a foreign object in the eye to fractures (often suspected to be caused by child abuse) and hair tourniquet syndrome. In *hair tourniquet syndrome*, a piece of hair (or string from clothing), becomes wrapped tightly around the baby's finger or toe, or penis, as in one case. Five infants had gastrointestinal problems such as constipation and gastrointestinal reflux. Three suffered from problems associated with the central nervous system such as encephalitis or subdural hematoma caused from child abuse. Two babies were suffering from drug overdoses, 2 had behavioral concerns (1 night terrors, the other had just been overstimulated), 2 others had cardiovascular concerns, and 1 had a metabolic concern. The remaining 10 infants in this study were diagnosed with idiopathic crying, meaning the child experienced a single, self-limited episode of crying for which the cause could not be determined. These infants had cried for 1 to 3 hours then suddenly stopped. They were observed briefly in the emergency room to be sure the crying did not indicate any other serious problem (Poole & Magilner, 2000).

Parents can investigate themselves to find the cause of their baby's crying: look the baby over carefully to determine if there is something wrong with, or in, her eye, or whether a string or hair has wrapped itself around her fingers or toes.

Crying Out of Frustration

Newborns rarely cry because they are frustrated. This changes at about 2 months old when babies becomes more interested in their environment and makes attempts (usually unsuccessful) to reach out and grasp things (Brazelton, 1992; Leach, 1997). Parents can offer their baby assistance by helping her explore the toy or by using toy links to position the toy to be within his reach. At 3 months, babies notice when parents leave them, and they may begin to protest. Placing the baby where she can see her parent can help lessen crying at this age. Whenever the baby is crying out of frustration, it is helpful to verbalize what the baby might be trying to communicate. Parents can also try to distract the baby, especially if the object she wants to explore is not really appropriate or safe.

Stress-Related Crying

Parents should be advised to avoid events or situations that may cause their baby to be startled or become fearful. Because babies have individual thresholds for stimulation, parents will need to observe their own baby's reactions and gain a sense of the baby's responses. Stress-related crying often occurs at the end of the day, when the baby becomes tired from processing and responding to many stimuli. Creating a calm atmosphere is key. Parents should learn to evaluate environments and situations that seem pleasing and calming to their baby (Brazelton, 1992; Sammons, 1999).

Crying for Attention and Out of a Desire to Interact

By about 4 months old, babies develop a keen interest in interacting with their parents or other familiar adults. They coo and gurgle to attract attention and get the adult to respond to them. When the baby doesn't get the desired attention, she may cry. This cry is quite distinct from a pain or hunger cry. Crying for attention stops as soon as interaction begins—in fact, the baby may immediately shift from the crying state to a broad smile. Because the young baby can't move herself toward the parent, her only options to get attention are to coo, "talk," or cry. Paying attention to the baby who is asking for it does not spoil the baby, but rather brings the baby interaction and, typically, a chance to practice reciprocal interchanges (Brazelton, 1992; Greenspan & Greenspan, 1985). Many parents report that a demanding baby can be stressful. During this period of the baby's development, parents can try putting the baby in a position where she can easily see the parent and talk to the baby while they are completing tasks. Varying what the baby has to look at can help as well; the baby may enjoy studying something new. Playing music for the baby may also entertain him in such a way that the parents can complete household tasks.

What Is Colic?

A baby who cries excessively, and whose crying does not lessen in response to any attempt to calm her, may have "colic." Typically, parents make repeated attempts to establish a diagnosis and find a cure. Crying from colic is very disruptive to families. It can strain relationships and elicit feelings of guilt and concerns about losing control (Long & Johnson, 2001). Although colic is a common concern of parents of young infants, no effective treatment has been identified, and the criteria for defining colic are vague (Evanoo, 2007). Parents often receive confusing and contradictory information, and there is little evidence-based practice upon which to rely. Colic may be described as "inconsolable crying," or crying that occurs 3 or more hours per day, three or more times per week. Other experts have defined colic as 3 hours of crying per day for 3 days in 1 week and appearing in "seemingly healthy infants less than four months of age" (Brazelton, 1992; Leach, 1997).

Due to the potentially devastating consequences, it is very important that educators be attentive and supportive to parents who have a baby who cries (or is perceived to cry) excessively. Persistent infant crying is one of the leading causes of child abuse and SBS or AHT (Barr, 2012) which can result in death or a lifelong disability (Altman et al., 2011). In an investigation, "Current Beliefs and Management Strategies for Treating Infant Colic," Lobo et al. (2004) found that the cause for colic continues to be debated, and that "with a lack of understanding of the cause of colic comes a lack of consensus on the definition and management strategies" (Lobo, 2004, p. 16). This study did find that the management of colic varied greatly and depended on what parents believed about its etiology. Because the baby's crying is so stressful to parents, and because prolonged excessive crying can put the baby at risk for nonaccidental injury, educators working with parents of colicky babies should be extra supportive and, when possible, take extra time with the parents to listen and problem solve (Evanoo, 2007).

SBS and AHT

A baby's excessive crying creates intense psychological stress, and prolonged inconsolable crying may trigger the adult to lose control. Parents and caregivers must be informed of the dangers of shaking a baby. The SBS campaign has been used for a number of years and is widely recognized. However, additional research has led to a deeper understanding of the broader range of pathologic methods that lead to injuries. Although it has been proven that shaking an infant can cause serious injury (Nakagawa & Conway, 2004), researchers have also found that blunt impact (striking, throwing, or dropping an infant) can also result in serious or terminal injuries.

The term *abusive head trauma* (AHT) includes all mechanisms of injury, including shaking (Barr, 2012; Christian & Block, 2009). AHT and SBS are both classified as nonaccidental injuries to infants resulting from impact to the head by either shaking or an impact to the head or both. Head trauma is the leading cause of death from child abuse in the United States. The first 6 to 8 weeks of life, when the infant cries the most, correlates to the timing of occurrences of SBS and AHT (Barr, 2012). The AAP recommends that AHT be used for legal and medical purposes, to avoid implying knowledge of injury mechanisms that cannot be demonstrated. SBS is thus a subset of AHT, which is in the category of physical abuse of infants and young children. The AAP continues to endorse using the terms "Shaken Baby" as they note the SBS campaign is widely recognized by the public.

Because babies have very weak neck muscles and a heavy head, even a second or two of violent shaking or striking head can cause serious injury or even death. Symptoms of SBS/AHT do not always include signs of external trauma. Internal symptoms that indicate AHT include intracranial bleeding, cerebral edema, and retinal hemorrhage. Because the anatomy of infants puts them at particular risk for injury from this kind of action, the majority of victims are infants younger than 1 year old. However, AHT can occur in children up to 5 years old—so all young children are at risk for this type of injury.

What to Look For

Although falls from beds or changing tables are common, studies indicate that falls from a height of less than 4 feet rarely cause serious injury to babies. If an injured child who is said to have fallen exhibits symptoms such as respiratory problems or cardiac arrest, professionals should also look for signs that the child has been violently shaken. Shaking alone can cause traumatic brain injury and is considered to be child abuse (Christian & Block, 2009). Infants who have suffered SBS/AHT may also sustain posterior rib fractures due to being forcefully grabbed. Parents or caregivers may claim that CPR (cardiopulmonary resuscitation) must have caused the rib fractures (Nakagawa & Conway, 2004), but studies (e.g., Hinds, Shalaby-Rana, Jackson, & Khademian, 2015) have found that critically ill children who receive CPR do not usually sustain rib fractures, and also that CPR does not result in posterior rib fractures (Hinds et al., 2015).

Infants who survive SBS/AHT may be left profoundly neurologically impaired and have cortical blindness, seizures, hydrocephalus, or learning disabilities, or a combination. Moreover, because the injuries associated with SBS/AHT include swelling in the brain and/or intracranial bleeding, the prognosis for a full recovery is poor. There is often a delay in seeking treatment following the injury, which further jeopardizes recovery (Altimier, 2008, Nakagawa & Conway, 2004).

If you suspect an infant has been a victim of SBS/AHT, seek medical help immediately. Following are some possible indicators of SBS/AHT:

- lethargy
- irritability
- vomiting
- poor sucking or swallowing
- decreased appetite
- lack of smiling or vocalizing

- rigidity
- seizures
- difficulty breathing
- blue color due to lack of oxygen
- altered consciousness
- unequal pupil sizes
- inability to lift the head
- inability to focus the eyes or track movement

Who Is at Risk for Becoming a Perpetrator?

Anyone can be at risk for causing injury to a young baby in her care. Sleep deprivation, coupled with an infant who cannot be soothed, put both the caregiver and infant at high risk. In studies of SBS perpetrators, factors included high stress, isolation, and low income. In the cases of infants who suffer SBS in the first 6 to 8 weeks of life, mothers had returned to work and the infants were left with fathers or male caretakers who had little prior opportunity to learn how to care for a baby. In fact, biological fathers, stepfathers, and mother's boyfriends make up the majority of perpetrators in several studies (Hinds et al., 2015). However, it is essential that all caregivers be educated about SBS (Altimier, 2008).

Preventing SBS/AHT

Remind parents that caring for a baby along with trying to balance other obligations in life can be overwhelming. When the feeling of being overwhelmed begins to increase, they need to know it is a sign of strength to ask for help or to arrange to have time away from the baby. A key message for parents and caregivers is that the safest place for an inconsolable infant is in the crib, not in the parent's or caregiver's arms (Barr, 2012; Nakagawa & Conway, 2004). Tips for parents who feel like they may harm (shake) the baby include: offering the baby something to eat or suck on, going out for a walk with the baby, placing the baby in a safe place such as her crib and stepping into another room for a period of time and letting the baby cry, calling a friend or relative for assistance, or taking the baby to a local crisis nursery, if such a resource is available (Altimier, 2008). Crying in and of itself does not physically harm the baby.

The Period of PURPLE Crying

The National Center on Shaken Baby Syndrome has created intervention booklets and videos designed to encourage the widest distribution possible to health care facilities and the general public. The center seeks to educate parents about the "period of PURPLE crying." PURPLE is an acronym for the six properties of normal crying that are typical in the first few months of life:

- **P** for crying peak

- **U** for the unexpected timing of prolonged crying bouts
- **R** for resistance to soothing
- **P** for a pain-like face even when they are not in pain
- **L** for long crying bout
- **E** for evening clustering of crying

The Period of PURPLE Crying program (purplecrying.info) teaches new parents about crying and provides strategies to deal with a crying baby. On the website, educators will find program materials that include an 11-page booklet and a 12-minute video designed to educate parents. Emphasize to parents that this information should be shared with all of the baby's caregivers, especially information about the dangers of becoming overwhelmed and injuring the baby and strategies of comforting/calming—and the recommendation to simply walk away. The Period of PURPLE Crying program encourages parents and all caregivers to use these three strategies:

1. Increase their contact, carry, walk, and talk responses that will help reduce crying, although they may not stop it altogether.
2. If the crying becomes too frustrating, they should be assured that is it acceptable and advisable to walk away, put their baby in a crib for a few minutes, and calm themselves.
3. Never shake or hurt their baby.

Parent educators should become familiar with these materials so they can promote and use them, as well as teach prevention strategies to all parents of newborns.

Community Resources

Educators should be sure to have the phone number of their local crisis nursery or other agency that can respond by giving the parent time away from the baby. Consider giving out this type of information on a routine basis to all new parents. In Minneapolis, MN, the Crisis Nursery offers respite care on an immediate basis for parents who indicate they feel like they may harm their child, and the staff provides follow-up services and parent counseling.

The parent–infant activity found in Pathway 4—The Crying Baby is designed to generate a discussion with parents about infant crying and inform them about the serious injuries that can occur when a baby is shaken. Within this Pathway are directions for teaching the Flex/Hold (Pearson, 1999), a particularly effective way to help calm a newborn. A key message included in this Pathway is to advise parents to practice self-care so they can handle the acute stress of parenting an inconsolable baby (Sears & Sears, 1996).

Recommended Reading:

Altman, R. L., Canter, J., Patrick, P. A., Daley, N., Butt, N. K., & Brand, D. A. (2011). Parent education by maternity nurses and prevention of abusive head trauma. *Pediatrics, 128*(5), e1164–e1172. http://doi.org/10.1542/peds.2010-3260

Barr, R. G. (2012). Preventing abusive head trauma resulting from a failure of normal interaction between infants and their caregivers. *Proceedings of the National Academy of Sciences, 109*(Suppl. 2), 17294–17301. http://doi.org/10.1073/pnas.1121267109

Educator Tools:

It is recommended educators visit and explore these websites.

- The Period of PURPLE Crying—New Ways to Understand Your Baby's Crying
  www.purplecrying.info
- The National Center on Shaken Baby Syndrome
  www.dontshake.org
  Training modules for providers, outreach materials, and training modules.
- The Centers for Disease Control—Injury Prevention and Control: Traumatic Brain Injury
  www.cdc.gov/violenceprevention/childmaltreatment/abusive-head-trauma.html

  The section on SBS has research-based information, media guides for journalists writing about SBS/AHT and downloadable public service announcements.

Parent Education Activity

Welcome Baby Level 1

Purpose:

To frame crying as a powerful way an infant communicates that can also cause stress in adults

Instructional Content/Strategies:

- Discuss reasons why babies cry.
- Demonstrate techniques that can be used to calm a crying baby.
- Warn parents about the stress they may experience when their baby cries and is not consolable.
- Provide anticipatory guidance about the developmental course of crying.
- Describe the harm a baby can suffer when shaken or handled roughly
- Educate parents about the three strategies of the PURPLE program.

Materials:

- Teaching Teddy
- Teaching Photographs:
  Figure 4A: Baby crying intensely
  Figure 4B: Baby positioned in the Flex/Hold—held facing outward, flexed forward, hands to mouth and legs flexed.

Ask:

"What is your baby's crying like?"

Some parents will have experienced a crying episode in which they couldn't effectively soothe the baby or they weren't sure why the baby was crying (or both), leading to tension and stress. Parents sharing their experiences can be a springboard for the educator to affirm what the parents have already learned, to add additional information or insight, and at times, to correct misinformation.

Infant Observation/Activity A (when a baby begins to cry during class):

The educator should immediately focus on the crying baby and her parent, because the session cannot be effective in the presence of an unhappy, crying baby. You can use this as a teachable moment. The educator might say, "A baby's cry is meant to let adults know they need something. Let's see what [name of baby] might need." By stopping and attending to the baby and parent, the educator demonstrates flexibility in changing the class agenda to meet the needs of the baby. Her response models the responsiveness and adaptability that sensitive parenting requires, and she can highlight this by saying, for example, "Many times parents find it necessary to be flexible and change their plans because the baby needs something. The baby's cry right now gives us a chance to practice being flexible."

The educator should observe what the parent is doing to calm the baby and encourage her to pick the baby up if she hasn't done so. Mothers who have just given birth may be in extreme physical discomfort, especially those who delivered by Caesarean section or had an episiotomy. They may not be able to easily stand in order to get their baby out of the bassinet. Assist them by asking "Would you like me to get the baby for you?" If prepared, the educator may also ask, "May I try to calm your baby as part of a teachable moment for the class?"

If the parent grants the educator permission to get the baby for her, the educator should model the following sequence, adapted from the NBAS (Brazelton & Nugent, 1995). This sequence gives the baby a chance to practice self-regulation and to calm down just by seeing a face or listening to a voice rather than being picked up and rocked.

1. Talk to the baby in a soft, steady voice, saying, "If you hear my voice, will it help you calm down?" Repeat this several times. In other words, the content of what you say to the baby will be narrating the intent of the interventions.

2. Place a hand on the baby's stomach and say, "Do you feel my hand on your tummy? Will this help you calm down?"
3. If the baby's arms are flailing, inhibit the baby's flailing hands and continue speaking, saying, for example, "Sometimes newborns feel out of control. In the womb, the baby moved, but movements were always eased by contact with the womb wall." Continue saying to the parents and baby, "I am using my hands to help you find a boundary—like you had in the womb."
4. Pick the baby up and continue talking to her while placing her in the parent's arms. "Babies usually begin to calm down when they are picked up. Let's see if this is helpful." Narrate what occurs. This allows the baby a chance to calm to a less intensive action such as being picked up, and may allow the baby to find her hands and fingers to self-soothe. More information about this is found Pathway 6—The Dexterous Baby.
5. If placing the baby in the parent's arms doesn't help and the baby continues crying, suggest other interventions to try, such as talking to the baby, standing up and rocking the baby, or trying to burp the baby. If the baby seems to be hungry, inquire if the parent is comfortable feeding the baby in class or if she would rather return to her room to feed the baby.

There is a delicate balance between allowing the parent to do what she senses intuitively and using the parent's actions to illustrate teaching points. If the educator senses the parent is getting stressed, or the baby isn't calming down through the interventions the parent is trying, the educator may ask if she might try to settle the baby. If the parent gives the educator permission, the educator can proceed with putting the baby in the position called the Flex/Hold.

The Flex/Hold technique (see photos below and on the next page) is so effective that it should be taught to every parent. It can be effectively taught using the Teaching Teddy.

1. **To begin, place the baby on her back** on a blanket on the low table and remove anything that is covering the baby's hand, like mittens, which are often part of newborn T-shirt sleeves.
2. **Use one hand to secure baby's hands,** positioning them so they are resting near the baby's mouth.
3. **Slide the other hand under the baby's back and gently roll the baby over into a prone position.** The baby's weight and gravity should keep the baby's hands in contact with the baby's mouth.

Photo Flex/Hold 2

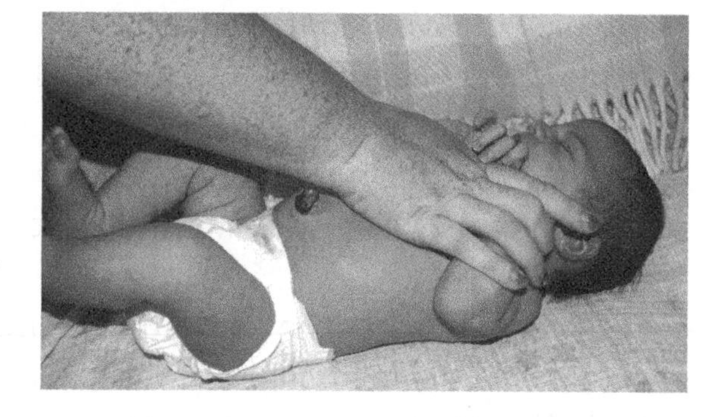

4. **Bring the baby upright with the baby's back to the educator's chest,** letting the baby naturally flex over the hand that is containing the arms and maintaining the baby's hand-to-mouth position.
5. **Use the other hand to press the baby's legs into a flexed position.**

Photo Flex/Hold 3

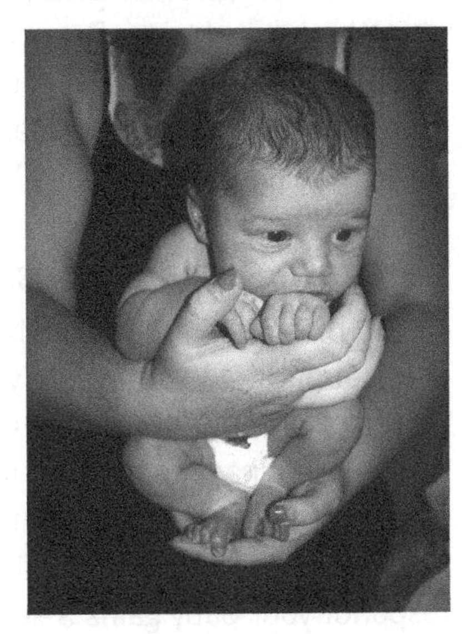

The educator should describe each step to the parents. A baby in the Flex/Hold position will usually calm down quite quickly and will sometimes begin suckling very loudly on his fist. If the baby continues to fuss or cry, the educator should add gentle vertical movement by doing knee bends. Always check to ensure the baby's hands are maintained in the hand-to-mouth position. If the baby continues to cry despite all these interventions, determine with the parent if the baby might be hungry and needs to be fed. If this is the case, determine with the parents whether they are comfortable feeding the baby in class or would like to return to their room.

Because this is such an unusual position, it might cause some parents to be concerned. The educator should explain that this position mimics the baby's flexed position in the womb and that no head support is needed when the baby is flexed forward. See Teaching Photograph Figure 4B, Baby positioned in the Flex/Hold. Never use this position with a baby who was born prematurely or who is ill—even if the baby is older and appears strong. Prematurely born babies (and babies with other conditions) often have less muscle strength or tone and could flex their neck forward, interfering with their breathing.

Infant Observation/Activity B (when there is no crying baby in class):

Using the Teaching Teddy positioned on its back on the table, ask the parents to imagine that this is a very upset crying baby, and proceed as described in the preceding section. Use *Pathways* Teaching Photographs Figure 4A and 4B. Be sure to demonstrate each step of the Flex/Hold, using the Teaching Teddy. Follow the above protocol for the Flex/Hold.

Developmental Context:

"Your baby's cry is a powerful form of communication. It is the baby's best way of signaling a need for help. It focuses your attention on the baby in an immediate way, alerting you that she is hungry, cold, wet, needs to burp, is tired, overstimulated, and so on. The baby helps you know when your attention and assistance are necessary.

"As upsetting as it can be for you to deal with your crying baby, it is helpful that the baby can let you know when she needs something. Babies who have a weak cry or who rarely cry can present another challenge. These infants don't call for help and may not get enough to eat or let their parents know they need their diaper changed.

"Responding to your baby's cries of distress teaches the baby you will provide security, warmth and nurturing. Responding to your newborn's cries will not spoil her; rather it teaches her to trust you as a caregiver and to trust her own ability to ask for and receive help. Babies need attention and help from their parents in order to develop emotionally, physically, and intellectually."

Caregiving Implications:

"By responding to your baby's cries, you are letting her know you understand she is upset and that you will do your best to help her. This repeated helpful assistance builds your baby's sense of trust and helps foster a positive relationship between you. Researchers have found that infants who had this type of responsive care in early infancy cried less and were more confident in their interactions with others. Far from spoiling your baby, responsive care strengthens the relationship between you and your baby. When you respond, your baby gains a sense of security, comfort, nurturing, and warmth.

"As you respond to your baby's cries over the next several weeks, you may note the baby has different types of cries. Listen to the crying for these differences. For example, a cry of pain is usually shrill and sharp. The baby will also have distinct cries that are associated with hunger or being tired. As you come to know your baby's cries and crying patterns, you will find it easier to know how to respond best. In the first weeks, most parents find their baby's crying very distressing—some even describe crying along with their baby.

"If you have tried a number of strategies, such as burping, feeding, changing, rocking, or holding your baby, and she continues to cry, she might be overstimulated, and your best efforts to help might only be contributing to further overstimulation. You might try putting the baby in the crib or bassinet or other safe place and letting him cry for a while to release tension. It will not physically harm a baby to cry on her own for a while when other efforts haven't helped. Parents are sometimes surprised to see that, once put down, that their baby cries loudly for several minutes and then falls asleep."

Anticipatory Guidance:

"While you are still in the hospital, your baby may mostly sleep, cry only a bit, awaken to be fed, and then return to sleep. Once you are at home, your baby's crying will likely increase. This increased crying is normal, because your baby is becoming hungrier and more alert and is dealing with discomforts such as gas and fatigue. When babies are tired, hungry, lonely, uncomfortable, or overstimulated, they cry. There are many reasons why a baby may cry, and it may not always be apparent to you why the baby is crying. By responding to your baby's crying, you will learn more about why she is crying.

"As your baby becomes more alert at a few weeks old, she may begin to fuss and cry for extended periods in the late afternoon and early evening. This is because as your baby takes interest in the world and is more alert, she may become overstimulated. The world is just so interesting she takes in as much as she can and then suddenly realizes she is overwhelmed. Fussing and crying signal a need for a change of pace.

"If you find your baby's pattern of fussiness is consistently occurring in the late afternoon and early evening, try planning ahead for this difficult time of day. For example, try feeding the baby before she becomes too tired and too hungry. If your baby enjoys a bath, give a bath before the typical time she begins to cry. If your baby responds well to music and rocking, set up a routine of soothing music and rocking before your baby's fussy time. You may want to try taking a class on infant massage to learn how to use massage to relax your baby. There are many options, and you will need to learn which works best for you and your baby."

Parent Care:

"When your own nervous system is overloaded, or when you get tense and perhaps even feel angry with the baby, just put the baby down and let her cry. Stepping away from your crying baby for a few minutes, perhaps doing some deep breathing, deciding if you might need something to eat or drink—taking care of your own needs—are ways to cope with this situation. Many parents of young babies find they have skipped meals or haven't had a chance to get enough fluids and are actually dehydrated. Breastfeeding mothers, especially, should eat nutritious snacks throughout the day, in addition to balanced meals. If you are feeling very tired, lie down and take a nap. If necessary, ask someone to watch the baby for a short time.

"Never take out your frustration or anger by hitting, yelling at, or shaking the baby. Shaking a baby *even for a few seconds* can cause permanent brain damage or death. Grabbing the baby roughly can cause internal injuries and broken bones. Be sure to inform anyone who takes care of your baby how dangerous it is to shake a baby.

"If your baby's crying is very difficult for you to deal with, ask a friend or a family member for help or hire someone who can take over for a while and give you a break. Plan outings. Being home all day with a young baby can be a very isolating experience. Going out for a short walk can be extremely helpful and give you renewed energy to cope. Try to partner with your spouse or a relative or friend so that the baby's care is shared. Don't neglect your relationship with your spouse or partner."

Welcome Baby Level 2

See Welcome Baby Level 1.

Welcome Baby Level 3

Materials:

- Teaching Teddy
- Teaching Photographs Figures 4A and 4B: The Crying Baby

Baby:

In a full state of crying. (If there is no baby crying, give a verbal description of a crying baby based on what the parents have said about their baby's crying.)

Ask:

See Welcome Baby Level 1.

Infant Observation/Activity:

See Welcome Baby Level 1, Part A.

Facilitation Tip:

Add commentary on the individuality of consoling, the ways the baby might self-quiet, and the rationale for graded intervention with crying.

PATHWAY 5

The Oral Baby

> *Sucking is probably your infant's most common behavior, but within that behavior he has many variations. Beyond sucking on the nipple, you will see him suck on his hand, his arm, his toes, his lips, and just about any other object available.* (Sammons, 1999, p. 117)

What You Will Learn in This Pathway:

- the relationship between suckling and self-soothing
- why breastfeeding should be encouraged and supported
- understanding and identifying cues of hunger
- how to elicit the rooting reflex for good feeding positioning, whether breastfeeding or bottle-feeding
- identifying the suckling and swallowing pattern
- bottle-feeding tips
- pacifier use and problems associated with pacifiers

Why This Pathway Is Important:

- Breastfeeding can be challenging, and many new mothers do not receive the information, support, or encouragement they need to continue.
- Knowledge of proper positioning in feeding will contribute to the success of the feeding.
- With an understanding of the ways in which an infant uses suckling, parents can determine whether their baby is hungry or is self-soothing.

Key Information

Feeding Skills Begin to Develop Before Birth

In the womb before birth, babies engage in suckling on their fists and fingers, and occasionally a thumb or even a toe! Through sonographic studies, researchers have learned that the fetus shows swallowing movements around 11 weeks gestation; by 15 weeks gestation, the fetus shows suckling movements. These movements increase with intensity throughout the pregnancy. Amniotic fluid contains important proteins for growth, and swallowing helps the fetus to regulate the volume of fluid it ingests (Levy et al., 2005). By 20 weeks gestation, the fetus is skilled at suckling on its fingers and thumbs and practices the coordinated movements that will be needed for feeding (Levy et al., 2005). In the womb, suckling is not due to hunger; it is how the fetus occupies itself. Suckling has been noted to correlate with the fetus becoming calm. Similarly, the newborn uses the hand-to-mouth and fist- or finger-suckling strategy to help him cope with new stimuli (Brazelton & Nugent, 1995; deVries et al., 1985).

The Association Between Suckling and Self-Soothing

Many parents wonder about the meaning of suckling, or whether allowing suckling on the fist and fingers could be the start of a bad habit. "He is sucking on his hand. I just fed him! How can he still be hungry?" "Does this mean he is going to be a thumb-sucker?" Suckling on his fist or fingers might be a sign he is hungry, but a baby needs and desires opportunities for nonnutritive suckling as well. Nonnutritional suckling is important. It provides extra practice for suckling and usually helps the baby become or stay calm (Brazelton & Nugent, 1995; Sammons, 1999). For the breastfeeding baby, nonnutritive suckling at the breast increases the mother's milk supply (Kitzinger, 1998; Younger, 2002).

Encourage parents to observe their infant's hand-to-mouth activity and to help their baby find his fists and fingers. The fetus, in a flexed position, has easy access to his hands and fingers, and they are never far from its face or mouth. The newborn, without the boundaries of the womb, has more difficulty bringing his hands and fingers to his mouth. Parents can promote their newborn's self-soothing by replicating the womb environment and swaddling the baby with hands up and out of the blanket, or by placing the baby in position to easily find his hand and fingers.

With hands out of the swaddling blanket, the baby's fingernails may scratch his face on the way to his mouth, so parents can file the nails to help avoid scratches. Working with the baby's nails when the baby is in deep sleep will make it easier; when alert, the infant moves when he feels stimulation to his hands or fingers. Clipping the nails of a newborn is difficult, and not advised, because the nail is not well defined and usually still attached firmly to the nail bed, making it easy to accidentally clip the skin. Washing the baby's hands a few times per day will help prevent the transfer of germs from the hands to the mouth—especially important if other adults or children have been touching the baby's hands.

Nonnutritive self-soothing by suckling gives the baby a sense of mastery and helps him comfort and calm himself (Brazelton & Nugent, 1995; Sammons, 1999). Babies who can self-soothe reward their parents by suckling their fist or fingers and putting themselves back to sleep when they rouse in the night. Parents get more rest, and the baby learns to self-regulate.

Rooting and Suckling to Meet Nutritional Needs

Babies are born with the skills needed to breastfeed. When skin-to-skin, many can find the breast and self-attach without assistance. *Skin-to-skin* contact takes place right after birth: The naked baby is placed on the mother's bare chest for an uninterrupted period of time. During this time, babies exhibit the behaviors and skills that lead to their first breastfeeding (Phillips, 2013).

Suckling and Swallowing

Once colostrum from the breast or formula comes into the baby's mouth, the baby displays the familiar pattern of suckling and swallowing practiced before birth. However, the newborn now has to coordinate breathing with suckling and swallowing (Colson, Meek, & Hawdon, 2008). The baby usually does *not* follow a continuous pattern of suckling and swallowing, but rather suckles, suckles, suckles, and then pauses. During this pause the baby is taking a breath. After the breath, the baby resumes suckling again, with more suckles and pauses following. This is the baby's first task, to learn to coordinate suckling, swallowing, and breathing to be successful in taking in nourishment, either from the breast or bottle (Huggins, 1990; Kitzinger, 1998). Feeding requires a complex synchrony of the tongue, larynx, and laryngeal muscles (Woolridge, 1986). Parents should be taught to expect the pauses and not remove the source of food because they take the baby's pausing a sign that he is finished feeding.

Positive Feeding Sessions Nourish More Than the Body

Feeding a baby contributes to the infant's physical growth, and the feeding experience also contributes to a baby's psychological development. Feeding times provide important opportunities for the newborn and his parents to be close to one another. Feeding nourishes the baby with more than food; it provides comfort as well as physical and social stimulation. A baby's olfactory and taste senses are quite developed at birth and the baby comes to recognize the particular scent of his mother's milk within days of birth (Lipchock, Reed, & Mennella, 2011). In the *Guide to Understanding Your Child*, the Yale Child Study Center (Mays & Cohen, 2002) recommended that during feedings, a baby's nutritional intake should include pleasant sights and sounds.

An infant experiences feelings and stores memories even before he develops words. If feeding time is pleasant and provides comfort and caring, a child will associate all the cues with feeding (and the person feeding him) as a positive experience (Barnard et al., 1993; Shelov & Hannemann, 2004). Parents should be encouraged to make feeding times pleasurable, to hold their baby close and engage in eye contact, if the baby is alert and can manage to look and eat at the same time. The frequent feedings that take place in early infancy provide multiple opportunities for the parent and infant to interact and, through these interactions, develop a positive relationship (Barnard et al., 1993). Babies who are fed in this positive manner begin to trust their environment and find enjoyment in eating (Kitzinger, 1998).

How a Baby Lets You Know He Is Hungry

The *New Mother's Guide to Breastfeeding* (Younger Meek & AAP, 2011) recommended that parents learn to read their infant's cues of hunger and begin a feeding before a baby is crying for food. Crying is a very late cue for hunger. Once a baby has reached the level of distress in which he cries, he may latch onto the bottle or breast and gulp, rather than pace the flow of milk into his mouth, and begin to choke.

An infant's early cues for hunger include:

- increased movement of the arms and legs (active alert; fussing)
- looking around
- rooting and suckling behaviors, such as bringing a hand or fingers to the mouth and trying to suckle

Parents should be encouraged to note the particular signals their baby uses to communicate hunger. In the first weeks of life, infants will need to be fed anywhere from 8–12 times per day (Martin, 2000; Shelov & Hannemann, 2004; Younger Meek & AAP, 2011). Parents may need to awaken newborns for feedings if they do not actively seek to eat after 3½–4 hours. Pathway 2—The Sleeping Baby includes information regarding when and how to try to waken a sleeping baby. A healthy baby will typically awaken for feeding regularly as his body senses hunger. A baby may need to be awakened for feedings if he has an infection or is taking medications that make him extra sleepy. To waken a very sleepy baby for a feeding, advise parents to:

- Change the baby's diaper.
- Talk to the baby while positioning him in a semi-upright position.
- Bathe the baby.
- Undress the baby down to his diaper.
- While holding the baby on your shoulder, massage his back using circular motions.
- Sit the baby up on your lap while supporting his chest and neck.

The Rooting Reflex and Feeding Positioning

Whether a parent chooses to breastfeed or bottle-feed, knowing how to best position the infant for feeding can make the feeding experience more successful. First, parents should learn how to stimulate the baby's rooting reflex, which is particularly observable when a baby is hungry: When the cheeks or lips of a hungry newborn are stroked or touched, the infant will turn in that direction, opening his mouth in search of food. This reflex serves to orient the baby's mouth toward the breast or bottle. The rooting reflex can be stimulated from all four quadrants of the baby's mouth (Brazelton & Nugent, 1995; Prechtl, 1977); if the stimulation is from the side, the baby will turn his head toward that side and then latch onto the breast or bottle.

Problem With Rooting to the Side

Try turning your own face to one side and then try to swallow. You will notice that it is difficult. Now turn your head so you are looking straight ahead to swallow. It is so much easier. This is what the newborn experiences when the rooting reflex is stimulated on a side of his mouth—he will turn and then latch on. With the first swallow, he discovers that latching this way is difficult, and may let go of the nipple and try to latch again. However, repeated latching attempts can damage the nipple of a breastfeeding mother and result in acute pain. To avoid this situation, the caregiver should stimulate this reflex from the center of the baby's bottom lip—this will make the baby open his mouth without turning his head. He can then latch onto the nipple and begin to both suck and swallow smoothly (Huggins, 1990; Martin, 2000, Younger Meek & AAP, 2011).

Lactation consultants often advise feeding in the tummy-to-tummy position. Observe a baby breastfeeding tummy to tummy with his mother, and you will note his mouth is positioned straight onto the breast and not turned to the side. This important piece of information can make a significant difference in a mother's ability to get her baby to feed optimally, and thus to feel more successful (Colson et al., 2008).

Benefits of Breastfeeding

"The American Academy of Pediatrics reaffirms its recommendation of exclusive breastfeeding for about 6 months, followed by continued breastfeeding as complementary foods are introduced, with continuation of breastfeeding for 1 year or longer as mutually desired by mother and infant" (AAP, 2012, p. e827). The AAP policy statement asserted that breastfeeding and human milk are the normative standards for infant care and, given the documented short- and long-term benefits of breastfeeding, it should be considered a public health issue, not just a lifestyle choice. The AAP (2012) reported the following findings regarding the health benefits of breastfeeding:

- An infant exclusively breastfed for 4 or more months has a 72% lower risk of being hospitalized for a respiratory tract infection.
- In a meta-analysis of data on breastfeeding and SIDS, breastfeeding was associated with a 36% reduced risk of SIDS.
- For infants who are breastfed exclusively for 3 to 4 months, the incidence of clinical asthma, atopic dermatitis, and eczema were reduced by 27% in infants at low risk for these conditions and by as much as 42% for infants with a family history of these conditions.
- Premature infants who were fed exclusively a human milk diet had a 77% reduction in developing necrotizing enterocolitis than babies who were fed cow's-milk-based formula. Necrotizing enterocolitis causes babies to develop a tear in their intestines, allowing bacteria in, which then causes a widespread infection. This is considered to be a medical emergency.

- Breastfeeding appears to have long-term benefits for the individual as a protective factor in becoming obese. In individuals who were breastfed, research indicates there is a 15% to 30% reduction in adolescent and adult obesity rates.

Breastfeeding also has benefits for the mother, including:

- Decreased postpartum blood loss and a more rapid involution of the uterus.
- Continued breastfeeding leads to increased child spacing secondary to lactational amenorrhea (AAP, 2012).
- For mothers who exclusively breastfed there was a lower likelihood of getting pregnant again—thus there was increased spacing between the births of children.
- Lower rates of PPD when compared with mothers who did not breastfeed, or who weaned their baby early.

Many Economic Benefits!

Breastfeeding has benefits for the broader community, including decreased loss of parental employment time due to children not getting sick as often, decreased environmental burden due to reduced disposal of formula cans and bottles, and decreased energy costs for transporting artificial feeding products (AAP, 2012; Bartick & Reinhold, 2010).

Promoting Breastfeeding as a Cultural Norm

A brief review of the history of breastfeeding in the United States reveals that in the early 1900s nearly all babies were breastfed, with more than half the babies breastfeeding up to 1 year. When glass bottles and rubber nipples became more available, breastfeeding decreased. World War II took many women away from home and put them in the workplace, where they were unable to breastfeed. By 1966, only 18% of babies were being breastfed when discharged from the hospital, and even fewer were breastfed for any length of time. In the 1970s there was a push for more natural childbirth practices, and breastfeeding rates rose. By 2000, the rate had increased to about 68%. Still, a steep decline in breastfeeding occurs by 6 months; only 31% of babies 6 months old or older are still being breastfed (Younger Meek & AAP, 2011). Challenges to breastfeeding include returning to work, lack of support and education about breastfeeding, and a lack of knowledgeable professionals to assist new mothers during the critical first weeks of initiating breastfeeding. Healthy People 2020 (U.S. Department of Health and Human Services, 2012) aims to increase the proportions of infants who:

- ever breastfed to 81.9%,
- are still breastfeeding at 6 months to 60.6%,
- are still breastfeeding at 1 year to 34.1%,
- are breastfed exclusively through 3 months to 46.2%, and
- are breastfed exclusively through 6 months to 25.5%.

In 2013, the Centers for Disease Control and Prevention "Breastfeeding Report Card" noted that 77% of all infants began breastfeeding. There is continuing concern that infants are not breastfed for as long as recommended, but progress has been made in the past 10 years. For example, of infants born in 2010, 49% were breastfeeding at 6 months, up from 35% in 2000. The breastfeeding rate at 12 months increased from 16% to 27% during that same time period (Centers for Disease Control and Prevention, 2013). Professionals working with parents in the prenatal period have an excellent opportunity to educate parents about the many benefits of breastfeeding and to give parents "food for thought," as pregnant parents make choices about feeding their babies.

The oral suction a baby has right after birth is especially strong. Parents who are planning to breastfeed should be informed about this, so as to take advantage of the suckling instinct. When a baby is put to a breast as soon as possible, the instinctive strong suckling helps trigger the production of milk.

Mothers who are breastfeeding should be made aware of breastfeeding support groups, such as La Leche League, and trained lactation consultants who can provide one-to-one assistance and appropriate information. The National Women's Health Information Center (www.womenshealth.gov/breastfeeding) has developed a national helpline (with the tagline "Best for Baby; Best for Mom") to offer parents information and support in their communities.

Breastfed Babies and Bottles

As the newborn gets more practice with feeding, he learns more about the feel and shape of the nipple and the amount of strength needed to extract the milk. Many experts advise against the use of pacifiers (see next page) or introducing bottle-feedings in the first weeks of establishing breastfeeding patterns, so that the baby learns to be an effective breast-feeder (Gartner & Eidelman, 2005; Victoria, 1997). When expressed breast milk is used for a feeding, bottles that are harder to get milk from are preferred because they make the baby work to feed in a similar manner to feeding from the breast. Because taking milk from a bottle is a new experience for the breastfed baby, parents should be informed that it may take some time and effort. However, the AAP (2012) cautioned:

> *Breastfed infants self-regulate intake volume irrespective of maneuvers that increase available milk volume, and the early programming of self-regulation, in turn, affects adult weight gain. This concept is further supported by the observations that infants who are fed by bottle, formula, or expressed breast milk will have increased bottle emptying, poorer self-regulation, and excessive weight gain late infancy (older than 6 months) compared with infants who only nurse from the breast.* (AAP, 2012, p. 830)

Bottle-Feeding

Babies who are bottle-fed should enjoy a similar close positioning to their parents while feeding. Never prop up a bottle or leave a baby alone with a bottle; this is a choking hazard. Putting a baby to bed with a bottle in his mouth promotes tooth decay—even before the baby has teeth erupting (Mayes, Cohen, Schowalter, & Granger, 2003; Shelov & Hannemann, 2004). Parents who bottle-feed should be advised to alternate the hand used to hold the bottle; this helps stimulate the baby's brain in the same way alternating orientation in breastfeeding does. Alternating sides when the baby is bottle-feeding can also give the baby practice in being oriented in both directions and decrease the likelihood of the baby developing torticollis, a condition which the baby is "stuck" looking in one direction because of positioning over time that results in the muscles in the neck becoming shortened on one side (the side the baby looks toward) and elongated on the other side.

To bottle-feed, parents should seat themselves in a comfortable chair. The baby can be pulled in snugly, cradled in the parent's arm, resting in the crook of the parent's elbow. The baby should be in a semi-upright position, which makes it much easier to swallow. Touch the bottle nipple to the baby's lower lip. A hungry baby will open his mouth in search of food, and the bottle nipple can be inserted. Be sure the baby is getting milk and not air. This can be accomplished by holding the bottle at about a 45-degree angle (Elbrit, 2000; Mayes et al., 2003).

If the baby swallows air, it can cause discomfort and disruption to the feeding session. If the nipple flattens, pull the nipple out of the baby's mouth slightly and milk will flow back into the nipple. It is important to hold the bottle steady, so that the baby can apply suction to the nipple. If the bottle is held too loosely, the nipple will slide out of the baby's mouth. Holding the baby during feedings provides rich interaction and stimulation for the baby's development beyond simply nourishing his body.

Benefits to and Cautions of Using a Pacifier

In Pathway 2—The Sleeping Baby, you learned that pacifiers appear to be beneficial in lessening the risk of SIDS. Because of this finding, the AAP has endorsed the use of a pacifier on a limited basis, with the following guidelines (Hauk et al., 2005):

- Pacifier use for breastfed babies should be delayed for the first month, or until the baby's breastfeeding is established.
- The pacifier should not be used as a substitute for feeding.
- The pacifier should be used when placing the infant down to sleep (day or night). The pacifier should not be reinserted once the child falls asleep.
- Pacifier use should not be forced if the baby refuses it.
- Pacifiers should not be coated with any sweet solution.
- Pacifiers should be cleaned and replaced regularly.
- Pacifier use should be discontinued at 1 year, when the risk of SIDS declines but the risk of otitis media (ear infection) increases.

The Effect of Pacifier Use on Breastfeeding

Parents should know that pacifier use is detrimental to the continuation of breastfeeding. The waning and cessation of breastfeeding may occur soon after beginning pacifier use. Many lactation educators and breastfeeding consultants either recommend that parents avoid introducing pacifiers for a specified period of time, or recommend avoid pacifiers altogether. Avoidance of pacifiers has been shown to be important to the successful establishment of breastfeeding (Cinar, 2004; Gartner & Eidelman, 2005; Howard et al., 2003).

Pacifiers and Otitis Media (Ear Infection)

In an article that appeared in *Pediatric Nursing*, Garrelts and Melnyk (2001) examined the relationship between pacifier usage and acute otitis media (ear infection) in infants and young children. Health care providers are concerned about otitis media (and parents should be informed about it) because it affects about 70% of children under 3 years old and is one of the primary reasons that children receive antibiotics. Untreated otitis media can lead to hearing loss, middle-ear disorders, and delays in speech development (Jackson & Mournio, 1999; Niemela, 2000), but child overuse of antibiotics has led to increasing antibiotic resistance. This poses a real danger to a child who needs an antibiotic for a serious or life-threatening illness (Niemela, 2000).

The biological mechanism that links pacifier usage and otitis media is the increased activity between the eustachian tube and nasopharynx in babies that use pacifiers (Hanafin & Griffiths, 2002). Suckling on a pacifier lifts the soft palate in the mouth, causing the tensor veli palatine muscle to contract. The eustachian tube thus becomes actively patent (open), providing a pathway through which bacteria and viruses from the nasopharynx reach the middle ear (Jackson & Mournio, 1999). Suckling on a pacifier also increases the production of saliva in the mouth, providing a favorable medium for microorganisms to grow. Thumb suckling does not produce the same mechanisms, nor is it related to an increased incidence of acute otitis media (Neimela, 2000).

Alternative Ways to Provide Supplemental Feedings

Supplemental feedings by bottle are often given to primarily breastfed infants (Howard et al., 2003). Because the mechanisms involved in breastfeeding differ from bottle-feeding, concerns have been raised about giving a breastfed baby a bottle during the newborn period. At the same time, breastfed infants (or newborns just beginning breastfeeding) may need some type of supplemental feeding. If a breastfeeding mother is unable to produce enough milk or a baby's medical condition impedes breastfeeding, babies can be fed human donor milk. Mothers who have an abundant supply of milk donate to milk banks, where the milk is tested and made available to babies who need it. Donor milk is more commonly used for infants born prematurely, but it can be used with full-term infants.

Cup-feeding, used when a baby needs supplementation but there is a desire to avoid artificial nipples, involves using a very small cup to provide the infant with sips of breast milk or formula. However, there is little basis for concern about "nipple confusion," the notion that because the sucking mechanisms between breastfeeding and bottle-feeding are different, a baby exposed to both may become confused. The mechanisms between breastfeeding and bottle-feeding do differ significantly, but there is no evidence to bear out the idea that babies get confused. Some babies who are exposed to both breastfeeding and bottle-feeding find that bottle-feeding requires much less effort and tend to prefer it over breastfeeding.

A randomized trial (Howard et al., 2003) found that supplemental feedings, regardless of the method (cup or bottle) had detrimental effects on breastfeeding duration. For infants delivered by Cesarean section, cup-feeding significantly prolonged exclusive, full, and overall breastfeeding duration. Exclusive breastfeeding at 4 weeks was far less likely among infants exposed to pacifiers. These researchers (Howard et al., 2003) also found that there were different outcomes when the pacifier was used early versus later; early use shortened the overall duration of breastfeeding (Gartner & Eidelman, 2005; Victoria, 1997). The researchers concluded that cup-feeding with infants who may need multiple supplemental feedings was useful. Pacifier use in the neonatal period was detrimental to breastfeeding overall.

Problems Associated With Pacifiers

For the prematurely born baby, pacifier use can be a necessary intervention to stimulate their suckling reflex and strengthen the muscles involved in suckling (Linden et al., 2013). Parents of full-term babies, however, often use pacifiers to calm their infants rather than to provide an extra nonnutritive suckling experience. Degan and Puppin (2004) studied the prevalence of nutritive and nonnutritive feeding habits and linked the habits to a variety of outcomes. They found that the more a child was breastfed, the less the pacifier was used. They pointed out that pacifier use alters occlusal development (depending on the intensity, frequency, and duration of the habit), and prolonged suckling can also cause an open bite. The most effective and commonly used method of eliminating pacifier use was abrupt interruption. The authors raised the concern that "every time a child is irritated, if the pacifier is offered as a form of amusement and a panacea, the child develops a strong attachment to the sucking object" (p. 148).

There are many opportunities to observe both rooting and suckling behaviors in the very young infant. These observations set the stage for engaging in conversation with parents about nonnutritive suckling needs, the possible undesirable outcomes from introducing a pacifier (other than when given just as the child is laid down to sleep), ways to help the baby with self-soothing, and for reminding parents that their own nutritional needs are important as well.

Recommended Reading:

American Academy of Pediatrics. (2012). Policy statement: Breastfeeding and the use of human milk. *Pediatrics, 129*(3), e827–e841. doi:10.1542/peds.2011-3552

Educator Tools:

- **The National Woman's Health Information Center**
  (www.womenshealth.gov/breastfeeding)
  Explore this website to find a fact sheet on breastfeeding and many topics that arise in breastfeeding such as challenges, finding support, special circumstances, pumping and storage of breast milk and returning to work, and continuing to breastfeed.
- **La Leche League International**
  Phone Number: 800-525-3243 • www.llli.org
  The Mission of La Leche League is to provide support, encouragement, information, and education that promote a better understanding of breastfeeding. The website provides information to find groups and their locations, podcasts, a mother-to-mother forum, and information about breastfeeding laws. The site is international and has information in many languages.
- **The Australian Breastfeeding Association Videos**
  This website provides helpful videos for parents who are visual learners.
  https://www.breastfeeding.asn.au/bf-info/videos

Parent Education Activities

Welcome Baby Level 1

Purpose:

To help parents understand the infant's need for nonnutritive suckling (self-comforting) and to learn how to capitalize on the newborn's rooting and suckling behaviors in feeding.

Instructional Content/Strategies:

- Observe and discuss baby's need for nonnutritive suckling.
- Demonstrate optimal positioning for feeding.
- Alert parents to the possible negative effects of pacifier use and discuss alternatives.

Materials:

- Teaching Teddy with his "hands" inside the mittens that are extensions of the sleeves of a newborn t-shirt often used in the hospital, or use newborn mittens
- Blanket for swaddling Teaching Teddy
- Teaching Photographs:
  Figure 5A: Baby breastfeeding, positioned well
  Figure 5B: Baby suckling on her hands and fingers

Ask:

"How does your baby let you know he is getting hungry?"

Listen to and affirm what the parents have noticed, and add cues that are not mentioned:

- an increased movement of the arms and legs (active alert—fussing)
- the baby is looking around
- rooting and suckling behaviors, such as bringing his hand or fingers to his mouth and trying to suckle them

Remind parents that crying is a late cue—a baby may not be able to feed well if he is crying from being hungry; and that in the first weeks of life, infants will need to be fed anywhere from 8–12 times per day.

"Did see your baby suckling on his fingers or thumb in an ultrasound?"

"After birth, have you noticed your baby suckling on his fist or fingers, or attempting to? Did you allow the baby to suckle? Were you wondering if you should?"

Typically parents will notice the baby trying to suckle on hands and fingers. Some parents may observe the baby sucking his thumb right after birth. Many parents may already be concerned about thumb-sucking, as they believe it will become a "bad habit" if they allow the baby to do it. They may deliberately cover the baby's hands with mittens to prevent the baby having any access to them.

Infant Observation/Activity:

Teaching Photographs:
Figure 5A: Baby breastfeeding, positioned well
Figure 5B: Baby suckling on her hands and fingers

Rooting:

Stroke the cheek of the Teaching Teddy and describe how a hungry baby would respond by turning his head in that direction and opening his mouth in search of something to suckle. Turn the teaching teddy's head to the side that was stroked. Explain to the parents that the rooting reflex can be triggered by stroking the corners of the baby's mouth, the middle, or either the top or bottom lip. Stroking any of these areas will cause the baby to turn in the direction of the stimulation.

Turn your own face to one side or the other and ask the parents to also turn their face to one side—then ask them to try to swallow. Note that although it is possible to swallow, it is very difficult. If the baby latches on to breast or bottle by rooting and turning in such a manner that his head is turned to the side, the baby will likely let go of the nipple when he has to swallow.

Ask the parents to look straight ahead and swallow. Note how much easier it is. The same is true for the baby. If he latches on and keeps his head centered with his body, it is much easier to coordinate sucking and swallowing. This is true whether bottle or breastfeeding. Use Teaching Photograph Figure 5A to point out how this baby is in a good breastfeeding position.

With the Teaching Teddy, demonstrate stimulating the mid-section of the lower lip, which also stimulates the rooting reflex without causing the baby to turn his head or neck. A hungry baby will open his mouth while maintaining his head in the midline position. When the baby is hungry and the rooting reflex is elicited in this way, the baby opens his mouth, providing an opportunity to have the baby latch on in the correct position. Explain that this can be an excellent way to elicit the baby's rooting response and help him open his mouth for feeding.

Encourage the parents (especially the fathers) to experience the strength of a baby's suckling by inserting a finger into their baby's mouth (pad side of the adult's finger toward the roof of the baby's mouth) and allowing the baby to suckle. Fathers are typically impressed by the strength of the baby's suckling.

"Eliciting the rooting reflex by stimulating the middle of the bottom lip is a helpful way to encourage the baby to open his mouth for feeding without turning to the side."

Suckling for Comfort:

Observe to see if the baby engages in suckling on his fist, fingers, or thumb. Point this out as an example of the way the baby comforts and calms himself. Show and discuss Teaching Photograph Figure 5A. Observe the baby's attempts to bring his hands to his mouth, which may be unsuccessful due to misguided attempts or inaccessibility of the hands.

Begin with the Teaching Teddy on his back with his T-shirt mittens covering his hands. Point out that after birth a baby no longer has the womb wall keeping his arms flexed and his hands near her face. Model with the Teaching Teddy how the uterus wall did this before birth by flexing the Teaching Teddy and positioning its arms near its face.

Explain that, in addition to the loss of positioning of the hands near the face, newborns are often dressed in T-shirts that cover their hands. Demonstrate with the Teaching Teddy that even if the baby managed to bring his fist to his mouth, he would find a barrier of cloth. Explain that a baby can chafe his face by frantically trying to find his fist and rubbing against the cloth.

Expose the Teaching Teddy's "hand" by rolling back the T-shirt and cradling the Teaching Teddy, guiding the Teddy's "hand" to its "mouth." Show and discuss *Pathways* Teaching Photograph Figure 5B. Describe how a baby might respond by suckling vigorously and calming down, or might simply enjoy suckling and maintaining his hand-to-mouth position.

Wrap (swaddle) the Teaching Teddy so that his arms are flexed and his hands are positioned near his face. This allows the baby access to his hands and self-comfort. The educator will demonstrate how wrapping the baby in this manner can help a baby maintain his hand-to-mouth position. Make sure to note to parents that swaddling should not be too tight, because it can interfere with the baby's breathing and even cause hip dysplasia. The swaddling should be removed when the baby is laid down to sleep, because it often loosens and becomes a safety hazard (Oden et al., 2012).

Discuss the recommended use of pacifiers to prevent SIDS. Review the guidelines and emphasize the delay of the pacifier for breastfed babies.

Developmental Context:

"Before birth, your baby held his hands near his face and suckled on his fist or thumb. (You might have seen your baby suckling on an ultrasound.) This suckling was not due to the baby being hungry. In the womb, your baby was nourished by the placenta and had a tummy full of amniotic fluid and didn't experience hunger. Babies suckle to comfort and calm themselves.

"Sometimes the suckling will indicate your baby is hungry, sometimes not. Your baby may often use suckling to calm himself. Suckling is soothing to your baby. When your baby can calm himself by suckling on his fingers it is termed self-comforting.

"Pacifiers can be useful for giving a baby an opportunity to suckle. However, the particular way in which a baby suckles on a pacifier is quite different from the type of suckling a baby needs to breastfeed. The American Academy of Pediatrics recommends limited use of the pacifier for helping prevent Sudden Infant Death Syndrome. If you are breastfeeding you should delay use of the pacifier until your breastfeeding is established.

"A newborn must learn how to adjust the suckling he did before birth to meet a new challenge—using the suckling reflex to get food. Some newborns who are given pacifiers have difficulty using the suckle pattern needed to feed at the breast. A baby can also become tired by suckling on the pacifier and have less energy to put into breastfeeding. One additional item to note: pacifiers have also been linked to increased ear infections."

Caregiving Implications:

"A baby whose hands are wrapped into the blanket when swaddled or whose T-shirt has mittens is unable to use suckling on his hands for a self-comforting measure. If his arms are flexed and wrapped firmly (as in the demonstration), your baby is not likely to scratch his face and will have an opportunity to use his fist and fingers for suckling, just as he did before birth. Sometimes a baby just likes to have a hand resting on his face.

"It is important to support your newborn baby's efforts to self-calm. Suckling is comforting to babies. Fingernails can be filed for now and clipped later, when the nail bed is more separated from the finger. The baby's fist and fingers have already been the baby's best 'pacifier' and are always there when the baby needs them.

"The way a baby suckles on a pacifier is very different from the manner in which a baby must suckle on the breast for feeding. A commercially made pacifier will give a baby an opportunity to suckle, however, when it falls out of his mouth, the baby cannot retrieve it and cannot self-regulate through suckling on his fist or finger. In suckling on a pacifier a baby only needs a suckling motion, whereas in breastfeeding the baby must learn to suckle and compress the nipple. Studies have found that early use of the pacifier can interfere with breastfeeding, for example, when a baby learns to suckle on a pacifier or bottle successfully but then cannot adjust the suckle pattern to be successful at the breast. Other studies have shown that babies can obtain food more easily from the bottle and then refuse the breast primarily because it is harder work. A hungry infant who is given a pacifier may show less interest in breastfeeding. A baby may suckle long and hard on the pacifier and not have enough energy for the suckling work involved in breastfeeding.

"Some research links the use of pacifiers to a 40% increase in ear infections, as well as to tooth decay and thrush. Parents may want to have a pacifier to use when their baby needs additional soothing, but parents should use it only occasionally, for brief periods, and not as the only way to calm their baby.

"Suckling does not always indicate the baby is hungry—but it is an often an early cue of becoming hungry. So look for other signs that the baby is getting hungry, such as his arms and legs becoming active, and looking around. He may just want to suckle as a way to calm down and relax. A baby who is positioned in such a way to be able to suckle on his fists or fingers is more likely to self-comfort.

Parent Care:

"Do not wait to seek help if you find breastfeeding painful or challenging. Contact a breastfeeding consultant immediately. When breastfeeding, initially you may experience discomfort in your breasts, especially the nipples. While some of this can be typical, extreme pain at any time or pain during the entire feeding often indicates a problem.

"Sometimes the baby needs to be positioned differently on the breast to relieve pressure, or the baby needs to modify his suckling pattern. There are devices that can help you ease the discomfort and become successful at breastfeeding. Mothers who experience discomfort at each feeding begin to become anxious about feedings or even dread the idea of having to feed the baby again. This can cause the mother to discontinue breastfeeding. Seeking help from a lactation consultant may help the mother over the initial discomfort and identify any special help that is needed.

"Often, as a new mother, you are so busy feeding the baby you forget your own need for nutrition. In order to keep up with your baby, take time to eat well. Stock up on foods you enjoy and can be easily prepared or need no preparation at all. Fathers or partners can help to nourish mothers by preparing meals."

Welcome Baby Level 2 and Welcome Baby Level 3 use the same protocols.

Materials:

- Teaching Photographs
  Figure 5A: Baby breastfeeding, positioned well
  Figure 5B: Baby suckling on her hands and fingers

Baby:

In a fussing or crying state.

Ask:

See Welcome Baby Level 1.

Infant Observation/Activity:

Suckling for Comfort:

Observe the baby. If he tries or is suckling his fist, fingers, or thumb, point this out as an example of the way a baby comforts and calms himself. If there is a baby who has begun to fuss or cry, ask permission to calm the baby by helping the baby maintain a hand-to-mouth position (see Figure 5B). If the baby has T-shirt mittens on, ask permission to slide them up so that the baby will have access to his hands.

Wrap (swaddle) the baby in such a manner that the baby can more easily maintain the hand-to-mouth position on his own.

Rooting:

Observe whether the baby is showing signs of hunger. He may try to suckle his fists, fingers, or thumb and may also be rooting. Point this out. Ask permission to demonstrate the rooting reflex with the baby. While cradling the baby in your arm, with a gloved finger stroke the right or left side of the baby's face, starting near the corner of the mouth and stroking in the direction of the cheek. If the baby is hungry, this simple stroke will elicit the rooting reflex. Point out that the baby is using this reflex to search for food.

First ask the parents to turn their heads to one side and try to swallow, while demonstrating yourself. The parents will find it is very hard to swallow. Now ask the parents to look straight ahead and swallow and note how much easier it is. The same is true for the baby. If he latches on, and keeps his head in alignment with his body, it is much easier to coordinate suckling and swallowing. This is true whether bottle or breastfeeding.

The educator should then demonstrate stimulating of the mid-section of the lower lip, which also stimulates the rooting reflex. It is an ideal way to get the baby to open his mouth without turning his head. When the baby is hungry and the rooting reflex is elicited, the baby opens his mouth (again without turning his head). Explain how this can be an excellent way to elicit the baby's rooting response and coax him to open his mouth for feeding. In addition, using this correct alignment information makes any position that is comfortable for the parent a success for the baby.

Encourage the partner to experience the strength of a baby's suckling by inserting a finger into the baby's mouth (pad side of the adult's finger toward the roof of the baby's mouth) and allowing the baby to suckle.

Developmental Context:

See Welcome Baby Level 1.

Caregiving Implications:

See Welcome Baby Level 1.

Parent Care:

See Welcome Baby Level 1.

PATHWAY 6

The Dexterous Baby

> *All the changes in man's environment are brought about by his hands. Really, it might seem as if the whole business of intelligences is to guide their work.* (Montessori, 1964, p. 151)

What You Will Learn in This Pathway:

- how grasping and holding facilitates the process of attachment
- the important ways a baby uses her hands—to soothe herself and explore
- the developmental progression from grasping, to swiping to reaching, holding, and manipulating objects

Why This Pathway Is Important:

- Observations can be used to educate parents about their infant's fine motor skills.
- Perceived problems with the baby "pinching" can be reframed as a reflex.
- Educate parents about the importance of self-soothing and non-nutritive suckling.
- Provide parents with ideas for simple toys that help increase fine motor skills.

Key Information

Once a baby learns to reach, grasp, and hold objects, she becomes much more independent and able to explore the world around her. She can choose the toys with which she wishes to play and manipulate them. The ability to manipulate objects with the hands and fingers is called *fine motor development* (Liddle & Yorke, 2004). There are many important steps involved in the development of a child's fine motor skills. Parents can be very effective in giving their child experiences and activities that enhance fine motor development.

Fetal Tactile Sensation and Grasping

Touch is one of the first senses to develop in the fetus; touch in the fingertips is evidenced from 7–8 weeks gestation. With the sense of touch and the ability to coordinate arm movements and hands, the fetus appears to stroke its own body, the uterine wall, and its umbilical cord. Ultrasound has revealed that fetuses also grasp their umbilical cords (deVries et al., 1985; Vergara & Bigsby, 2004).

The grasp reflex develops before birth and is evident in the fetus between 14–16 weeks gestation (Piontelli, 2015). The grasp ability of a tiny baby often evokes emotion and feelings of connection as parents of premature babies have reported (Linden et al., 2013). This is an example of what it meant for photographer Michael Clancy to witness the grasp reflex in a fetus: In 1999 photographer Michael Clancy was asked to photograph a surgery in which the fetus was being operated on while still in the womb at 21 weeks gestation. To the amazement of the photographer, once the surgeon made an incision in the uterine wall, the fetus's hand protruded and appeared to grasp the surgeon's finger. *USA Today* editors titled the photograph "The Hand of Hope" and the photograph can be viewed at www.michaelclancy.com. The photo first appeared on September 7, 1999, in *USA Today*. This is what the photographer wrote about how he captured this photo: "Out of the corner of my eye I saw the uterus shake, but no one's hands were near it. It was shaking from within. Suddenly an entire arm thrust out of the opening, then pulled back until just a little hand was showing. The doctor reached over and lifted the hand which reacted and squeezed the doctor's finger. As if testing for strength, the doctor shook the tiny fist. Samuel held firm and I took the picture." (National Right to Life News, October 2003)

The Start of Dexterity of the Hands

Grasping is the beginning of being able to hold and manipulate objects. The grasping a baby does helps her to explore the tactile features of her world, and this grasp becomes more voluntarily and purposeful. Yet, when a baby is born, she has very little control over her arms and hands. Her arms wave randomly and her hands are typically in a fisted position. However, a healthy newborn has a viselike grip. This grasping is an involuntary reflex (Prechtl, 1977). The newborn's little fingers close tightly around anything that comes in contact with the palm of her hand, and the movements involved in the newborn's grasp help to build up the muscles in her hands. The baby is unable to let go of objects caught in her grasp.

What Grasping May Mean to Parents

- "My baby is stronger than I thought!"
  In the hours after birth, many parents discover their newborn's viselike grip and are surprised the baby is so strong. This grasp is in fact so strong that a baby can be lifted using this grip.
- "My baby wants to connect with me."
  Many parents also find it endearing that the baby will grasp their finger. It is a tangible, visible way they experience their baby reaching out to them and holding on to them. For parents of prematurely born infants, the ability of their infant to grasp their finger is a powerful connection (Barsuhn, 2008).
- "My baby is annoyed."
  In an effort to "help" during feedings—especially breastfeeding—the newborn will often attempt to grasp the mother's nipple or insert her fingers into her mouth,

thus disrupting the mother's attempts to get the baby to latch on. The baby's fingers or hand comes between the nipple and the baby's mouth, and some parents perceive this as the baby being difficult. Some mothers have expressed that they believe their baby is "pinching" them, and may interpret this as the start of naughty behavior.

Working With Grasping

In the beginning, the newborn will tightly grasp anything that comes in contact with her palm and will be unable to release it. Mothers sometimes find their newborn grasps their hair, and they have to work to help the baby uncurl her fingers to release the hair. Grasping on to something may help the baby may feel calmer and be less fussy. So, when the newborn is fussing, try offering her a finger to grasp. When breastfeeding, have another adult with a finger out for the baby to grasp until the baby is successfully latched onto the breast. As the mother becomes more competent with breastfeeding, she may find she can offer her own finger while maintaining a good feeding position.

Self-Soothing

In a home visit session using the *Pathways* curriculum, an educator observed a 4-week-old baby wearing mittens. The father described the reason the baby had mittens on: that she had scratched herself and pulled her own hair. The home visitor shared information about the grasp of a young baby—that a newborn doesn't have the ability to let go. She also shared that a baby tries to get her fingers to her mouth in order to calm herself down or indicate she is getting hungry. The educator offered the parents more information without downplaying their concerns. She effectively used both the *Pathways* Teaching Photographs and the Teaching Teddy. During the visit the baby tried several more times to get her hands to her mouth but was unsuccessful due to the mittens. The educator demonstrated the foot grasp. This demonstration intrigued the parents. The mother then decided to remove the baby's mittens and both parents began experimenting with the grasp reflexes of their baby. The baby brought her hands to her mouth and inserted two fingers and began happily suckling away, becoming very calm and focused. The parents remarked she was able to calm herself.

A baby's fine motor skills develop gradually. In the first 3 months, the grasp reflex, which causes the baby to curl the fingers and clench any and all objects that are placed in the hand, is dominant. But by the end of the first year, the baby can choose the most suitable method to grasp an object and will be able to manipulate the object to explore it and play with it. It is important to note that awake prone time ("tummy time") contributes to helping the baby open the hands. When the young infant is on her tummy, she pushes her hands down on the floor in order to lift herself up. The pressure of pushing helps open the hand and contributes to developing strength in the baby's fingers.

Developmental Trajectory

The intentional grasping done by a baby between 2 and 4 months old is quite different than the newborn grasping. In intentional grasping, the baby deliberately grips objects placed in her hands. At first, this way of grasping is quite primitive. The baby opens her hand wide and then closes it, with the object being held by the part of the palm farthest from the thumb (Bly, 1994). Fingers and thumb act as if they were all the same. The baby has little ability to manipulate or explore the object grasped in this way; and babies at this stage have yet to develop the ability to release an object they have grasped.

By about 5 months old, the baby begins to use her thumb in partial opposition, to help hold things in her hands (Liddle & Yorke, 2004; Mays & Cohen, 2002). This allows the baby to hold things much more securely and begin to pass items from one hand to the other. At around 6 months, the baby will use her hands not only to grasp objects but also to explore them. She will feel the texture of toys, sense their weight and size, and learn that banging things creates sounds. As use of the baby's hands is refined, she will learn to use a pincer grasp when attempting to pick up small objects. The *pincer grasp* is a uniquely human skill, using one finger in opposition to the thumb. This gives the infant much improved precision (Bly, 1994). It has been found that around the time a child develops a pincer grasp there is also a time of increased intellectual milestones (Liddle & Yorke, 2004; Ramey & Ramey, 1999). The baby no longer passively looks at things but initiates contact by reaching out and grasping them. Babies who are developing their pincer grasp will attempt to pick up any and all small objects and bring them to their mouth to explore. This is a time parents must be vigilant and ensure small objects are cleared away or inaccessible to the baby. By 9 months old, the baby will be able to pass a small toy back and forth between the hands. Toys that encourage simple problem solving, such as a container to drop smaller toys into, will intrigue the baby. Primitive reflexes are typically present in childhood and are integrated (suppressed) as more complex development occurs (Schott & Rossor, 2003).

Swiping

From the moment of birth, the healthy full-term baby makes swiping motions with her arms. These may or may not be directed at anything at all at first. In the first weeks, as a baby gains more visual information, the baby's swiping motions begin to demonstrate rudimentary eye–hand coordination (Alexander, Boehme, & Cupps, 1993). When swiping, the baby uses mainly her shoulder and elbow to try to make bodily contact with something she sees. Parents can be advised that lowering a mobile so that the baby has a chance to make contact with it when she swipes will encourage the baby to try again and again, thus gaining more experience and practice. When the baby makes contact with the mobile or toy and a movement or sound occurs, the baby learns about the positive consequences of this behavior; she can make things happen! This type of positive reinforcement results in the baby becoming even more attentive to and curious about the world around her. A baby practicing swiping is improving motor control and learning about the consequences of actions (Liddle & Yorke, 2004).

Learning to Reach to Build Eye–Hand Coordination

Reaching is a much more controlled form of swiping that begins when the baby is between 2 and 3 months old. For about the first 2 months of life, babies engage in swiping at desired objects. The experience they gain from swiping helps them learn which arm movements give them success and which do not. When a baby is successful, she repeats the successful movement over and over, eventually becoming more accurate at reaching for objects she has learned are within his reach (Alexander et al., 1993).

How the baby is positioned determines the limitations of her reaching. For example, a baby who is sitting with support will generally use a two-handed reach. A baby who is without support will usually use a one-arm reach in order to use the opposite arm for support and balance. By 5 months, babies have fairly good eye–hand–arm coordination. They are able to accurately reach for things, giving them a good measure of control over their play. Babies reach out and grab toys and objects that interest them. They look back and forth between the toy and the hand as they learn to plan and coordinate their movements. To help a baby develop this skill, parents can offer the toy in such a way that the baby must reach out to grab it (Liddle & Yorke, 2004). Parents can alternate the hand to which they offer the baby the toy. In a study of 275 infants followed from 6 to 14 months (Babik, Campbell, & Michel, 2014), infants showed hand preferences between 6 and 11 months of age but decreased the preference in the following months. It was theorized that because infants are learning to crawl, sit, stand, and walk during this period, each postural change and positional development causes them to explore new ways of using their hands. Thus, handedness continues to develop throughout the first year of life.

Important and Useful

The newborn uses her hands to serve an important function in the first weeks and months of life: self-soothing. Babies suckle on their hands and fists as a way to regulate themselves. (See Pathway 5—The Oral Baby for more information about self-soothing.) By 2 months, the infant's hands change from being stuck in fists to being more relaxed and open. Once the hands can open and close more voluntarily, the baby begins to use them to explore the environment and make things happen (Bly, 1994). Babies need a variety of objects to touch and hold to continue to develop their hands and explore the world around them. Parents can encourage fine motor development by allowing their child to grasp and experience a variety of items providing different sizes and textures. As the infant becomes increasingly adept at picking up small objects, parents must be careful to remove or be wary of small objects that could be harmful if the child swallowed them.

Almost all parents notice the strong grip with which their babies are born. It is endearing to parents when their newborn grasps the parents finger tightly. This readily observable newborn reflex becomes the backdrop for this Pathway, The Dexterous Baby.

Recommended Reading:

Liddle, A. & Yorke, L. (2004). *Why motor skills matter.* New York, NY: Contemporary Books.

Educator Tools:

Explore the Pathways.org website. The site provides motor milestone schedules and also notes red flags in motor milestone development.

Parent Educator Activities

Welcome Baby Level 1

Purpose:

To educate parents about how their newborn's reflexes will become more purposeful and voluntary and how young babies both soothe and explore their world through their hands.

Instructional Content/Strategies:

- Identify the newborn's grasp reflex in both hands and feet.
- Provide anticipatory guidance about acquisition of fine motor skills.
- Give parents suggestions on how to enhance the development of their infant's fine motor skills.

Materials:

- Teaching Teddy
- Two or three small, lightweight rattles (suitable for a newborn to grasp and an older infant to safely explore orally), or simple toys that promote fine motor development (such as plastic toy rings that can be hooked together), for the baby to explore or to hang toys in an infant gym. Other simple toys, such as an O Ball, can be displayed.
- Teaching Photographs:
  Figure 6A: Baby grasping an adult's finger
  Figure 6B: Baby grasping with toes

Baby:

In a drowsy, quiet alert, or active alert state.

Ask:

"Have you noticed how your baby can grasp? Have you noticed your baby grasping at the nipple or clutching the blanket?"

Typically, mothers who are breastfeeding will report frustration at the baby putting his hands in between the breast and the nipple. Many parents are surprised at the strength of the baby's grasp. Some parents have interpreted this grasping reflex to be intentional pinching on the part of the baby.

Infant Observation/Activity:

Using the Teaching Teddy, press your finger into the Teddy's palm and describe how a baby would then grasp the finger. Show the photograph of the hand grasp (Figure 6A). Encourage parents to do this with their baby.

Then press a finger on the ball of the Teddy's foot, describing how the toes will grasp your finger. Show the photograph of the toe grasp (Figure 6B).

Invite the parents to try this with their babies during class. To elicit the toe grasp, be sure the baby's leg is flexed (see Figure 6B). It can sometimes take a few seconds of gentle pressure to elicit the toe grasp, although sometimes the baby's toes grasp immediately.

Additional Infant Observation/Activity:

Show parents a set of small, developmentally appropriate, lightweight rattles and a set of hard plastic toy rings. Explain that when babies are allowed to explore the toy rings and rattles by mouthing them and manipulating them they learn to reach, coordinate their hands and eyes, and discriminate various textures. Allow parents to explore the toys.

Developmental Context:

"Babies are born with reflexes that help them survive. The strong grasp the baby has literally helps her 'hold' on to the parent. Babies participate in holding their parents by curling into their mom or dad's body or literally grasping with their hands. Note how whenever a finger is put into the baby's palm, the baby wraps her finger around it. This grasping reflex was present even before your baby was born. During surgery on a fetal baby at 21 weeks gestation, the fetal baby's arm reached out of the incision in the womb and when the doctor placed his finger in the fetus's palm, the fetus's hand grasped it. You may have noticed your baby grasping her umbilical cord in an ultrasound.

"In the beginning, the reflex is so strong the baby is able to hang on to whatever is grasped. This includes the mom's nipple during breastfeeding or perhaps the parent's hair when being help upright. When a baby is holding on to your finger, the hair on dad's chest or his blanket, it may also make her feel secure and calmer. Babies also like to bring their hands to their mouth and suck on their fingers. This is similar to the way a baby self-soothed in the womb. Allowing your baby to put her fingers in her mouth and suck encourages self-soothing, which builds her capacity to self-regulate. File her nails so she won't scratch her face.

"As your baby develops, this grasping reflex is replaced by the ability to voluntarily reach for and grasp toys. One of the normal developmental stages is when your baby's hand is always open (at about 2 months) and it seems that the baby cannot grasp as strongly as she was as a newborn. Parents sometimes wonder about this seeming loss of strength; but really, your baby is losing the reflex grasp in order to develop the ability to grasp at will, called voluntary control. At about 3 months, the baby will both grasp and let go of a small rattle put in her hand. By 4 months, the baby can purposefully reach out and grasp an object and will also drop the object in a more voluntary way. If you have a toy gym, be sure to hang toys over the middle of the baby's body. This encourages the baby to bring her hands together in the middle (an important skill). As your baby is able to reach to the middle, bringing both hands together, she can use both hands to explore objects. Once your baby is good at this, try moving the toys to one side, then the other. While your baby is on her tummy, put the toy just a little out of reach, and she will stretch to get it. [Each of these ideas can be demonstrated with the Teaching Teddy.] As your baby reaches out for toys, place them within her reach or just a little out of reach. This helps the baby develop hand–eye coordination as well as do a little problem solving by needing to move. This allows her to bring an object to her mouth: This is how babies explore their first toys. (Washing toys frequently can help cut down on germs.) By the end of the first year your baby will be able to coordinate play using both hands. This is quite an accomplishment and allows her to do so many new things."

Caregiving Implications:

"While trying to latch on, the breastfed baby will want to 'help' by bringing her hand up to the breast or grabbing the nipple of the bottle. In the beginning, this is not exactly helpful; often the hand comes between the breast and the baby's mouth and the baby may pinch you, though not on purpose. In the meantime, you might want to have your partner hold the baby's hands until she is latched on, or wrap the baby so her hands are not able to come between the breast and her mouth or pinch you. With practice and experience the baby will learn to rest her hand upon the breast rather than grasp at the nipple.

"Allowing your baby to grasp your finger helps your baby feel connected to you and often makes the baby calmer. You may also place a small rattle or a bit of blanket into her hand to give your baby experiences with a variety of textures. Be sure to give your baby opportunities to grasp and hold using both the right and left hands.

"Provide opportunities for your baby to look at and bat toys placed within reach. A toy bar or toys attached to an infant gym are good ways to provide this kind of experience. At about 3 months old the baby will again grasp and then let go of a small rattle put in her hand. By 4 months, the baby can purposefully reach out and grasp an object. Be sure the toys are within reach or the baby may become frustrated."

Parent Care:

"As we discussed, babies are born with the skills to grasp and hold, a way to maintain closeness to you. (In Pathway 1—The Transitioning Baby, we discussed the use of an infant carrier, like a sling, that can keep your baby close but give you some freedom.)

Welcome Baby Level 2

Ask:

See Welcome Baby Level 1

Infant Observation/Activity:

Observe an infant in a drowsy, alert or fussy state:

- Elicit the grasp in the hand and then the foot.
- Show parents some developmentally appropriate lightweight toys, such as rattles, that can be given to a young baby to explore.

Developmental Context:

See Welcome Baby Level 1.

Implications:

See Welcome Baby Level 1.

Parent Care:

See Welcome Baby Level 1.

Welcome Baby Level 3

Ask:

See Welcome Baby Level 1.

Baby:

In a drowsy, alert, or fussy state.

Infant Observation/Activity:

Elicit the Babinski reflex just prior to eliciting the plantar grasp and show parents how it is done.

Elicit the Palmer grasp. If the baby demonstrates a firm grasp, allow the baby to continue to grasp while you pull gently upward (but not in a full pull-to-sit NBAS maneuver). This adds further demonstration regarding the strength of this reflex in the newborn. Place your hand behind the baby's head and shoulders to catch her if she releases her grasp.

Demonstrate developmentally appropriate baby toys that build a baby's fine motor skills.

Developmental Context:

See Welcome Baby Level 1.

Caregiving Implication:

See Welcome Baby Level 1.

Parent Care:

See Welcome Baby Level 1.

PATHWAY 7

The Strong Baby

> *Tummy Time is an important activity for your baby's development and is endorsed by the American Academy of Pediatrics (AAP). The AAP recommends that babies sleep on their backs for safety reasons; however, babies need enough supervised Tummy Time during the hours they are awake to strengthen head, neck, and upper body muscles. Tummy Time helps to build the strength and coordination needed for rolling over, crawling, reaching, and playing. Remember that all babies benefit from Tummy Time, including newborns.* (American Occupational Therapy Association, 2015)

What You Will Learn in This Pathway:

- the capabilities of a newborn in prone (tummy)
- why prone positioning (being on the tummy) is so important to a child's future development
- the confusion leading parents to misinterpret the Back to Sleep recommendation
- when and how to position a baby in prone
- detrimental effects of too much time in supine positioning (on the back)
- cautions regarding overuse of infant equipment

Why This Pathway Is Important:

Much of a baby's physical development depends on spending time in prone (tummy) play.

- Prone play involves working against gravity, a key way to stimulate both the *vestibular* (movement sensation) and *proprioceptive* (pressure sensation) systems.
- Prone play helps develop the neck muscles, which results in head control.
- Prone play encourages muscle development in the lower abdomen, which is necessary for developing balance in both sitting and standing.
- Prone play encourages babies to bear weight on their hands and arms, thus developing finger, hand, arm, and shoulder strength.
- Serious developmental problems have resulted from spending too much time in supine or infant positioning equipment (such as car seats).
- Lack of experience in prone positioning can result in significant delays in attaining motor milestones such as rolling, sitting, creeping, crawling, pulling to stand, and walking.

When parents are educated about the importance of tummy time, parents can prevent cranial malformations (flat heads) that require intensive intervention at great expense. Education about tummy time will also lead to a reduction in the number of children with deficits in fine motor skills.

Key Information

Before Birth

As early as 7–8 weeks gestation, limb buds have changed into hands and feet with fingers and toes. Between 10 and 13 weeks gestation, general movements can be seen through ultrasound. By 14 weeks and going forward, the legs and feet are the primary way the fetal body is set in motion. As the fetus performs these movements, the *vestibular* sense (movement and balance) is developed. The vestibular sense is foundational to neuromotor development; it gives us information about where our head and body are in space (Vergara & Bigsby, 2004). It allows us to stay upright while we sit, stand, and walk. As the fetus moves about and comes in contact with the womb and his own umbilical cord, he develops proprioception, a body awareness sense that tells us where our body parts are relative to one *another*. During this development, the fetus gets feedback from both his own movements and the movements of his mother.

Developing Strength and Control

Babies develop strength and control from their heads to their toes. A baby develops shoulder strength before developing strength in her hands and hip strength before foot strength. Gross motor skills (large muscles) develop before fine motor (small muscle) skills, another general principle in the development of movement patterns (Alexander et al., 1993). The vestibular and proprioceptive systems that began developing in the womb continue to develop; together, both systems support the baby's early reflexive movements. Later in development, these systems work together to support purposeful movement (Bly, 1994).

A newborn becomes stronger and develops more bodily control and strength primarily by working against gravity in the prone (tummy) position, which involves further development and stimulation of both the vestibular and proprioceptive systems. As the newborn lies on his tummy he is able to turn his head from side to side. Some newborn babies can even raise their heads momentarily. Repeating these actions activates the neck muscles, which become stronger and allow the baby to raise his head and maintain this position. The shoulders and arms also become stronger (Liddle & Yorke, 2004).

The *awake prone position* is wording developed to clearly describe the fact that babies need prone (tummy time) when awake and alert. By 2 to 3 months, a baby who has adequate time in the awake prone position will begin to prop himself on his arms, in addition to lifting his head. At first he will prop his arms behind his shoulders (Bly, 1994). As he increases his ability to bear weight, his elbows will be in front of his shoulders. Weight-bearing in this position helps extend the baby's wrist muscles. When the wrist flexor muscles are stretched, the baby's hands open (Alexander et al., 1993). Babies who do not spend time in awake prone play sometimes show delayed fine motor skills later on in their development (Salls, Silverman, & Gatty, 2002). One of the reasons for this may be the lack of weight-bearing experience and strengthening of shoulders and arms that also help the wrist, hands, and fingers develop (Liddle & Yorke, 2004).

Tummy play also encourages muscles in the lower abdomen (pelvic area) to strengthen and develop flexibility. In the prone position the pelvis tilts forward; in supported sitting, the pelvis tilts backward. This type of flexible back and forth movement of the pelvis is important for balance in sitting and standing. The proprioceptive system develops through the sensory information coming from the skin, tendons, and muscles (Bly, 1994; Liddle & Yorke, 2004). The prone play position gives proprioceptive input to the baby's shoulder, hip, and knee joints through weight-bearing and muscle-stretching sensations.

The prone position of an infant for play when awake promotes upper extremity strength and stability and general overall motor skills. In prone play, a baby will turn his head to look at something, and when his head is turned, he automatically places more weight on the side he is looking toward. As he turns his arms rotate, giving him the experience of supination (turning out) and pronation (turning in) of the forearm (Bly, 1994). This movement further supports fine motor development and helps develop the baby's sense of his body's position in space. Carrying, rocking, and moving a baby all provide input movement sensations to the baby's vestibular system. Movement can be both calming and alerting, depending on the speed and rhythm of the movement. Movement experiences help shape a baby's muscle tone, strength, coordination, and balance (Liddle & Yorke, 2004).

Awake Prone Play Promotes Optimal Development

Awake prone positioning for play—tummy time—provides essential experiences for a baby's optimal development. Many parents are not informed about the need to give their baby opportunities to play in the prone position (Beard & Dallwitz, 1995; Salls et al., 2002). Moreover, some parents believe they should not position their baby in a prone position (Kitzman, 2011). Once they discover that awake prone time is a desired activity, parents may try to place their infant (who is now a bit older and has never experienced the prone position) in a prone position but give up because the baby "doesn't like it" and fusses if left in the position. Parents should be encouraged not to give up. Shorter periods of tummy time make it tolerable for the infant. As the baby tolerates short periods, the time can be increased. Parents need to be willing to tolerate some of the baby's fussing.

Prone positioning provides many developmental benefits to the baby. Therefore it is important that educators pass along information about the need for awake prone play and inform parents about techniques that help babies tolerate and enjoy it (Miller, Johnson, Duggan, & Behm, 2011). It has been found that babies who sleep in supine (as is recommended) and do not receive awake prone time are at risk of developing acquired torticollis (neck tightness on one side with over-stretching of neck muscles on the opposite side), plagiocephly (a flat area on the head), and gross motor delays (delays in the ability to roll over, sit up, and walk; Jantz, Blosser, & Fruchting, 1997; Lennartsson, 2011). Why is there confusion and reluctance about placing infants in prone? Why are babies spending so little time in the prone position for play when they are awake?

AAP Recommendations for Infant Positioning

In April 1994, the AAP issued a task force statement on infant positioning and SIDS (Willinger, Hoffman, & Hartford, 1994). The AAP introduced the recommendation to place babies on their backs to sleep. That recommendation and the resulting change in parents' practice led to a dramatic 50% decrease in the incidence of SIDS. Because of these dramatic decreases in SIDS deaths, the AAP issued a position statement in 2002 endorsing the Back to Sleep campaign (Moon, Gingras, & Erwin, 2002) Research conducted after 2002 revealed many other dangers that parents must be made aware of, and the Back to Sleep campaign became the Safe to Sleep campaign (Flook & Vincze, 2012).

Although the decrease in the incidence of SIDS was cause to celebrate, a new challenge has arisen. Studies (Davis, Moon, Sachs, & Ottilini, 1998; Jantz et al., 1997) indicate that infants who are placed in supine for sleep are also placed in supine for play. This has resulted in delays in development compared to expected norms. By studying prone and supine sleepers, B. Davis et al. (1998) found that infants who sleep in the recommended supine position show "a significant difference in the attainment of rolling prone to supine, tripod sitting, creeping, crawling, and pulling to stand" (Davis et al., 1998, p. 1). The same year, Dewey, Fleming, and Golding (1998) investigated whether supine sleeping positioning had adverse effects on the child's motor development. More recent studies (Dudek-Shriber & Zelazny, 2007) have found important differences in development between those babies who get tummy time versus those who do not. In addition, some physical and occupational therapists believe subtle differences remain and can cause developmental challenges at later stages (Dudek-Shriber & Zelazny, 2007; Zelazny, 1999). Weighing their findings against the adverse health effects demonstrated with prone sleeping, the AAP concluded that the message of the Safe to Sleep (Back to Sleep) campaign should not be changed; instead, they added a recommendation to address the adverse effects of babies not getting tummy time (Kinney & Thach, 2009):

> *Supervised, awake tummy time is recommended to facilitate development and to minimize development of positional plagiocephaly. "Although there are no data to make specific recommendations as to how often and how long it should be undertaken, supervised, awake tummy time is recommended on a daily basis, beginning as early as possible, to promote motor development, facilitate development of the upper body muscles, and minimize the risk of positional plagiocephaly."*
> (R. Y. Moon 2011, p. 1035)

Confusion Around the Back to Sleep/Safe to Sleep Message

In earlier research, Mildred, Beard, Dallwitz, and Unwin (1995) found that sleep positioning recommendations influenced how parents positioned their infants for play. Of the 100 caregivers in Mildred et al.'s study, 93% reported that their knowledge of SIDS influenced sleep positioning, and 84% reported they never put their baby in prone for sleeping. Thirty-seven percent reported that SIDS knowledge did influence play positioning, with 27% percent reporting that they never placed their infants in prone for play. Educators who give parents Safe to Sleep/Back to Sleep information must also give parents the key message that babies need to spend time in awake prone play (Salls et al., 2002).

Zachry and Kitzmann (2011) conducted a study to discover why some parents do not give their babies tummy time. They learned that 25% of caregivers were not aware of the recommendation that babies need tummy time. Of that group, 25% were not aware of the complications that can arise if tummy time is limited or not given at all (Zachry & Kitzmann, 2011). Of those infants whose parents provided tummy time, 53% of the infants were in prone position fewer than 30 minutes per day. Thirty-five percent of parents reported that their infants were intolerant of tummy time. The researchers urged that parents be educated about the importance of prone play and ways to increase infants' tolerance of this position, to prevent serious medical issues from arising (Zachry & Kitzmann, 2011).

Cranial Malformations Are Related to Lack of Awake Prone Positioning

Delayed acquisition of motor skills was not the only risk of excessive supine positioning. Therapists have seen a dramatic increase in the incidence of deformation of the occipital skull, which can cause significant posterior cranial asymmetry, malposition of the ears, distortion of the cranial base, deformation of the forehead, and facial asymmetry (Argenta, David, Wilson, & Bell, 1996; Hutchinson, Thompson, & Mitchell, 2003). It is not unusual for new parents to have heard that someone's baby had to wear a helmet to fix a flat head. Although the damage to the skull can be fixed, it is costly, time consuming, and mostly unnecessary if parents simply place their infants in awake prone to play (Graham, 2006). Education is key to prevention; parent educators should be prepared to emphasize that infants must spend supervised play time on their tummies and that awake prone positioning is not a risk factor for SIDS (Hutchinson et al., 2003).

Additional Risks

When a baby's breathing is occluded, he will work to free his airway (Brazelton & Nugent, 1995; Prechtl, 1977) in a survival reflex seen even in a newborn. Babies who are always on their backs (supine) will learn to roll into prone and may not be able to roll back to supine. Without early, adequate awake prone play experience, they will not develop the strength and motor skills to move out of danger, for example, to avoid suffocation if they have rolled into a blanket or other soft material (Miller et al., 2011).

When and How Can Parents Begin Tummy Time Play With Their Baby?

Right from day one! Many parents are not aware that it is possible to place their newborn baby in prone. Being prone will not harm the umbilical cord. Diaper changes are ideal for tummy time—parents can place the baby on his tummy for a few minutes while they are right at hand. Parents should be alerted, however, that a newborn in awake prone position can scoot forward using a crawling reflex, so tummy time must always occur in a safe place, while the baby is supervised.

Newborns feel secure in prone because the position limits their movement—similarly to the confines of the womb. In addition, babies in prone can easily engage in hand-to-mouth behavior, which is self-soothing. Parents should be advised that awake prone playtime is essential for their infant's development and be encouraged to place their awake infant in prone as often as possible, beginning with a few minutes per day and gradually increasing the prone time.

Here are some tips to help parents get started with prone playtime, or tummy time: Parents can lie on their backs or be semireclined and place the baby on top of them. Babies typically enjoy looking at their parent's face as well as being in full-body contact. A parent can also place the baby on his tummy and then lie next to the baby so they are face to face. Some babies may need a small blanket rolled and placed under their chests to assist them in lifting and propping. Parents can sit on the floor with their legs out in front of them, placing baby down over one thigh. Like the blanket roll, the elevation of the parent's thigh helps the baby lift his head and look around. Placing a favorite toy or infant-safe mirror in front of the baby will also entertain the baby while he is on his tummy. During a tummy time session, parents can play music or sing to their baby, making the experience especially enjoyable (Liddle & Yorke, 2004).

How Much Time Does a Baby Need in Awake Prone Positioning?

Once parents understand the need for prone play, the inevitable question will be: how much time? There are no formal guidelines, but Salls et al. (2002) found that 2-month-old infants who spent more than 15 minutes per day in prone playtime showed gross motor skill development at normative levels. Infants who were in prone position fewer than 15 minutes per day passed the gross motor milestones at significantly lower percentages than the normative population. Based on this study, it appears that in order to show benefit, ameliorate developmental differences, and avoid developing a flat head, infants younger than 2 months need a minimum of 15 minutes per day. By 3 months, the length of tummy time should be increased to at least 1 hour per day.

Pathways.org is an organization dedicated to empowering parents and health professionals with free tools and resources to maximize a child's motor, sensory, play, and communication development. The leading physicians, therapists, clinicians, nurse practitioners, and lay advisors who comprise the organization are sensitive to the medical and emotional needs of infants, children, and their families. They recommend that "your baby should work up to an hour of Tummy Time per day by 3 months of age" (see www.pathways.org). Parents can begin with a few minutes at a time, several times a day. Experts at Pathways.org also suggest that after routines such as diapering or bathing parents place their baby on their tummy, even for a short time, to get the baby used to this position. The Pathways.org website provides tips and videos to help parents make tummy time successful.

Additional Benefits of Awake Prone Play

Tummy time play has been shown to help avoid head flattening associated with supine sleep positioning. Recommendations for reducing the likelihood of positional torticollis include alternating the baby's head position so that he is not always sleeping on the same side, as well as increasing his awake prone time (AAP, 2000).

Equipment that sits an infant in an upright position can also contribute to this problem. Not only can a baby develop a flat head, but he can also acquire stiffness in his neck that will interfere with development (Graham, 2006; Hutchinson et al., 2003). Some babies show real preferences for a particular side, and parents will need to provide interventions such as:

- Alternating the direction the baby is placed to sleep in the crib.
- Alternating sides on which an infant is fed by bottle (switching sides is inevitable with breastfeeding).
- Alternating the side on which the car seat is placed to encourage looking in both directions.
- Limiting the use of infant seats and car seats when the baby is not in the car.

Tummy time reduces head flattening and neck tightness because it takes pressure off the back of the baby's head and encourages development of neck and shoulder muscles.

Limiting the Use of Infant Positioning Equipment Is Also Important

Parents have many types of infant equipment to choose from, including baby carriers that attach to the parent, infant seats (some that vibrate or play music), swings, exersaucers, baby jumpers that attach to door frames, infant walkers, and more! Some infant car seats can be removed from the car and used as baby carriers. Many babies stay in their car seats for long periods of time in the car; some are also left to sleep in their car seat at night (most often the car seat is put into the crib or rests on the bedroom floor).

Some pieces of infant equipment are marketed to give the impression they will contribute to the infant's development, and parents may not know about their potential negative effects. Parents may believe that a baby "walker" will help their baby learn to walk, when in fact the opposite is true: A baby walker supports a baby in all directions, so the baby does not develop the necessary balance for walking. When positioned in a walker the baby does not learn to control his center of gravity, and he will still need to learn this skill when not in a baby walker. Abbott and Bartlett (2001) found that infants who used walkers "demonstrated decreased knee flexion and stride length, and greater forward lean when walking independently" (p. 296). Babies who used walkers were also found to develop a stiff-legged gait. Because a walker allows the baby to move independently to places parents may not consider safe, babies who use infant walkers are more prone to have accidents such as falling down stairs. Some countries have banned this equipment; "Canada became the first country to ban the sale, importation, or advertisement of baby walkers because of concerns that babies who are put in them can fall down stairs and reach dangerous objects when out of the sight" (The New York Times, 2010, p. 1824).

Other infant equipment, such as baby bouncers, were found to reinforce primitive responses and delayed acquisition of voluntary movements (Pin, Eldridge, & Galea, 2007). In their study, Abbott and Bartlett (2001) used a parental survey to determine the amount of infant equipment in the home when the babies were 8 months old. There was a significant correlation between higher use of infant equipment and lower scores on infant motor development. The authors suggested that parent education focus on informing parents that they should make only moderate use of infant equipment and provide their infants with adequate floor time in which to practice and learn motor skills. An analysis (Garrett, McElroy, & Staines, 2002) of research on the effects of baby walkers on locomotor milestones showed that children who used walkers were delayed in achieving walking by 11 to 26 days, on average, compared to their peers who did not use baby walkers.

Beginning With the Very Young Infant

Educators can provide information to parents about the benefit and necessity of placing their baby in the awake prone position to play. Parents may be surprised to note that their newborn, when placed in prone, can turn his head from one side to the other, pick up his head briefly, and scoot forward (Brazelton & Nugent, 1995). The newborn can demonstrate his ability not only to tolerate the prone play position but to show enjoyment in the position, in which a newborn can more easily get his hands and fingers into his mouth to supply his need for nonnutritive sucking. Some babies will tolerate being in the awake prone position for only a short time unless they are given experience early on, starting when they are newborns. To introduce the prone position to an older baby who has not had much previous experience in prone will take patience, creativity, and tolerance for hearing the baby fuss. With time and practice, even older babies will come to enjoy and benefit greatly from playing in the prone position.

Recommended Reading:

Liddle, T. A., & Yorke, L. (2004). *Why motor skills matter.* New York, NY: Contemporary Books.

Educator Tools:

Explore Pathways.org. The website provides printouts for parents on a variety of topics, downloadable brochures, and videos demonstrating how to make tummy time more enjoyable.

Parent Education Activities

Welcome Baby Level 1

Purpose:

To explain the importance of having an infant spend time in the prone (tummy) position.

Instructional Content/Strategies:

- Demonstrate and discuss the ability of the newborn to tolerate the prone (tummy) position.
- Inform parents of the skills a baby develops when in the prone play position.
- Describe the negative consequences of overuse of infant equipment or supine positioning.
- Encourage optimal infant care practices.

Materials:

- Teaching Teddy
- Two baby blankets
- Small colorful toy
- Teaching Photographs:
  Figure 7A: Very young baby in prone assisted by a blanket roll
  Figure 7B: Baby on caregiver's chest lifting her head

Ask:

"Have you heard that it is important to place your baby on his back to sleep?"

Typically all parents will say yes. Be prepared to give information about Safe to Sleep (previously called Back to Sleep) to anyone who has not heard this current recommended practice.

Then ask, "Have you been told that playing on the tummy is important for your baby?"

Someone in the group may have heard about the problem of a baby being on his back too much and that having tummy time is important. A parent may share knowing a baby whose development was delayed because she didn't have enough tummy time or that an infant's lack of tummy time was so severe the baby's head became very flat or asymmetrical, with a helmet needed to correct the problem. Use whatever the parents share to guide the conversation about the importance of tummy time.

Infant Observation/Activity:

Place the Teaching Teddy on its tummy. Describe the baby's ability to move forward and turn his head from side to side. Show the *Pathways* Teaching Photograph Figure 7B of a baby in a beginning prone position resting on his caregiver's chest. Explain that in this position, a baby can become used to the prone position. Show *Pathways* Photograph 7A and describe that when a baby practices lifting his head in this way, he strengthens his neck muscles and develops head control. Explain that the small blanket roll is used to assist the baby in making the prone position more comfortable and tolerable for some babies. With the Teaching Teddy on his belly, put the small toy about 10 inches from the Teddy's face and explain that the baby may enjoy tummy time more if he has something to look at. Demonstrate getting down to the baby's eye level and talking.

Developmental Context:

"A newborn placed on his tummy will move about using a crawling reflex and can lift and turn his head from side to side. He often finds his fist and fingers more easily when he is on his tummy. When placed on his tummy, a baby is also bearing weight in his shoulders, wrists, and hip and knee joints. This ability to bear weight on the joints will be important in the development of other skills such as rolling over, crawling, and sitting.

"By 2 months old, the baby who has not had previous experience in playing on his tummy will be very unhappy when placed on his tummy. This is because the 2-month-old baby's experience of the world has been from only the back lying position. The baby's weight has increased, thus taking more effort to rise up and look around when he is on his tummy. Older babies who have not had tummy playtime become even more frustrated and demand to be placed on their backs.

"Pediatricians have noted that parents are not giving their babies tummy play time and, as a result, some babies are delayed in being able to control their heads, are not rolling over or crawling at the times expected, and develop flat spots on their heads so severe they need to be treated. Although most of these babies will eventually be able to roll over and crawl, they are often frustrated by not being able to roll or sit at earlier ages when they want to be able to play and move. Some babies with flat spots will need to wear a helmet to help reshape their heads. This type of intervention is intensive and expensive, and can be avoided if babies are simply given adequate time to play in awake prone.

"Give your newborn baby opportunities at least two to three times a day to be on his tummy for short periods that add up to at least 5 minutes per day (you can also count time spent with baby chest to chest). Between 6 weeks and 2 months, babies need at least 15 minutes per day of prone play. When the baby is around 4 months old, tummy time should increase to at least 1½ hours per day. These are minimums—if your baby enjoys tummy time, give him more time! If your baby cries or fusses during tummy time, try to make it a bit more interesting by placing a colorful toy or baby mirror in front of his face while he is lying on his belly. This will also encourage him to lift his head and reach. Or get down on your baby's level and sing and talk, which will keep his interest and prolong tummy time."

Caregiving Implications:

"Most new parents know that the baby MUST sleep on his back, but many are not aware that tummy playtime (when the baby is alert) is also important. When your baby has tummy time, he strengthens neck muscles by lifting the weight of his head. Development of neck muscles in turn helps your baby develop head control. When your baby plays on his tummy he bears weight on his joints. The ability to bear weight will be a part of your baby learning to roll and sit.

"If a baby is positioned on his tummy, be aware of how even a newborn baby can use the crawl reflex to scoot forward. Make sure your baby's tummy playtime is in a safe place, and do not leave the baby alone: Infants can fall off a bed or changing table or become wedged under pillows or blankets. Make sure the baby remains alert when you give him tummy time, and clear the surface of any hazards."

Anticipatory Guidance:

"Once your baby can roll from his back to his tummy, you may find the baby rolls to his tummy during sleep, or even prefers this position. The American Academy of Pediatrics currently does not advise using devices to keep your baby on his back. Instead, ensure the crib or sleeping area is free of blankets, toys, and bumper pads that could be a hazard. If your baby's ability to roll to his tummy at night concerns you, discuss this with your baby's doctor."

Parent Care:

"This is also a time when parents need opportunities to change their 'positions' as well. The early days of parenting are exhausting. Parents often report being totally homebound or even couch-bound. It is easy to feel lonely and have little energy. A new mother should be encouraged to take a short walk outdoors daily. Stretching and deep breathing can contribute to lessening stress and helping a mother regain her strength and energy. Mothers who were used to exercising intensely should be advised to check with their doctor before returning to this type of routine."

Welcome Baby Level 2

Ask:

See Welcome Baby Level 1.

Materials:

Three blankets spread smoothly for a firm but padded surface

Baby:

In active alert, fussy, or crying state.

Infant Observation/Activity:

Place an alert or fussy baby in prone position. Observe the baby's response and describe what the baby does. Discuss the Developmental Context and Caregiving Implications as described in Welcome Baby Level 1.

Developmental Context:

See Welcome Baby Level 1.

Implications:

See Welcome Baby Level 1.

Parent Care:

See Welcome Baby Level 1.

Welcome Baby Level 3

Materials:

See Welcome Baby Level 2.

Baby:

In active alert or crying state.

Infant Observation/Activity:

With the baby suspended over the educator's hand, the educator taps along one side of the spine to elicit the incurvation (Gallant) response. This will usually elicit the baby's bottom to curve to the stimulated side. Always do this maneuver over the table or bassinet, because some babies may have a very robust response and move off of the educator's hand.

Explain that this is a response to stimulation of the central nervous system. The baby will lose this response over time. It is useful in labor when the uterus contracts and tactile pressure is brought to bear on the spine, causing the baby to move in the same manner demonstrated. Babies use this fishtail movement to move through the birth canal during labor.

A related reflex behavior is crawling. A baby must be in a quiet alert, active alert, or crying state to demonstrate this reflex. The educator should elicit the incurvation response and immediately place the baby in a prone position on a firm surface covered by baby blankets. Emphasize that you can't always predict whether the baby will crawl, otherwise parents may be concerned or alarmed if the baby chooses to lie quietly on his tummy.

Place the baby near the bottom of the blankets on a low table. The educator should place her hands firmly (light pressure) against the baby's feet. Sometimes the baby will provide an excellent lesson by dramatically pushing off the educator's hands, crawling forward, and even lifting and turning his head. Some babies may almost roll over. Be sure the baby is safely positioned before engaging in this demonstration.

If the baby is crying or begins to cry, the educator should attend to the crying, although there are times when a parent may allow the educator to place the crying baby in a prone position before attempting to comfort and calm the baby. This should be done thoughtfully and with the consent of the parent. Once the baby has demonstrated the prone behaviors, be sure to immediately comfort and calm the baby.

Developmental Context:

See Welcome Baby Level 1.

Caregiving Implications:

See Welcome Baby Level 1.

Parent Care:

See Welcome Baby Level 1.

PATHWAY 8

The Premature Baby

"Just make it through the first year and everything will become much easier." How many health professionals have said this to parents of premature infants as they prepare to leave the neonatal intensive care unit (NICU)? In my 12 years of experience working as an NICU nurse, I said it to many parents. Yet it wasn't until I delivered my premature daughter, weighing 790 gm at 26 weeks, that I began to understand the reality of the crisis that parents endure in the first year of their premature infant's life. There is a wonderful illusion presented by the medical staff and believed by parents: When a premature infant is discharged home, family life will settle in, calm down, and become somewhat "normal." However, the crisis that begins in the NICU often continues after discharge, as a result of the overwhelming medical needs of the infant, and the recurring grief and emotional devastation that the family of a chronically ill child must cope with. This continuing crisis is frequently unrecognized by professionals. (Maroney, n.d., p. 1)

What You Will Learn in This Pathway:

- when a baby is considered premature
- differences in premature infants' behavior and development
- early parenting experiences that are different for parents of premature infants.

Why This Pathway Is Important:

- Parents of premature infants need information and support, tailored to individual situations.
- Early interactions between parents and their premature infants can be stressful.
- Professionals must be ready to listen to parents' concerns while recognizing they may not fully understand all that the parents have gone through.
- Professionals must be aware of and alert parents of premature babies to early intervention opportunities in their communities.

Key Information

This Pathway reveals some of the developmental differences of premature babies, as well as differences in early parenting experiences when a baby is born prematurely. Educators can use this information to customize their work with parents and their premature babies. Some information contained in *Pathways* applies to all parents, such as PPD, SBS, Safe to Sleep, self-soothing, and tummy time. However, babies born prematurely have a different beginning to life, and their parents need additional insight from educators with the appropriate information and support.

When Is a Baby Considered Premature?

The World Health Organization defines *prematurity* as when a newborn's gestational age is less than 37 weeks. The typical full-term baby is born between 38 and 40 weeks gestation; a few babies are born as late as 42 weeks. Some babies are born at 24 weeks, which means that they enter the world a full 4 months early. Premature babies miss time to develop in the womb and often come into the world in a very fragile condition. They are born with or develop complications such as impaired heart and circulation functioning; lung dysfunction or disease; an inability to breathe independently; problems with feeding and digestion; very low birthweight and lack of weight gain; brain hemorrhage; and an immature immune system, which increases their vulnerability to bacteria and viruses. The Born Too Soon campaign was described in the *Global Action Report on Preterm Birth*, (March of Dimes, PMNCH, Save the Children, & WHO, 2012). It is an effort to reduce the rate of premature birth in the United States from 11.4% in 2014 (one of the highest rates among industrialized nations) to 9.6% or less by 2020. Globally, premature birth is the number-one cause of death of children under 5 years old (March of Dimes, 2015).

Contrasting the Experience of a Full-Term Birth With That of a Premature Birth

A full-term pregnancy allows parents time to prepare physically, mentally, and in practical ways for the birth of their baby. There is a sense of anticipation leading up to the birth and a sense of accomplishment when the baby is delivered. Parents often experience a positive surge of emotions, a combination of feelings of success and fulfilled expectations. Parents are able to hold and caress their newborns. Mothers are able to attempt feeding in the first hours. Parents look forward to bringing their baby home within a short period of time. The baby, even within minutes after birth, shows responsiveness and is socially engaging, as described in previous Pathways. Families of full-term babies typically plan time to adjust to being a parent and learn to care for their baby. New parents find support and integrate their baby into their lives by preparing to take parental leave to care for their baby, having grandparents or other family around who will be available to help, enrolling in parent education programs, enjoying sharing their baby with friends and coworkers, and getting together with friends who have babies (Kitzinger, 1995; Klaus & Kennell, 1995).

Premature Birth Is Often an Unexpected Event

Premature labor is often unexpected and is usually charged with feelings of fear and tension. In many cases, it is a medical emergency. If the labor cannot be stopped from progressing, the medical team prepares for the birth of a baby who will need immediate medical attention in order to survive. A premature birth is often the beginning of an unanticipated, sometimes frightening, journey. Stages in pregnancy are marked by emotional milestones, which lead to the parents being prepared both physically and emotionally for the pregnancy to end. For parents of premature babies, that emotional preparation has not fully taken place, and they are typically in shock that the pregnancy is over (D. Davis & Stein, 2004).

Once the baby is delivered, the medical team takes over the baby's care and the parents are often worried and frightened about their baby's well-being. Premature babies are typically taken to the neonatal intensive care unit (NICU), where specially trained professionals use a variety of technological devices and interventions to help the baby survive (Linden et al., 2013). Parents may first meet their baby attached to monitors and a breathing apparatus, with an IV protruding from the head, and a nasogastric tube taped to the face for feeding. If a mother has planned to breastfeed she will need to establish a routine of expressing and storing milk until her baby can feed from the breast. Parents have to give over care of their infant to the medical staff for a few days to several months, depending on the baby's medical conditions and maturity.

Parents have described leaving their baby in the hospital as painful and traumatic, even though they know they are welcome to "visit" at any time (Cantle, 2013). Although parents typically are immensely grateful this medical care is available for their premature baby, they feel, at first, uncomfortable and unsure of their role. They leave the hospital no longer pregnant, but without a baby and with professionals taking over their baby's care—as well as with many unanswered questions about their baby's future.

Coping After the Birth of a Premature Baby

In the days and weeks after a premature birth, parents do their best to adjust their schedules to include time to be with the baby in the hospital. They are inundated with new information, are called upon to make critical decisions for their baby, and must stand by and watch others do for their baby what they cannot do. Most parents are unprepared to care for a hospitalized baby (D. Davis & Stein, 2004). Mothers may feel a sense of failure because the labor and birth process did not meet their expectations (Green, Darbyshire, Adams, & Jackson, 2015). Mothers, especially, often have feelings of guilt and wonder if they could have been responsible for the premature birth (D. Davis & Stein, 2004). They may also experience a sense of loss, because the pregnancy has ended earlier than expected, yet there is no baby to care for.

Mothers and fathers whose babies are admitted to the NICU are at increased risk for PPD. Studies have found that mothers whose infants were hospitalized in the NICU were between 28% and 70% more likely to suffer from PPD than were mothers who had full-term births (Blucker et al., 2014). Parents whose babies are admitted to the NICU experience increased family, relationship, and financial stresses when compared to families with healthy term infants.

Parenting a Different Way, in a Different Place

Parents of premature, hospitalized infants begin their parenting journey facing many obstacles. Their experiences include separation and reduced opportunities to interact with their infant, and dependent relationships with the medical team who cares for their baby. Parents' feelings about the medical team can swing from deep gratitude to resentment as parents meet, depend upon, and interact with a multitude of staff who care for their baby. Psychological challenges may include feelings of disappointment in not achieving the expected pregnancy outcome and fears regarding the infant's survival. Parents must balance between two intense psychological processes: attachment and grief. These are difficult and often painful psychological experiences for parents.

The sights and sounds of the NICU, the infant's physical appearance, intimidating equipment, and relationships with health care personnel in the unit are all factors that impact parenting behavior (Barsuhn, 2008). Not only must parents adapt to a high-tech hospital environment, they must begin their parenting experience in a very public place. These experiences can interfere with a parent's ability to achieve and feel successful in the parental role. When parents are limited in interacting with their infant, they sometimes feel they are "less than parents." (D. Davis & Stein, 2004)

Behavioral, Developmental, and Caregiving Differences in Premature Infants

Behavioral and developmental differences between a full-term healthy newborn and a premature newborn must also be considered. The full-term healthy baby comes into the world ready to communicate her needs and interact with her parents. A full-term baby has six defined levels of alertness, as well as behavioral cues that parents can readily observe and understand. A baby displaying quiet, focused, alert behavior invites parents to talk to her and interact with her. Lusty crying communicates to her parents that she needs help and might be hungry, cold, or tired. Parents of full-term babies have many opportunities to interact with their babies, can minister to their infant's needs, and in this way learn about their baby's individual likes and dislikes. They also begin experiencing a sense of competency in taking care of their baby, which builds parental confidence.

Premature or medically fragile babies have less organized levels of alertness, often making it difficult to tell whether they are truly awake or asleep (Legendre, Burtner, Martinez, & Crowe, 2011). This creates confusion for parents about when to interact with the baby and how to interpret the baby's responses to them. Fragile babies often lack the ability or energy to cry, although they definitely display many signs of being stressed: turning bright red or becoming very pale, startling, splaying their fingers, and extending their limbs in unusual ways. Very early preemies do not have an audible cry, so parents must learn to read more subtle cues to know when their baby is distressed or overstimulated. Babies born at 23 and 24 weeks gestation may still have their eyelids fused, and it will be several days before a parent may even see the baby's eyes. Once the baby's eyes are open, it may be several more weeks before the baby can sustain even the slightest visual contact with his mom or dad (Als, 1982; Als & Gilkerson, 1995).

Full-term and preterm infants have contrasting competencies and challenges. The full-term baby has a responsive attention system, respiratory control, the ability to regulate her temperature, an operational digestive system, a balance of flexor/extensor postures, and a range of states and the ability to smoothly transition from state to state. The full-term infant's main agenda is to stabilize the alert state in order to attend to the environment. Conversely, the prematurely born infant is often less alert and less responsive, has poor state modulation, lacks distinctive cues, displays irregular behaviors, and has abnormal movement patterns. The premature infant's agenda is to coordinate many systems in order to survive, rather than interact with the environment. The premature infant has the most difficulty in displaying behaviors that promote and sustain interaction and reciprocity.

A premature infant's states of consciousness may differ from those observed in a full-term healthy newborn, with different implications for parental response:

- Prematurely born infants have more transitional states of consciousness, so it can be more difficult to judge what state they are actually in. Whereas the full-term baby has six states of consciousness, researchers who study premature infants describe 12 states that differ qualitatively from the full-term baby's states of consciousness (Als, 1982). In fact, premature infants can appear drowsy when they are in fact alert and carefully absorbing stimuli in their environment. They may become stressed if someone looks into their eyes and talks to them at the same time.
- In the first weeks (especially if born very prematurely), premature infants who are able to come to an alert state have trouble maintaining this state for more than a few minutes. Thus, parents do not have that initial, reassuring eye contact with their baby.
- Prematurely born infants have more difficulty achieving and maintaining a longer period of sleep (the deep sleep state). NICU personnel make extra efforts to create a quality sleep environment, such as by covering the baby's isolette, dimming lights, and having quiet times. Lack of deep sleep can be dangerous; a preemie who is overly tired may have difficulties feeding and gaining weight.
- Babies born prematurely may not have a lusty, robust cry for the first weeks or months. Rather than cry, premature babies signal distress with more subtle cues, such as body color changes due to increased or decreased blood pressure. They may also develop hiccoughs, begin gagging, or strain as if they are having a bowel movement.
- Once these babies are able to cry, they tend to cry more than full-term infants. This creates additional stress for parents who note this difference from a typical baby.

NICU personnel educate parents to read their premature baby's transitional states of consciousness and cues and to note when the baby is showing stability and approachability, in contrast to disorganization and stress (see box Regulatory Stability Signs and Stress Signs).

Premature babies are less likely to organize stimuli, thus, they can easily become overstimulated. With a preterm baby, one may need to not talk or move in order for the baby to organize her attention or focus. Overall, premature infants' signals and behaviors are often unpredictable, making it challenging for parents to know how to interpret their infants' cues and respond appropriately (Kynø et al., 2013).

This stands in stark contrast to the visual capabilities of the full-term newborn described in Pathway 3—The Social Baby. Fragile babies are less able to reach out to their parents visually through sustained eye contact. This does not mean the parents cannot connect and communicate with their premature baby. The approach to interaction must be gentle, because the premature baby will show cues of engagement and cues of stress in much more subtle ways, as noted above. Techniques such as "kangaroo care" (skin-to-skin contact) bring parents and their premature babies together, providing the close contact that parents long for and the ideal environment for the premature baby to rest peacefully (Tallandini, 2015). This way, given the right information, opportunity, and support (Als & Gilkerson, 1995), parents can still experience caregiving for and interaction with their baby.

Regulatory Stability Signs and Stress Signs

Self-Regulatory Signs

Stability/ Approachability	Disorganization and Signs of Stress
• Regular respiration • Good color • Stable digestion • 6 states of consciousness • Smooth transitions between states • Prolonged shiny-eyed alertness • Smooth motor movements • Balanced tone	• Irregular breathing • Poor color • Unstable digestion • Jerky movements • Overuse of extensor movements • Narrow range of states • Consciousness • Strained alertness

The care of a prematurely born baby calls for different recommendations than caring for a full-term baby. Early in their hospital stay, many preemies are placed in prone to sleep. Why? In prone, prematurely born infants are less stressed, conserve their limited energy, and breathe more easily. As the baby approaches what would have been her full-term birthday, she is trained to sleep on her back like her full-term counterparts. Preemie babies are born with a suckling reflex. To sustain this reflex and strengthen suckling for oral feedings (which may not be given for several weeks), preemies are often given pacifiers. Pacifiers serve an important function for preemies that a full-term baby does not need. (See Pathway 5—The Oral Baby for the recommended limited use of pacifiers with full-term infants.)

A Different Kind of Support

It may be difficult to know what to say to parents who have just given birth prematurely. Should you congratulate them? Should you tell them how sorry you are? Listening to their concerns and offering companionship and practical help are best. Many times, in an effort to be supportive, friends—and even professionals—say things to these families that are emotionally painful. By understanding some of the challenges families of premature babies face, it is possible to offer positive support and understanding and avoid making comments or suggestions that can add to the parents' burdens (D. Davis & Stein, 2004; Lau & Morse, 1998), such as the following:

It will all work out. Medical staff members do not make guarantees, nor should anyone else. For a very early born premature infant, the outlook given by medical professionals can be very bleak and frightening. Parents are informed about the many serious conditions their child could develop (or may have developed), as well as possible future negative outcomes. It is difficult for the parents to focus beyond what is in front of them. Saying, "It will all work out" is not helpful, because it does not acknowledge the parents' many real concerns.

I know someone else with a preemie and they are doing fine now. Parents of a premature baby currently residing in the NICU feel disconnected from the experiences of other families. They can't imagine their baby will ever get bigger, or leave the NICU unscathed, given all of the developmental and medical information they are learning about preemies. They can't gain perspective from someone else's experience when they are so embedded in their own.

Why don't you take a break and get your mind off the situation? Parents of hospitalized infants feel the need to spend long hours at their baby's bedside. Mothers, especially, relate that they don't feel at peace anywhere else except at their baby's bedside. There is no such thing for these parents as "taking their minds off the situation."

What to Understand About Parents of Preemies

There are many rules about visitation and limitations to the number of visitors allowed in the NICU. Parents often feel even they are not able to spend enough time with their baby, let alone share their baby with friends and family. Do not be offended if you are not invited to meet the baby in the NICU. If you are invited to visit, it is important to respect all of the rules. Do not expect to touch or hold the baby.

Parents have little time or energy to keep friends and family members updated about their baby's condition. Be patient and wait for them to be able to give you information. Find out if they have established a website for their baby: Some NICUs offer this service to parents, and parents report finding it very helpful for sharing information about their baby and staying in touch. Offer to help with older siblings. Parents often feel guilty about their older children because they cannot give them attention. Offer to help with home chores, run errands, or make phone calls.

Once the baby comes home, parents are often told to limit visitors and avoid having others touch or handle the baby. Friends and families often think the parents are being overly protective—but they have to be: The common cold can place a prematurely born baby at risk for rehospitalization, or even death. Respect the parents' need to keep their baby healthy (D. Davis & Stein, 2004).

Corrected Age Versus Chronological Age

Premature babies generally develop on a different timetable from their full-term peers. Their development will be influenced by both by their chronological age and their corrected age. This means that if a child is born 2 months prematurely and is currently 6 months old chronologically, he is 4 months corrected age. His developmental milestones will likely emerge and be mastered using his corrected chronological age of 4 months versus his chronological age of 6 months. This information is important to share with parents as they may otherwise worry that their child seems "behind." Many preemies catch up developmentally within the first 2 years, meaning that developmental differences between them and their peers born full-term are less evident, although they may not truly be caught up in every skill area.

Some preemies never catch up to their peers. A prematurely born infant who suffered from intraventricular hemorrhages, feeding problems, or lung disease may have additional developmental challenges that slow or impede the rate of developmental progress (Linden et al., 2013). Some preemies show a definite pattern of developmental delays that should be addressed as early as possible. Having a premature beginning puts children at risk for long-term physical, cognitive, and social-emotional challenges that contribute to difficulty in school. Early intervention can help to reduce this risk. Early Intervention programs provide an array of services designed to enhance children's development while informing and supporting the parents, addressing their concerns long past the initial hospitalization (Kynø et al., 2013). Many new parents are not aware of Early Intervention services, so educators should be prepared to share information about and make referrals to the Early Intervention programs in their community.

Suggestions for Parents

There are many books available for parents of premature or medically fragile babies. These books inform parents about the capabilities and special communication skills of their baby, affirm the important role they play while their child is hospitalized, give tips and insights about taking the baby home, and help them understand that they are not alone in their experience. As one mother of a baby born at 28 weeks gestation said, "Information is power and helps you feel like you understand what is going on."

Learn about the common emotional reactions that are normal for parents when their baby comes prematurely. The March of Dimes Share Your Story site can be a good place to begin: http://share.marchofdimes.org

Encourage parents to talk about their feelings and concerns. Some communities offer parent groups, and some clinics are willing to pair parents up with a parent with a similar experience. Share with parents the following advice:

- Talk with your health care provider about parent-to-parent support.
- Seek information about your baby's development and ask questions.
- Take care of yourself by getting good quality sleep and good nutrition.
- Keeping a journal can help you track your thoughts, feelings, and questions.
- Do not hesitate to seek mental health help if you find you are feeling down and anxious.

Educator Tools and Parent Resources:

This Pathway does not include any Teaching Teddy activities or *Pathways* Teaching Photographs. It is highly recommended that, instead, educators explore the following resources for sharing with parents.

Books:

VandenBerg, K., & Hanson, M. (2013). *Coming home from the NICU: A guide for supporting families in early care.* Baltimore, MD: Brookes.

Websites:

- **Understanding Your Premature Infant**
  www.marchofdimes.org/flash/modpreemie/preemie.html
  This March of Dimes program has information and short videos that cover the topics of stories, infant cues, body movements, sleep and awake, feeding, interaction, crying, and fussing. This site is informative for both parents and educators
- **March of Dimes—Premature Birth Report Card**
  www.marchofdimes.org/mission/prematurity-reportcard.aspx
  Check the statistics for your state.
- **Preemie Voices**
  http://preemievoices.com/resources
  Provides both professionals and families with sources and a variety of printouts that can be downloaded.
- **My Preemie App** (available in English and Spanish)
  https://itunes.apple.com/app/id931150109
  This is an app for both iPhone and iPad that features:
  - — Pocket Guide to Preemies—information on more than 100 health, developmental, and parenting issues of prematurity;
  - — Suggested Questions—to help you ask doctors and nurses about your baby;

— Our Diary—an illustrated Baby Book with prompts focusing on the experience of prematurity, to make it easy for you to document daily events, your feelings, and photos;

— Trackers—records your baby's daily weight, length, and head size and shows where your baby's growth falls on preemie growth charts;

— Remember to Ask List—automatically logs the Suggested Questions you tag, with space to add your own, so they're handy when the doctor comes around;

— Remember to Do List—keeps your tasks organized;

— Treasured Mementos—a checklist of objects for you to gather as precious keepsakes;

— Share—easily update family and friends by sharing any page of MyPreemie by email or Facebook. You can also print pages as PDF to save. This app was developed by authors of the book *PREEMIES: The Essential Guide for Parents of Premature Babies.*

- **Part C of the Individuals With Disabilities Act (IDEA) is focused on Early Intervention Services for infants and toddlers**
  http://ectacenter.org/contact/ptccoord.asp

  The Federal Early Childhood Technical Center's website provides contact information for each state's Part C lead coordinator as well as other helpful information about the services that are offered and eligibility. Become knowledgeable regarding the Early Intervention criteria for infants born prematurely in your state.

Part 5
Appendices

Appendix A: Infant States of Consciousness

An infant's *state of consciousness* refers to the varied levels of alertness that can be observed in a very young infant. The healthy full-term newborn enters the world with six observable states of consciousness. Being able to identify these states in a young infant forms a foundation for using this guide to educate parents.

In two of the states the infant is asleep, in the other four states the baby is alert. Because babies have these varying levels of alertness, they are able to have some control over how much stimulation they receive. Depending on the baby's state, stimulation can be either appropriate or inappropriate (Brazelton & Nugent, 1995). Knowing about these states and the behaviors related to the them may help parents and caregivers be more successful and less frustrated in caring for the baby (Nugent, 1985). Learning about these states can give parents clues about what their baby needs or is interested in.

Summary

Sleep states: deep and light
Awake states: drowsy, quiet alert, active alert, and crying

Detailed Descriptions and Caregiving Implications

Deep sleep. The baby's eyes are closed and the baby's body is very still. Occasionally the baby may make suckling motions with his mouth at regular intervals. There is almost no body activity except for an occasional startle or twitch. The baby's breathing is slow and regular and almost undetectable. There may be very disturbing stimuli nearby, but the baby tends to respond maybe once or twice, then continues to sleep (Brazelton & Nugent, 1995; Nugent, 1985). Only very disturbing stimuli will rouse the baby, and even then the baby may quickly return to sleep. A parent attempting to rouse a baby from a deep sleep for a feeding may be frustrated because the baby will wake only briefly and fall back to sleep. If waking a baby for a feeding is needed, parents should be advised to wait until the baby is in light sleep or drowsy state. The baby will be more responsive, and it will be a more pleasant experience for both the baby and the parent. When a baby is in deep sleep, it is best not to disturb him. The baby is resting and growing.

Deep sleep

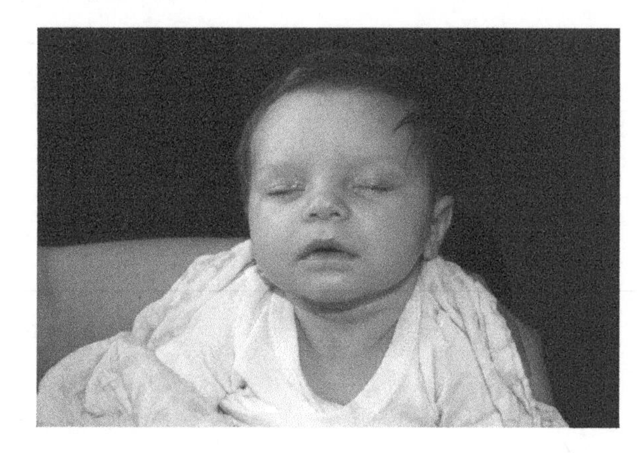

Light sleep

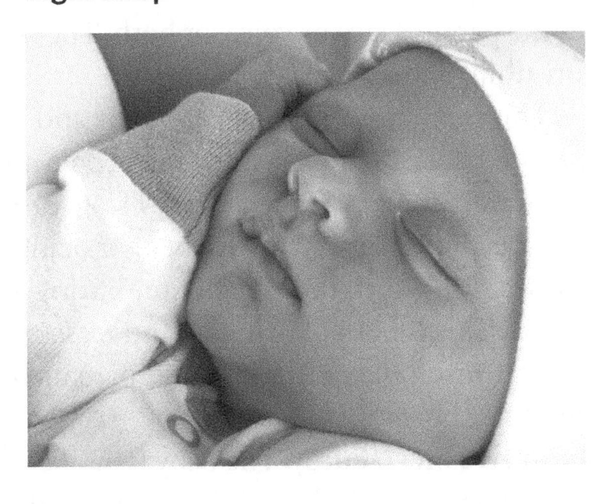

Light sleep. In the light sleep state, the baby is visibly still sleeping. The baby's face is slightly more animated, and the baby may smile briefly or fuss a little. The baby's body shows some slight movements. Rapid eye movements are seen under the closed eyelids. The breathing pattern is easily detected and is irregular. If there is sound or movement, the baby is more likely to respond by moving or grimacing but may not wake up. The baby also responds to internal stimuli. Light sleep makes up the highest proportion of newborn sleep and usually occurs before the baby wakes.

The fussing sounds the baby makes in light sleep can confuse caregivers. They may think the baby has awakened, yet the baby is not alert enough to feed or play with. It is best to let her continue to sleep. At times a baby goes into to a light sleep when she has had too much excitement and needs to lessen the stimulation she is taking in.

Drowsy

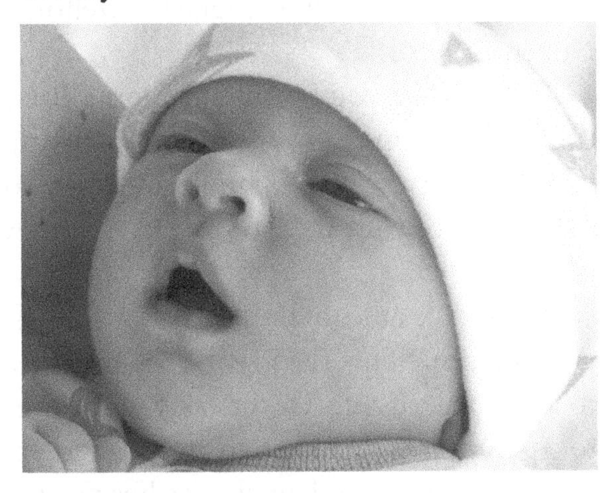

Drowsy. The baby's eyes open and close, but the look is rather dull and unfocused. There may be some facial movement such as yawning or stretching. The baby's activity level varies, with some mild startling or gentle movements. The breathing pattern is irregular. In the drowsy state, a baby may continue to increase his level of alertness, or return to sleep.

If a baby is left alone, he may fall back to sleep. If picked up and talked to, the baby becomes more alert (Brazelton & Nugent, 1995; Nugent, 1985). If it is about time for a feeding, picking up a baby in a drowsy state and getting him into an upright position while talking to him will usually bring him into a more alert state in which he is ready to eat and interact.

Quiet alert

Quiet alert. The baby's eyes are wide open and bright, and the baby's eyes widen in response to visual stimuli presented within 8–15 inches. The baby responds to sound by raising the brow and sometimes shifting the eyes or turning the head to locate the sound.

The baby is attentive to the environment and focuses attention on interesting stimuli, such as the parent's face or voice, or both. The baby's body is still (Brazelton & Nugent, 1995). Breathing has a regulated pattern.

This is an important time for baby and parents to spend in social interaction. An infant in a quiet alert state can study the people and things around her—this is an optimal learning time. An infant in a quiet alert state provides positive feedback and reassurance to parents that she is typical. Right after being born, many infants have a prolonged period of alertness in which they spend time gazing at their parents and responding (Klaus & Klaus, 1999). This is both pleasurable and reassuring for parents and reassuring to parents. When the baby is in the quiet alert state, parents begin to learn how responsive and interactive their newborn can be.

Active alert/Fussy. The baby is awake with open eyes. His body is in motion and his breathing patterns become more irregular. His arms and legs may be in motion. His face is much more animated. The baby becomes increasingly sensitive to disturbing stimuli such as excessive noise or handling, in addition to hunger and fatigue (Brazelton & Nugent, 1995).

Fussy

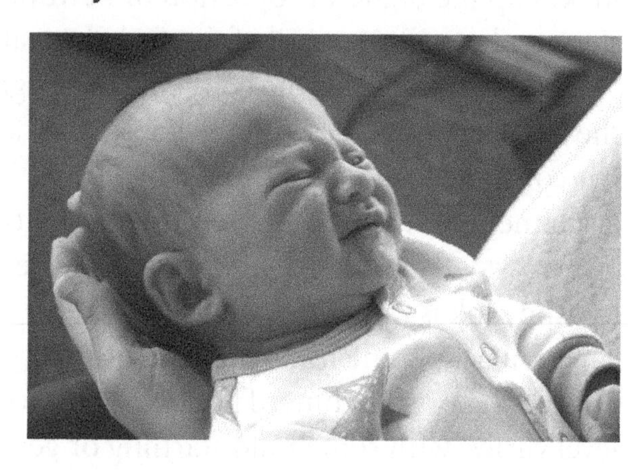

"I am telling you I would like some attention before I am really uncomfortable. I may be able to soothe myself, but I love when you help me with your voice or touch!" (Guiney, 2013, p. 10).

Crying

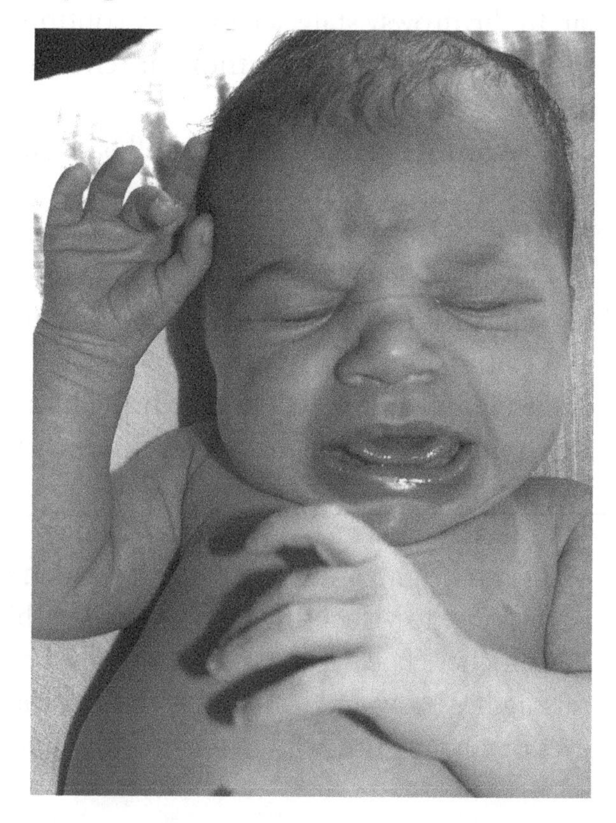

If a baby is able to find her fist or fingers and begin sucking, she may be able to return to a quiet alert state. Or the baby may tune in to a parent talking to her, focus on an interesting sight or sound, or change her position. These are ways a baby self-calms. If a parent intervenes at this point by picking the baby up, feeding the baby, or talking to the baby in higher pitched tones, the baby may return to a quiet alert state. Without intervention, the baby may begin full-blown crying. Sometimes crying is inevitable.

Crying. It would be hard to misinterpret the crying state. The baby is loud, and the sound of the cry evokes concern or anxiety in the parents. The baby's body movements increase dramatically. The baby's face may become very red, and her eyes are either tightly closed or open. Her face grimaces, and she responds to any unpleasant stimulation (Brazelton & Nugent, 1995).

"I am trying to tell you I've reached my limits. I need to know you're there for me. If you pick me up and walk with me, we can figure it out together" (Guiney, 2013, p. 13).

The baby's cry is his most powerful way to communicate that his limits have been reached or exceeded. Crying may indicate the baby is hungry, tired, cold, or uncomfortable in some way. A baby may make attempts (sometimes successful) to console himself by sucking on his fist or fingers. Typically, picking up and holding a crying baby begins to lessen the intensity of the crying. Other ways to comfort a crying baby are by talking, singing, gently touching, or rocking.

Appendix B: Infant Observation Guide

The observation activities are designed to assist Welcome Baby Levels 1 and 2 educators in being able to recognize and describe infant states and state-related behaviors based on first-hand experiences practicing identifying newborn states and key newborn behaviors.

Arrange opportunities to observe and interact with 8 to 10 very young infants. With this number, you are likely to see a full range of states and many infant cues and behaviors. Continue adding to your observation skills by learning from every parent and baby you work with. (Note that completion of Infant Observation Guides is not sufficient training for use of the Welcome Baby Level 3 protocols.)

Process for Learning

1. Study the Infant Observation Activity and Developmental Context sections in Pathways 1–7, walking through the activities with your Teaching Teddy before completing these exercises.
2. Study the descriptions of infant states of consciousness in Appendix A.
3. Arrange for observations of infants who are less than 3 months old. As a Welcome Baby Levels 1 and 2 educator, you should arrange 8 to 10 observations. These may be in the form of home visits.
4. Read the Infant Observation Guide thoroughly before you begin observing.
5. Specifically study the protocols for the crying baby in Pathway 4 and ask permission from the parents to practice getting the baby into the Flex/Hold position. Bring your Teaching Teddy to demonstrate the Flex/Hold before trying it with the baby.
6. The Infant Observation Guide includes activities to engage in along with the baby based on the baby's state of consciousness. These activities will help illuminate state of consciousness related behaviors and influences on state-related behaviors. Once you have identified the baby's state of consciousness, engage in the activity of that state. During a 30-minute period, you will likely observe the baby in at least two or three states. Keep in mind that if the baby changes states, you will need to change activities and be ready to observe for different behaviors.
7. Do not attempt to complete the Infant Observation Guide in detail during the time you are observing the baby, because writing will distract you from the observation. Have a pen and paper to jot down a few notes as you can during the observation.

Explain to parents you are in the process of learning about infant development and infant behavior by observing babies. Offer to share a copy of Infant States of Consciousness (Appendix A) and the Infant Observation Guide with parents. They may enjoy observing along with you, and it can become a learning experience for all. These sessions provide excellent opportunities to practice listening and responding to the parents' birth story. Use the opportunity to gain insights into the perceptions, thoughts, and questions of the parents. Allow every baby to teach you about the marvelous capabilities of the human infant!

Take time afterward to reflect and write. Be sure to complete an Infant Observation Guide form for each infant. After you have completed them all, read through them and reflect upon what you learned from these babies and the parents using the Reflective Practice Guide questions (Appendix D).

8. Make multiple copies of the Pathways Infant Observation Guide and keep one copy as a master. Refer to Appendix A: Infant States of Consciousness. Read the following descriptions of infant states of consciousness thoroughly, so as to be able to identify each one when you use the Infant Observation Guide to observe newborns.

Explain that it is normal to not see everything listed in the form in one observation session. Explain that there is no right or wrong way for the baby to behave, that all of the baby's ways of being will help you learn about newborn development.

Using the Guide

This guide is adapted from the Neonatal Behavioral Assessment Scale (NBAS; Brazelton & Nugent, 1995) for use by educators in self-guided observation of newborns and very young infants. This guide is intended to help you become familiar with newborn states of consciousness and infant behaviors and to assist you in practicing integration of these observations in your conversations with parents. Bring along your Teaching Teddy and Teaching Photographs to each observation session.

Explain to the parents what you will be looking for. These guided observation/interaction activities will give you insights into how to use the Teaching Photographs and Teaching Teddy by having witnessed first-hand the newborn's states, behaviors, and responses to selected stimuli. By focusing on these observations now, educators will be able to portray them through use of the Teaching Photographs and Teaching Teddy protocols later with details. Every opportunity to interact with parents and newborns can be an enriching experience for you as the educator. After each session, reflect on what you learned from the parents and baby and your interaction and conversation with them

Keep in mind that the baby might be crying when you arrive. You will need to be prepared to address and observe crying as your first activity (Pathway 4) versus observing a baby in deep sleep (Pathway 2). The key is to be comfortable starting wherever the baby is in terms of state of consciousness or with the topic the parent is immediately interested in talking about.

Pathways Infant Observation Guide

Today's date__________

Baby's Name:________________________________ Sex________ DOB ____________

Gestational age at birth__________Weight__________

Type of delivery: ____

Other important background information: ___________________________

____

STATE-RELATED BEHAVIORS/ACTIVITIES:

Activity 1: DEEP SLEEP

Observe the baby in deep sleep for at least 2 minutes, noting all the characteristics of deep sleep (body very still, breathing is regular and may be hard to detect, occasional startle movement). Describe:

If the baby wakes up, describe the baby's new state and the baby's behavior:

Activity 2: LIGHT SLEEP OR DROWSY

Observe the baby in light sleep for 2 minutes and note all the characteristics of light sleep (baby moves about a bit, breathing is irregular, while the eyes are closed you see them moving under the eyelids).

After a few minutes of observing in light sleep, ask the parent to dim the lighting and unwrap the baby. You may find the baby begins to waken or the baby's eyes open—or the baby returns to deep sleep. Describe the baby's response:

Activity 3: DROWSY

Ask the parent to pick the baby up and place the baby in an upright position, talk to the baby, and use gentle vertical movement to gently rock the baby while you demonstrate this with the Teaching Teddy. Describe what happens (baby becomes more alert, acts hungry, begins to cry?):

Activity 4: QUIET ALERT

Ask the parent to pick the baby up and hold the baby about 8–10 inches away from his/her face. Ask the parent to talk to the baby. If the baby focuses on the parent's face, ask the parent to (without talking), try slowly moving to the right or left to see if the baby will focus and follow. Demonstrate this for the parent first by using the Teaching Teddy.
Describe:

Activity 5: ACTIVE ALERT/FUSSY

In this state, the baby may be very animated and may begin to fuss. Ask the parent to wait a minute or two when the baby reaches this state in order to see how the baby manages. Ask the parent to not intervene unless the baby cries. Explain that you can both observe the ways the baby attempts to self-calm. Place a check mark by all self-consoling behaviors observed:

___Baby changes position

___Sucks on fists or fingers

___Suck on tongue

___Brings hands near the mouth

___Attends to sounds

___Pays attention to visual stimulation

___Other (describe):

Activity 6: CRYING

Talk about this activity before the baby cries. If the parent is comfortable with this activity when the baby cries, ask the parent to allow the baby to cry for 5 seconds before intervening. Note if the baby makes any attempts to soothe or calm himself before anyone intervenes. If not, then ask the parent to try this sequence to comfort the baby that you have demonstrated—talk them through the sequence: while demonstrating with the Teaching Teddy (see Pathway 4—The Crying Baby).

1. Place a hand on the baby's tummy.
2. Contain any flailing limbs.
3. Pick the baby up and talk to the baby.
4. Place the baby in the Flex/Hold position described in Pathway 4. Be sure you have practiced this with the Teaching Teddy so you can give an informed demonstration.

Describe what worked:

Activity 7: INFANT CAPABILITIES

Place a check mark next to each behavior observed. The baby was able to:

____self-soothe by suckling or by placing a hand on face

____turn toward the sound of a voice (quiet alert state only)

____focus and follow visually

____indicate a need by crying

____be consoled by an adult

____tune out stimulation when in a deep sleep

____other (Describe):

Infant States: Complete this section after you have finished observing. If completed at the end of the session with the parent this can serve as a review of all that was observed during the session.

Amount of time spent observing:

Make a check mark by each of the states you observed during this session and enter comments from your observation:

1.____ Deep sleep

2.____ Light sleep

3.____ Drowsy

4.____ Quiet alert

5.____ Active alert

6.____ Crying

Additional Notes

What did *you* learn from this session from the baby, parent, or both? What did you learn about yourself as an educator?

Appendix C: Working With a Distressed Parent

If you suspect a parent is distressed or depressed, talk with the parent directly about your concerns. You should repeat back to the parent what you heard her say that caused your concern: "I heard you say you feel you can't take care of your baby because you feel so overwhelmed. Is that right?" If necessary, ask more questions to be sure you have understood correctly and to gain an increased understanding of the parent's level of stress or distress. Have the parent sign a release form so you are able to contact the parent's doctor, social worker, or relative on her behalf and share your concerns, if it should become necessary or if the parent agrees it would be helpful.

Contact the parent the next day or sooner if it seems necessary. Be sure to verify the phone number where you can reach the parent and be sure they have phone access.

Remind the parent who is there to help them when you are not there. A friend? A family member? A crisis line? Does your community have a crisis nursery where the child could spend a few days to give the parent respite? Stay with the parent and encourage the parent to call 911 if she feels she will harm herself or the baby. Emphasize that many mothers and fathers experience PPD, and that it is a sign of strength to seek help and support. Offer to seek help on the parent's behalf by contacting the person(s) indicated on the release form the parent signed.

Ensure the child's safety. Is this a situation where a call to child protection is warranted? If so, let the parent know you think the situation is that serious and why. If you do need to take this step, try to have the parent(s) make the report, if possible, with your support. Monitor the child's well-being. Is the parent able to cope well enough to take care of the child? Perhaps with support she will be able to provide adequate care? Who can be that support? Arrange for the child to have a developmental screening (including social-emotional areas) if the child shows signs of stress or is delayed in his development.

If a source of stress for the parent has to do with a situation such as housing, child care, or finances, find someone who has expertise in that area and help the parent make a connection with that person.

After intervening or addressing the parent's distress, document the date, time, and details of the situation, and let your supervisor know there is a crisis situation with a family participating in your program. Alert other team members who work with this family that there is a serious situation or potential crisis. Encourage them to be supportive to the parent as well as vigilant. See if another staff member has a close relationship with the parent and can help provide follow-up and support. Continue to monitor the child's well-being.

Often when working with a distressed parent, educators take on the emotional burdens and may be unaware of the toll it takes on their own psyches. Be sure to talk about your experience with this family to a supportive colleague to identify feelings that may arise from dealing with a difficult situation and to decrease your personal burden if you are the only one dealing with the situation directly.

Appendix D: Reflective Practice Guide

This simple tool, presented as a series of questions, is intended to help you incorporate reflective practice in your work with infants and parents. Documenting your thoughts regularly will enable you to take a step back and examine your own thoughts and feelings about the work you are doing. Reflective practice routines can help you notice things that may not have been clear in the moment. Practitioners are constantly evolving and developing, just as the families and children they work with are evolving and developing. If you work in an agency or program where others do similar work, consider forming a reflective practice discussion group.

What did I learn today from interacting with this child?

What did I learn today from interacting with this parent?

What went well today in my interaction with the parents and infants? Why did it feel successful?

What interaction or situation made me feel uncomfortable or uncertain? Why was this uncomfortable?

What resources or support do I need to do this work?

Appendix E: *Pathways* in Context

There have been many adaptations of the Neonatal Behavioral Assessment Scale (NBAS; Brazelton & Nugent, 1995) for parent education (Beal, 1986; Higley & Miller, 1996; Hotelling, 2004; Nugent & Brazelton, 1989; Tedder, 2008; Worobey, 1985). Although *Pathways* utilizes the states of consciousness as a way to organize its content, *Pathways* techniques are markedly different from the work described by Nugent, and others, who have adapted the NBAS to educate parents and heighten their sensitivity to the infant (Blackburn & Kang, 1991; Worobey, 1985). As Nugent and Brazelton (1989) stated in an article titled "Preventive Intervention With Infants and Families: The NBAS Model," "Because the infant and his or her behavior are at the center of the intervention process, competence in administering the NBAS is a sine qua non for the clinician. . . . It is the sensitivity and appropriateness of the clinicians handling techniques that mediate full exposition of the infant's individuality" (p. 94). In other words, at the core of the NBAS is the direct handling of infants by clinicians trained to elicit and interpret behaviors. The focus is primarily on the immediate meaning of the elicited responses. Parents observe the clinician administer the exam to their baby. Efforts are made to cover as much of the NBAS assessment in order to have the fullest picture of the baby. Clinicians using the NBAS are trained to systematically administer the exam and provide a profile of an infant's individuality, strengths and/or concerns (Nugent & Brazelton, 1989).

In *Pathways*, Welcome Baby Level 1, the educator is not encouraged to handle the infant or elicit behaviors. The emphasis is on learning what the parent has observed and uses the baby's current state of consciousness as a starting point for a thoughtful conversation with the parent. The *Pathways* curriculum provides information to share about observations the parents may make about their infants or observations of behaviors the parent and the educator may share in the moment. *Pathways* Teaching Photographs help create teachable moments by portraying babies in various states so that the parents and educator have an opportunity to explore behaviors beyond the baby's current state of consciousness. The Teaching Teddy, a key educational strategy in *Pathways*, allows the educator to demonstrate techniques in a realistic way, without directly touching the baby— similar to how infant massage instructors use a baby doll to guide parents in working with their babies (because infant massage acknowledges that contact with the baby empowers the parent's care of their baby and promotes attachment; McClure, 1998). Although exploring each Pathway with parents is desirable, an educator may decide to cover only particular Pathways depending on the circumstances.

Pathways Welcome Baby Level 1 provides educators with ideas of how to engage parents in a conversation around their birthing experience, asking parents to share observations they have made about their baby. When appropriate, the educator may share additional information through the use of *Pathways* information, Teaching Photographs, and additional observations of the baby. By using the Teaching Photographs, the educator is also able to engage parents in conversations about social cues of babies—even though their baby may currently be sleeping.

In *Pathways* Welcome Baby Level 2, the assumption is made that these individuals are already, due to their professional role, engaged in handling the baby as part of the work. (For example, home visiting nurses, postpartum nurses, physicians, and those providing care to the infant.) In the course of handling the baby, Welcome Baby Level 2 provides ideas for how to capitalize on opportunities to have the baby respond, particularly to the parent, and to enhance interpretation of the infant's responses for the parent. These individuals may find all of the techniques in Welcome Baby Level 1 useful in their work. In addition, suggestions have been added in Welcome Baby Level 2 for ways to demonstrate infant behavior in the course of handling the baby as part of their role with the family. In some instances, the suggestions are drawn from techniques used in administering the NBAS (Brazelton & Nugent, 1995) and adapted to involve the parent.

For those educators already certified in NBAS, *Pathways* provides techniques and suggestions for modifying the NBAS to include parents and to expand on the information offered. Programs that use NBAS often have the parent observe the examiner interacting with the baby (Beal, 1986; Higley & Miller, 1996; Tedder, 1991). *Pathways* seeks to place the parent at the center of the activity. Welcome Baby Level 3 includes adaptations of selected items from the NBAS designed to promote more parent involvement. For example, in the NBAS, the examiner presents his voice to the baby in an effort to get the baby to turn toward it, thus demonstrating the infant's ability to use her auditory capacities to both orient and engage. In Pathway 3, Welcome Baby Level 2, the educator engages the parent in a short teaching session regarding the type of high-pitched speaking that appeals to the young infant. The educator then holds the baby in midline position and asks the parent to call to the baby, to observe how the baby responds to the parent's voice. In the NBAS, this activity is repeated two times to the baby's right and left sides by the NBAS examiner. Here, however, the intent is to capitalize on an opportunity to have the baby respond to the parent, and then talk more about this. The educator may expand the conversation to how the baby already responds to the parent's voice by alerting and calming and that talking to the baby will increase his opportunities to pay attention and learn to communicate. When the baby's eyes shift or head turns toward the parent, it provides an excellent opportunity to show the parent how the baby already knows his voice.

Another protocol that reframes the NBAS and adapts techniques for involving parents is the Family Administered Neonatal Activities (FANA; Cardone & Gilkerson, 1995). The FANA is an adaptation of the NBAS in which the educator helps the parents administer, observe, and interpret the observations. Like *Pathways*, the FANA emphasizes the parent's responses and values the opportunity to process the labor and birth experiences. The FANA facilitator integrates comments into a discussion of infant state, and parents help transition their infant in various states. The FANA has an element of psychodynamic interviewing and a strong family empowerment approach (Cardone & Gilkerson, 1995). A FANA facilitator, who is NBAS trained, guides the parents in administering the NBAS with the infant. Along the way, they ask the parents what they have observed as a way to heighten the parents' awareness of their baby's skills and to draw the parent into a dialogue about their baby and themselves.

Pathways is designed to be used in individual sessions or in parent groups. *Pathways* uses the framework of states of consciousness (Brazelton & Nugent, 1995; Wolff, 1959). For example, Pathway 2 focuses on the baby in the sleep states, Pathway 3 focuses on the the baby in a quiet alert state, and so forth.

Pathway 1—The Transitioning Baby explores both the baby's and parent's transitions after birth, with an emphasis on teaching parents about PPD, its effects on parents and babies, and how to encourage parents to seek help. Pathway 5—The Oral Baby highlights support for breastfeeding, feeding techniques, and the importance of interactions that occur during feeding. Pathway 6—The Dexterous Baby explores the initial reflexes of the baby's hands and feet, with a view to how these reflexes change and more advanced skills develop. Within Pathway 7—The Strong Baby, the focus is on ensuring parents understand how important awake prone positioning is to their baby's overall physical development.

Featured within each Pathway is a Parent Care section. For example, in Pathway 7, when discussing the importance of the baby getting awake prone exercise (tummy time) there are suggestions for bringing up a discussion of the need for parents to keep up their own strength by exercising. In Pathway 5—The Oral Baby, parents are encouraged to consider their own nutritional needs. Parent Care sections are embedded in each Pathway in order to address postpartum topics that are likely to impact new parents, such as the lack of sleep, frustration with the baby's crying, postpartum blues/depression, support for breastfeeding, and more. The *Pathways* content is well suited for postpartum programs because the topics and up-to-date content can provide a core curriculum, whether done individually or in a parent group setting.

The NBAS has inspired many to find ways to utilize the amazing capabilities of the newborn to help enhance the beginning of the parent–infant relationship. *Pathways* is no exception to the many parent-education programs that owe gratitude to Dr. Brazelton's groundbreaking work (Brazelton & Nugent, 1995).

Appendix F: A Brief History of the Development of *Pathways*

During my master's degree program at Wheelock College, I had the honor of completing an internship at the Harvard Child Development Research Unit then directed by Dr. Berry Brazelton. The time spent in the internship was pivotal in my career. During my internship I learned to administer the Neonatal Behavioral Assessments Scale (NBAS) and spent hours observing Dr. Brazelton talk with parents and coach others in his approach, the Touchpoint Model. Combining this information with my child development knowledge, I joined Joann O'Leary, who was also NBAS certified, in providing the Infant as a Person class for parents of newborns prior to discharge from the hospital, as well as a postpartum group for parents and babies. Joann and I adapted many of the NBAS items in our practice. With the explosion of research in the 1990s that confirmed the importance of getting parents and infants off to a good start, we had many come to observe our work. We realized, however, that it was unrealistic for the vast number of professionals who wanted to emulate our work to complete the NBAS training and certification. As I reflected on my own practice, I realized that I had interwoven many other ideas into each session.

The first version of the *Pathways* guide began its development in 2000 for the Minneapolis Early Childhood Family Education (ECFE) program. Thirteen individuals were initially trained to provide Welcome Baby classes at local hospitals. The medical staff welcomed the ECFE educators into the hospitals because they recognized the value of the information provided to parents. Parents also affirmed that what they learned was important and useful in. In 2006, a continuing education course was developed using *Pathways* at University of Minnesota through the Center for Early Education and Development. In 2009, another course was developed to adapt the *Pathways* information and strategies for working with parents of prematurely born infants. Between these two courses, a total of 270 professionals from diverse backgrounds (many of them with significant years of experience) wrote in their course evaluations that *Pathways* was both helpful and complementary to their work.

Appendix G: Creating Teaching Points

You can create a *Pathways* Teaching Photograph booklet by carefully removing the Teaching Photographs from the back of your book. Place them in sheet protectors and use a three-ring binder to display them, or purchase a presentation booklet that has sheet protectors bound into the booklet. You can incorporate your Teaching Points into this booklet.

To create Teaching Points, read and study the information found in each Pathway. Create a document that lists key points you want to cover when discussing the topics in each Pathway with parents. Place this page in your Teaching Photograph booklet, facing the correct Pathway. When you work with parents, the points will remind you of important content or resources you wish to share. Use PowerPoint to create the teaching points documents; this gives them a crisp, professional look and will automatically create the bullet points in a landscape document, which will then fit into the Teaching Photographs booklet. Include the details you think would be helpful to remember and helpful to parents. Parents generally don't read the Teaching Points, they look at the photos; the Teaching Points are prompts for you. As you gain experience using your Teaching Points, you can revise and update them.

Example:

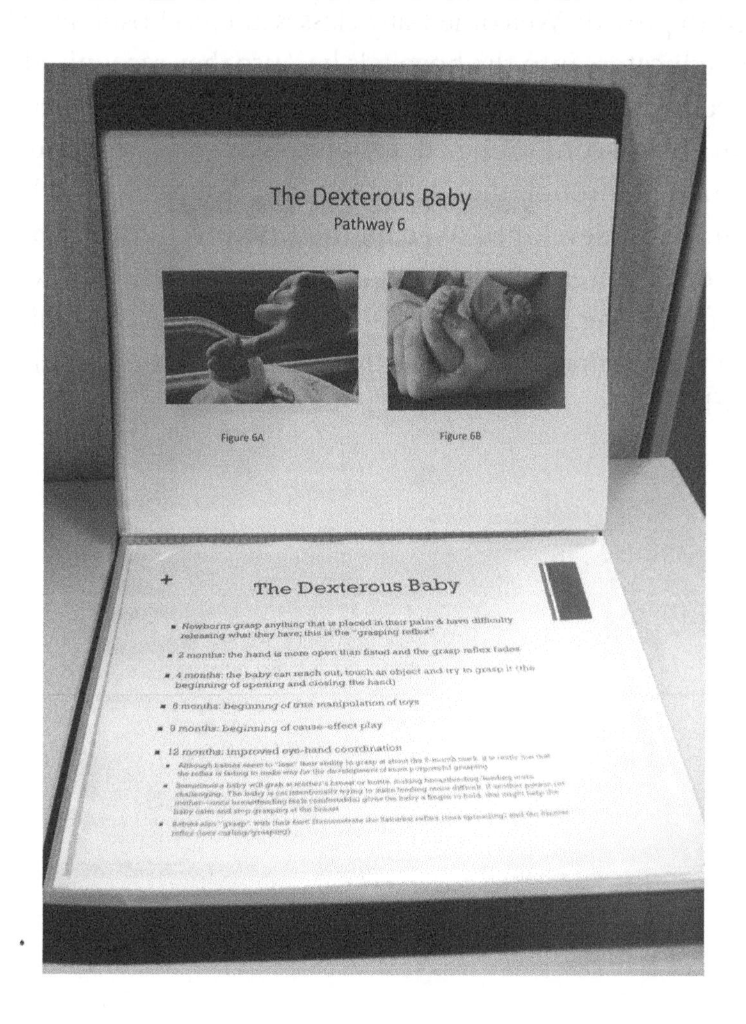

Part 6
References

Abbott, A., & Bartlett, D. (2001). Infant motor development and equipment use in the home. *Child Care, Health and Development, 27*(3), 295–304.

Ainsworth, M. D. (1969). Object relations, dependency, and attachment: A theoretical review of the infant-mother relationship. *Child Development*, 969–1025.

Ainsworth, M. D. (1985). Patterns of attachment. *Clinical Psychologist, 38*(2), 27–29.

Ainsworth, M., Blehar, M., Waters, E., & Wall, S. (1978). *Patterns of attachment: A psychological study of the strange situation.* Hillsdale, NJ: Erlbaum.

Alexander, R., Boehme, R., & Cupps, B. (1993). *Normal functional motor skills the first year of life.* Tuscon, AZ: Therapy Skill Builders.

Allen, K. A. (2012). Promoting and protecting infant sleep. *Advances in Neonatal Care: Official Journal of the National Association of Neonatal Nurses, 12*(5), 288–291.

Allen, M., & Capute, A. (1990). Tone and reflex development before term. *Pediatrics, 85*, 393–399.

Als, H. (1982). Toward a synactive theory of development: Promise for the assessment and support of infant individuality. *Infant Mental Health Journal, 3*, 229–243.

Als, H. (1993). *Newborn Individualized Developmental Care and Assessment Program (NIDCAP) guide.* Boston, MA: National NIDCAP Center.

Als, H., & Gilkerson, L. (1995). Developmentally supportive care in the neonatal intensive care unit. *Zero to Three, 15*(6), 1–10.

Altimier, L. (2008). Shaken baby syndrome. *Journal of Perinatal and Neonatal Nursing, 22*(1), 68–76.

Altman, R. L., Canter, J., Patrick, P. A., Daley, N., Butt, N. K., & Brand, D. A. (2011). Parent education by maternity nurses and prevention of abusive head trauma. *Pediatrics, 128*(5), e1164–e1172. doi:10.1542/peds.2010-3260

American Academy of Pediatrics. (2000). Changing concepts of sudden infant death syndrome: Implications for infant sleeping environments and sleep position (Policy statement). *Pediatrics, 105*(3), 650–656.

American Academy of Pediatrics, Committee on Environmental Health. (2003). *Handbook of pediatric environmental health* (2nd ed.). Washington, DC: Author.

American Academy of Pediatrics. (2012). Breastfeeding and the use of human milk (Policy statement). *Pediatrics, 115*(2), 496–506.

American Academy of Pediatrics. (2012). Breastfeeding and the use of human milk [Policy statement]. *Pediatrics, 129*(3), e827–e841. doi:10.1542/peds.2011-3552

American Occupational Therapy Association. (2013). *Establishing tummy time routines to enhance your baby's development*. Retrieved from www.aota.org/about-occupational-therapy/patients-clients/childrenandyouth/tummy-time.aspx

American Psychiatric Association. (2015). *Diagnostic and statistical manual of mental disorders* (5th ed.). Arlington, VA: Author.

Anders, T., Goodlin-Jones, B., & Zelenko, M. (1998). Infant regulation and sleep-wake development. *Zero to Three, 11*(5), 5–8.

Argenta, L., David, L., Wilson, J., & Bell, W. (1996). An increase in infant cranial facial deformity with supine sleeping position. *Craniofacial Surgery, 7*(1) 5-11.

Babik, I., Campbell, J. M., & Michel, G. F. (2014). Postural influences on the development of infant lateralized and symmetric hand use. *Child Development, 85*(1), 294–307. doi:10.1111/cdev.12121

Baranowski, M. D., Schilmoeller, G. L., & Higgins, B. S. (1990). Parenting attitudes of adolescent and older mothers. *Adolescence, 25*(100), 781–790.

Barnard, K., Morisset, C., & Spieker, S. (1993). Preventive interventions: Enhancing parent–infant relationships. In C. H. Zeanah Jr. (Ed.), *Handbook of infant mental health* (pp. 386–401). New York, NY: Guilford Press.

Barnet, A., & Barnet, R. (1998). *The youngest minds: Parenting and genetic inheritance in the development of intellect and emotion.* New York, NY: Simon & Schuster.

Barr, R. G. (2012). Preventing abusive head trauma resulting from a failure of normal interaction between infants and their caregivers. *Proceedings of the National Academy of Sciences, 109* (Suppl. 2), 17294–17301. doi:10.1073/pnas.1121267109

Barr, R., Fairbrother, N., Pauwels, J., Green, J., Chen, M., & Brant, R. (2014). Maternal frustration, emotional and behavioural responses to prolonged infant crying. *Infant Behavior and Development, 37*(4), 652–664.

Barsuhn, R. (2008). *Growing Sophia: The story of a premature baby* (2nd ed.). St. Paul, MN: Hummingwing Press.

Bartick, M., & Reinhold, A. (2010). The burden of suboptimal breastfeeding in the United States: A pediatric cost analysis. *Pediatrics, 125*(5), e1048–e1056. doi:10.1542/peds.2009–1616

Beal, J. (1986). The Brazelton Neonatal Behavioral Assessment Scale: A tool to enhance parental attachment. *Journal of Pediatric Nursing, 1*(3), 170–177.

Beard, M., & Dallwitz, A. (1995). Play position is influenced by knowledge of SIDS sleep position. *Journal of Pediatric Health, 31*(6), 499–502.

Beck, C. (2006). Postpartum depression: It isn't just the blues. *The American Journal of Nursing, 106*(5), 40–50.

Beckwith, L. (1990). Adaptive and maladaptive parenting: Implications for intervention. In J. P. Shonkoff & S. J. Meisels (Eds.), *Handbook for early childhood intervention* (pp. 53–77). Cambridge, United Kington: Cambridge University Press.

Beeghly, M., & Tronick, E. (2011). Early resilience in the context of parent-infant relationships: A social developmental perspective. *Current Problems in Pediatric and Adolescent Health Care, 41*(7), 197–201. doi:10.1016/j.cppeds.2011.02.005

Bennet, S., & Indman, P. (2003). *Beyond the blues: A guide to understanding and treating prenatal and postpartum depression.* San Jose, CA: Moodswings Press.

Birnholz, J. (1981). The development of human fetal eye movement features. *Science, 213*, 679–681.

Birnholz, J. (1983). The development of human fetal hearing. *Science, 222*, 516–518.

Blackburn, S., DePaul, D., Loan, L., Marbut, K., Taquino, L., Thomas, K., & Wilson, S. (2001). Neonatal thermal care, part III: The effect of infant position and temperature probe placement. *Neonatal Network, 20*(3), 25–30.

Blackburn, S., & Kang, R. (1991). *Early parent–infant relationships: Series 1. The first six hours after birth: Module 3.* White Plains, NY: March of Dimes.

Blackburn, S., & Vandenberg, K. (1993). Assessment and management of neonatal neurobehavioral development. In C. Kenner Brueggemeyer & L. Gunderson (Eds.), *Comprehensive neonatal care: A physiologic perspective* (pp. 1094–1133). Philadelphia, PA: W. B. Saunders.

Blucker, R., Gillaspy, J., Jr., Jackson, D., Hetherington, C., Kyler, K., Cherry, A., & Gillaspy, S. R. (2014). Postpartum depression in the NICU: An examination of the factor structure of the Postpartum Depression Screening Scale. *Advances in Neonatal Care, 14*(6), 424–432.

Bly, L. (1994). *Motor skill acquisition in the first year.* Tucson, AZ: Therapy Skill Builders.

Boukydis, Z. (2012). *Collaborative consultation with parents and infants in the perinatal period.* Baltimore, MD: Brookes.

Bowlby, J. (1969/1982). *Attachment and loss: Vol. 1. Attachment* (2nd ed.). New York, NY: Basic Books.

Braun, L., Coplon, J., & Sonnenschein, P. (1984). *Helping parents in groups: A leader's handbook.* Boston, MA: Wheelock College Press.

Brazelton, T. B. (1992). *Touchpoints: The essential reference.* Reading, MA: Merloyd Lawrence.

Brazelton, T. B., & Cramer, B. (1990). *The earliest relationship: Parents, infants and the drama of early attachment.* Reading, MA: Merloyd Lawrence.

Brazelton, T. B., & Nugent, K. (1995). *Neonatal behavioral assessment scale* (3rd ed.). Cambridge, MA: Cambridge University Press.

Brazelton, T. B., & Sparrow, J. (2003). *Calming your fussy baby the Brazelton way.* Cambridge, MA: Merloyd Lawrence.

Breastfeeding—Best for baby. Best for mom. (n.d.). Retrieved from www.womenshealth.gov/breastfeeding

Bromwich, R. (1997). *Working with families and their infants at risk: A perspective after 20 years of experience.* Austin, TX: Pro-Ed.

Brown, A. (2011). Media use by children younger than 2 years. *Pediatrics, 128*(5), 1040–1045.

Cantle, A., (2013). Alleviating the impact of stress and trauma in the neonatal unit and beyond. *Infant Observation, 16*(3), 257–269. doi:10.1080/13698036.2013.852723

Cardone, I., & Gilkerson, L. (1989). Family Administered Neonatal Activities: An innovative component of family-centered care. *Zero to Three, 10*(2), 23–28.

Cardone, I. A., & Gilkerson, L. (1995). Family Administered Neonatal Activities (FANA). *Clinics in Developmental Medicine,* (137), 111–116.

Carroll, L. (1953). *Alice in Wonderland.* Mount Vernon, NY: Peter Pauper Press.

Centers for Disease Control and Prevention. (2013). *Breastfeeding report card 2013.* Retrieved from www.cdc.gov/breastfeeding/pdf/2013breastfeedingreportcard.pdf

Centers for Disease Control and Prevention. (2014). *Compressed mortality file.* Retrieved from /www.cdc.gov/nchs/data_access/cmf.htm

Christian, C. W., & Block, R. (2009). Abusive head trauma in infants and children. *Pediatrics, 123*(5), 1409–1411.

Cinar, N. (2004). The advantages and disadvantages of pacifier use. *Contemporary Nurse, 17,* 109–112.

Colson, S. D., Meek, J. H., & Hawdon, J. M. (2008). Optimal positions for the release of primitive neonatal reflexes stimulating breastfeeding. *Early Human Development, 84*(7), 441–449. doi:10.1016/j.earlhumdev.2007.12.003

Davis, B., Moon, R., Sachs, H., & Ottilini M. (1998). Effects of infant sleep position on infant motor development. *Pediatrics, 104*(5), 1135–1140.

Davis, D., & Stein, M. (2004). *Parenting your premature baby and child: The emotional journey.* Golden, CO: Fulcrum Publishing.

Davis, K., Parker, K., & Montgomery, G. (2004a). Sleep in infants and young children: Part 1. Normal sleep. *Journal of Pediatric Health Care, 18*(2), 65–71.

Davis, K., Parker, K., & Montgomery, G. (2004b). Sleep in infants and young children: Part 2. Common sleep problems. *Journal of Pediatric Health Care, 18*(3), 130–137.

Degan, V., & Puppin, R. (2004). Prevalence of pacifier-sucking habits and successful methods to eliminate them—A preliminary study. *Journal of Dentistry for Children, 7*(2), 148–151.

DeLoache, J., Chiong, C., Sherman, K., Islam, N., Vanderborght, M., Troseth, G., & O'Doherty, K. (2010). Do babies learn from baby media? P*sychological Science, 21*(11), 1570–1574. doi:10.1177/0956797610384145

deVries, J., Visser, G., & Prechtl, H. (1985). The emergence of fetal behavior: II. Quantitative aspects. *Early Human Development, 12,* 99–120.

Dewey, C., Fleming, P., & Golding, J. (1998). Does the supine sleeping position have any adverse effects on the child? *Pediatrics, 101,* e5.

Dudek-Shriber, L., & Zelazny, S. (2007). The effects of prone positioning on the quality and acquisition of developmental milestones in four-month-old infants. *Pediatric Physical Therapy, 19*(1), 48–55.

Eagan, A. (1985). *The newborn mother: Stages of her growth.* Boston, MA: Little Brown & Co.

Elbrit, P. (2000). *Dr. Paula's house calls to your newborn: Birth through 6 months.* Tucson, AZ: Fisher Books.

Emde, R. (1980). Emotional availability: A reciprocal reward system for infants and parents with implications for prevention of psychosocial disorders. In P. Taylor (Ed.), *Parent–infant relationships* (pp. 87–115). Orlando, FL: Grune & Stratton.

Erickson, M., & Kurz-Riemer, K. (1999). *Infants, toddlers, and families: A framework for support.* New York, NY: Guilford Press.

Erickson, M., Sroufe, L., & Egeland, B. (1985). The relationship between quality of attachment and behavior problems in preschool in a high-risk sample. *Monographs of the Society for Research in Child Development, 5*(1–2), 147–166.

Eunice Kennedy Shriver National Institute of Child Health and Human Development. (2013). *Safe sleep for your baby.* Retrieved from www.nichd.nih.gov/publications/pubs/Documents/Safe_Sleep_Baby_English.pdf

Evanoo, G. (2007). Infant crying: A clinical conundrum. *Journal of Pediatric Health Care, 21*(5), 333–338. doi:10.1016/j.pedhc.2007.06.014

Ferber, R. (1985). *Solve your child's sleep problems.* New York, NY: Simon & Shuster.

Fiedler, A., Moseley, M., & Ng, Y. (1988). The immature visual system and premature birth. *British Medical Bulletin, 44*(4), 1093–1118.

Flook, D. M., & Vincze, D. L. (2012). Infant safe sleep: Efforts to improve education and awareness. *Journal of Pediatric Nursing.* doi:10.1016/j.pedn.2011.12.003

Friedman, S., Horwitz, S., Resnick P., (2005).Child murder by mothers: A critical analysis of the current state of knowledge and a research agenda. *American Journal of Psychiatry, 162*,1578–1587.

Galinsky, E. (1987). *The six stages of parenthood.* New York, NY: Addison-Wesley.

Garrett, M., McElroy, A. M., & Staines, A. (2002). Locomotor milestones and babywalkers: A cross sectional study. *British Medical Journal, 324*(7352), 1494.

Garrelts, L., & Melnyk, B. (2001). Pacifier usage and acute otitis media in infants and young children. *Pediatric Nursing, 27*(5), 516–519.

Gartner, L., & Eidelman, A. (2005). American Academy of Pediatrics policy statement on breastfeeding and the use of human milk. *Pediatrics, 115*(2), 496–506.

Gaziano, C., & O'Leary, J. (1998). Childbirth and infant development knowledge gaps in interpersonal settings. *Journal of Health Communication, 3*, 29–51.

Gerber, M., & Johnson, A. (1998). *Your self-confident baby: How to encourage your child's natural abilities from the very start.* New York, NY : John Wiley and Sons.

Ghasedi, G. (2004). *Recognizing postpartum depression: Signs, symptoms, and ways to help.* Minneapolis, MN: Family Information Services.

Goines, L. (2008). The importance of quiet in the home: Teaching noise awareness to parents before the infant is discharged from the NICU. *Neonatal Network, 27*(3), 171–176.

Gopnik, A., & Meltzoff-Kuhl, P. (1999). *Scientist in the crib: Minds, brains, and how children learn.* New York, NY: William Morrow.

Graham, J. M. (2006). Tummy time is important. *Clinical Pediatrics, 45*(2), 119–121. doi:10.1177/000992280604500202

Graven S. (2010). Sleep and brain development. *Clinics in Perinatology, 33*, 693–706.

Grazel, R., Phalen, A. G., & Polomano, R. (2010). Implementation of the American Academy of Pediatrics recommendations to reduce sudden infant death syndrome risk in neonatal intensive care units: An evaluation of nursing knowledge and practice. *Advances in Neonatal Care, 10*(6), 332–342.

Green, J., Darbyshire, P., Adams, A., & Jackson, D. (2015). Desperately seeking parenthood: Neonatal nurses reflect on parental anguish. *Journal of Clinical Nursing, 24*(13–14), 1885–1894. doi:10.1111/jocn.12811

Greenspan, S., & Benderly, B. (1997). *The growth of the mind and the endangered origins of intelligence.* Reading, MA: Perseus Books.

Greenspan, S., & Greenspan, N. (1985). *First feelings.* New York, NY: Viking Penguin Press.

Gross-loh, C. (2010, July/August). Babywearing is best for baby. *Mothering Magazine*, 44–56.

Gudsnuk, K. M. A., & Champagne, F. A. (2011). Epigenetic effects of early developmental experiences. *Clinics in Perinatology, 38*(4), 703–717. doi:10.1016/j.clp.2011.08.005

Guiney, J. B. (2013). *Read to me and I'll teach you about...my baby states.* Vienna, VA: The Center for Infant and Family Resources, LLC.

Gurian, A. (2003). Mother blues—Child blues: How maternal depression affects children. *New York University Child Study Center Newsletter, 7*(3), 7–11.

Hanafin, S., & Griffiths, P. (2002). Does pacifier use cause ear infections in young children? *British Journal of Community Nursing, 7*(4), 206–211.

Hauk, F. R., Omojokun, O. O., & Siadaty, M. S. (2005). Do pacifiers reduce the risk of sudden infant death syndrome? A meta-analysis. *Pediatrics, 116*, e716–e723.

Hernández-Martínez, C., Canals Sans, J., & Fernández-Ballart, J. (2011). Parents' perceptions of their neonates and their relation to infant development. *Child: Care, Health and Development, 37*(4), 484–492. doi:10.1111/j.1365-2214.2011.01210.x

Higley, A., & Miller, M. (1996). The development of parenting: Nursing resources. *Journal of Obstetric, Gynecological and Neonatal Nursing, 25*(8), 707–713.

Hill, B. (1999). *Hush little baby: Gentle ways to stop your baby from crying.* New York, NY: Avery.

Hilt, R. J. (2015). Adverse childhood experiences: What can we do? *Pediatric Annals, 44*(5), 174–175. doi:http://dx.doi.org/10.3928/00904481-20150512-02

Hinds, T., Shalaby-Rana, E., Jackson, A. M., & Khademian, Z. (2015). Aspects of abuse: Abusive head trauma. *Current problems in pediatric and adolescent health care, 45*(3), 71–79. doi:10.1016/j.cppeds.2015.02.002

Hogg, T. (2001). *Secrets of the baby whisperer.* New York, NY: Ballantine Books.

Hotelling, B. A. (2004). Newborn capabilities: Parent teaching is a necessity. *The Journal of Perinatal Education, 13*(4), 43–49. doi:10.1624/105812404X6225

Howard, C., Howard, F., Lanphear, B., Eberly, S., Oakes, D., & Lawrence, R. (2003). Randomized clinical trial of pacifier use and bottle-feeding or cupfeeding and their effect on breastfeeding. *Pediatrics, 111*(3), 511–518.

Huggins, K. (1990). *The nursing mother's companion* (rev. ed.). Cambridge, MA: The Harvard Common Press.

Hunziker, U., & Barr, R. (1986). Increased carrying reduces infant crying: A randomized controlled trial. *Pediatrics, 77*, 641–648.

Hutchinson, L., Thompson, J., & Mitchell, E. (2003). Determinant of nonsynstotic plagiocephaly: A case control study. *Pediatrics, 112*(4), 316–321.

Jackson, J., & Mournio, A. (1999). Pacifier use and otitis media in infants twelve months of age and younger. *Pediatric Dentistry, 21*, 256–260.

Jantz, W., Blosser, C., & Fruchting, L. (1997). A motor milestone change noted with a change in sleep position. *Archives of Pediatric and Adolescent Medicine, 151*, 565–568.

Karmiloff, K., & Karmiloff-Smith, A. (2004). *Everything your baby would ask: If only babies could talk.* Buffalo, NY: Firefly Books.

Karp, H. (2002). *The happiest baby on the block.* New York, NY: Random House.

Kinney, H. C., & Thach, B. T. (2009). The sudden infant death syndrome. *New England Journal of Medicine, 361*(8), 795–805. doi:10.1056/NEJMra0803836

Kitzinger, S. (1990). *The crying baby.* New York, NY: Penguin Books.

Kitzinger, S. (1995). *Ourselves as mothers: The universal experience of motherhood.* Reading, MA: Addison-Wesley.

Kitzinger, S. (1998). *Breastfeeding your baby* (rev. ed.). New York, NY: Alfred A. Knopf.

Kitzman, K. Z. A. (2011). Caregiver awareness of prone play recommendations (Brief report). *Journal of Occupational Therapy, 65*, 101–105.

Klaus, M., & Kennell, J. (1995). *Bonding: Building the foundation of secure attachment and independence.* Reading, MA: Adddison-Wesley.

Klaus, M., & Klaus, P. (1999). *Your amazing newborn.* Reading, MA: Merloyd Lawrence.

Knitzer, J., Theberge, S., & Johnson, K. (2008). *Reducing maternal depression and its impact on young children: Toward a responsive early childhood policy framework.* National Center for Children in Poverty. Retrieved from www.nccp.org/publications/pub_791.html

Kohlhoff, J., & Barnett, B. (2013). Parenting self-efficacy: Links with maternal depression, infant behaviour and adult attachment. *Early Human Development, 89*(4), 249–256. doi:10.1016/j.earlhumdev.2013.01.008

Kopp, C. (2003). *Baby steps: A guide to your child's social, physical, mental and emotional development in the first two years* (2nd ed.). New York, NY: Henry Holt.

Kunhaardt, J., Speigal, L., & Basile, S. (1996). *A mother's circle: Wisdom and reassurance from other mothers on your first year with your baby.* New York, NY: Avon Books.

Kynø, N. M., Ravn, I. H., Lindemann, R., Smeby, N. A., Torgersen, A. M., & Gundersen, T. (2013). Parents of preterm-born children; sources of stress and worry and experiences with an early intervention programme: A qualitative study. *BMC Nursing, 12*(1), 28–48. doi:10.1186/1472-6955-12-28

Lally, J. R. (2014). *The human brain's need for a "social womb" during infancy.* Retrieved from http://forourbabies.org/wp-content/uploads/2014/04/The-Human-Brains-Need-for-a-Social-WombFINALApril2014.pdf

Lau, R., & Morse, C. (1998). Experiences of parents with premature infants hospitalized in neonatal intensive care units: A literature review. *Journal of Neonatal Nursing, 4*(6), 23–29.

Leach, P. (1995). *Children first: What society must do—and is not doing—for children today.* New York, NY: Vintage Books Random House.

Leach, P. (1997). *Your baby and child: Birth to five years* (3rd ed.). New York, NY: Alfred A. Knopf.

Leach, P. (2013). *Your baby and child.* New York, NY: Knopf.

Legendre, V., Burtner, P. A., Martinez, K. L., & Crowe, T. K. (2011). The evolving practice of developmental care in the neonatal unit: A systematic review. *Physical & Occupational Therapy in Pediatrics, 31*(3), 315–338. doi:10.3109/01942638.2011.556697

Lennartsson, F. (2011). Developing guidelines for child health care nurses to prevent nonsynostotic plagiocephaly: Searching for the evidence. *Journal of Pediatric Nursing, 26*(4), 348–358. doi:10.1016/j.pedn.2010.07.003

Levy, D., Zielinsky, P., Aramayo, A. M., Behle, I., Stein, N., & Dewes, L. (2005). Repeatability of the sonographic assessment of fetal sucking and swallowing movements. *Ultrasound in Obstetrics and Gynecology, 26*(7), 745–749. doi:10.1002/uog.1868

Lickliter, R. (2011). The integrated development of sensory organization. *Clinics in Perinatology, 38*(4), 591–603.

Liddle, T., & Yorke, L. (2004). *Why motor skills matter.* New York, NY: Contemporary Books.

Linden, D. W., Trenti Paroli, E., & Doron, M. W. (2013). *Preemies: The essential guide for parents of premature babies.* New York, NY: Simon and Schuster.

Lipchock, S. V., Reed, D. R., & Mennella, J. A. (2011). The gustatory and olfactory systems during infancy: Implications for development of feeding behaviors in the high-risk neonate. *Clinics in Perinatology, 38*(4), 627–641. doi:10.1016/j.clp.2011.08.008

Lobo, M., Kotzer, A., Keefe, M., Brady, E., Deloian, B., Froese-Frenz, A., & Barbosa, G. (2004). Current beliefs and management strategies for treating infant colic. *Journal of Pediatric Health Care, 18*(3), 115–119.

Long, T., & Johnson, M. (2001). Living and coping with excessive infantile crying. Blackwell Science Ltd. *Journal of Advanced Nursing, 34*(2), 155–162.

Main, M., Kaplan, N., & Cassidy, J. (1985). Security in infancy, childhood, and adulthood: A move to the level of representation. *Monographs of the Society for Research in Child Development, 50*(1–2), 66–104.

March of Dimes. (2015). *2015 prematurity report card.* Retrieved from www.marchofdimes.org/materials/premature-birth-report-card-united-states.pdf

March of Dimes, PMNCH, Save the Children, & WHO. (2012). *Born Too Soon: The Global Action Report on Preterm Birth.* Eds CPHowson, MV Kinney, JE Lawn. Geneva, Switzerland: World Health Organization. Retrieved from www.who.int/pmnch/media/news/2012/201204_borntoosoon-report.pdf

Maroney, D. I. (n. d.). *Realities of a premature infant's first year: Helping parents cope.* Retrieved from www.pregnancy.org/article/realities-premature-infants-first-year-helping-parents-cope

Marshall, N., & Tracy, A. (2009). After the baby: Work-family conflict and working mothers' psychological health. *Family Relations, 58*(4), 380–391. doi:10.1111/j.1741-3729.2009.00560.x

Martin, C. (2000). *The nursing mother's problem solver.* New York, NY: Simon & Schuster.

Maurer, D., & Maurer, C. (1988). *The world of the newborn.* London, UK: Basic Books.

Mayo Clinic. (n.d.). *Postpartum depression: Symptoms.* Retrieved from www.mayoclinic.org/diseases-conditions/postpartum-depression/basics/symptoms/con-20029130

Mayes, L. C., Cohen, D. J., Schowalter, J. E., & Granger, R. H. (2003). *The Yale child study center guide to understanding your child: Healthy development from birth to adolescence.* New York, NY: Little, Brown and Co.

Mays, L., & Cohen, D. (2002). *The Yale Child Study Center guide to understanding your child: Healthy development from birth to adolescence.* Boston, MA: Little, Brown.

McClure, V. (1998). *Teaching infant massage: A handbook for instructors.* New York, NY: International Association of Infant Massage.

McGlaughlin, A., & Grayson, A. (2001). Crying in the first year of infancy: Patterns and prevalence. *Society for Reproductive and Infant Psychology, 19*(1), 47–59.

McMann, A. (2008). Babywearing: A natural fashion statement. *Natural Life Magazine.* Retrieved from www.life.ca/naturallife/0808/babywearing.htm

Mercer, R. (1986). *First time motherhood: Experiences from teens to forties.* New York, NY: Springer.

Mildred, J., Beard, K., Dallwitz, A., & Unwin, J. (1995). Play position is influenced by knowledge of SIDS sleep position recommendations. *Journal of Paediatrics and Child Health, 31*, 499–502.

Miller, L., Johnson, A., Duggan, L., & Behm, M. (2011). Consequences of the "Back to Sleep" program in infants. *Journal of Pediatric Nursing, 26*(4), 364–368. doi:10.1016/j.pedn.2009.10.004

Mitchell, E., Thach, B., Thompson, J., & Williams S. (1999). Changing infants' sleep position increases risk of sudden infant death syndrome. *Archives of Pediatric Adolescent Medicine, 153*, 1136–1141.

Montessori, M. (1964). *The absorbent mind.* Wheaton, IL: Theosophical Press.

Moon, C. (2011). The role of early auditory development in attachment and communication. *Clinics in Perinatology, 38*(4), 657–669. doi:10.1016/j.clp.2011.08.009

Moon, R. Y. (2011). SIDS and other sleep-related infant deaths: Expansion of recommendations for a safe infant sleeping environment. *Pediatrics, 128*(5), 1035–1039. doi:10.1016/j.ypdi.2012.02.005

Moon, R. Y., Gingras, J., & Erwin, R. (2002). Physician beliefs and practices regarding SIDS and SIDS risk reduction. *Clinical Pediatrics, 41*(6), 391–395.

Moon, R. Y., Patel, K. M., & Shaefer, S. J. M. (2000). Sudden infant death syndrome in child care settings. *Pediatrics, 106*(2), 295–300.

Moore, E., Anderson, G. C., & Bergman, N. (2007). Early skin-to-skin contact for mothers and their healthy newborn infants. *Cochrane Database of Systematic Reviews.* doi:10.1002/14651858.CD003519.pub2

Morse, C. (1971). *Whobody there?* Winona, MN: St. Mary's Press.

Nakagawa, T., & Conway, E. (2004). Shaken baby syndrome: Recognizing and responding to a lethal danger. *Contemporary Pediatrics, 1*(3), 37–57.

National Institute of Mental Health. (2004). *Depression: What you need to know.* Retrieved from www.nimh.nih.gov/health/publications/depression/index.shtml?rf=3247

National Right to Life News. (2003). *Hand of hope.* Retrieved from www.nationalrighttolifenews.org/news/tag/hand-of-hope/#.Vwgm4aT2YdU

National Scientific Council on the Developing Child. (2004). *Young children develop in an environment of relationships* (Working Paper No. 1). Retrieved from http://developingchild.harvard.edu/resources/wp1

Niemela, M. (2000). Pacifier as a risk factor for acute otitis media: A randomized controlled trial of parental counseling. *Pediatrics, 106*(3), 483–488.

Nordin, R. (2000). *After the baby: Making sense of marriage after childbirth.* Dallas, TX: Taylor Trade.

Nugent, J. K. (1985). *Using the NBAS with families: Guidelines for intervention.* White Plains NY: March of Dimes.

Nugent, J. K., & Brazelton, T. B. (1989). Preventive intervention with families: The NBAS model. *Infant Mental Health Journal, 10*(2), 84–98.

Oden, R. , Powell, C., Sims, A., Weisman, J., Joyner, B. , & Moon, R. (2012). Swaddling: Will it get babies onto their backs for sleep? *Clinical Pediatrics, 51*(3), 254–259. doi:10.1177/0009922811420714

Osterman, K. F., & Kottkamp, R. B. (1993). *Reflective practice for educators.* Newbury Park, CA: Corwin Press.

Ottolini, M., Davis, B., Patel, K., Sachs, H., Gershon, N., & Moon, R. (1999). Prone infant sleeping despite the back to sleep campaign. *Pediatric Adolescent Medicine, 153*(5), 512– 517.

Patel, A. L., Harris, K., & Thach, B. T. (2001). Inspired CO(2) and O(2) in sleeping infants rebreathing from bedding: Relevance for sudden infant death syndrome. *Journal of Applied Physiology, 91*(6), 2537–2545.

Pawl, J. (1995). The therapeutic relationship as human connectedness: Being held in another's mind. *Zero to Three, 15*(4), 1–5.

Pawl, J., & St. John, M. (1998). *How you are is as important as what you do: Making a positive difference for infants, toddlers and their families.* Washington, DC: ZERO TO THREE.

Pearlstein, T., Howard, M., Salisbury, A., & Zlotnick, C. (2009). Postpartum depression. *American Journal of Obstetrics and Gynecology, 200*(4), 357–364. doi:10.1016/j.ajog.2008.11.033

Pearson, J. (1999). Crying and calming: Effective techniques to teach parents of full-term newborns. *Mother Baby Journal, 4*(5), 39–41.

Peek, K., Hershberger, C., Kuehn, D., & Levett, J. (1999). Nursing practice and knowledge. *American Journal of Maternal Child Nursing, 24*(6), 301–304.

Peirano, P. C., & Uauy, R. (2003). Sleep-wake states and their regulatory mechanisms throughout early human development. *Journal of Pediatrics, 143,* 70–79.

Philbin, M., & Klass, P. (2000). The full-term and premature newborn: Hearing and behavioral responses to sound in full-term newborns. *Journal of Perinatology, 20,* S68–S76.

Philbin, M. K., & Gray, L. (2002). Changing levels of quiet in an intensive care nursery. *Journal of Perinatology: Official Journal of the California Perinatal Association, 22*(6), 455–460.

Phillips, R. (2013). The sacred hour: Uninterrupted skin-to-skin contact immediately after birth. *Newborn and Infant Nursing Reviews, 13*(2), 67–72. doi:10.1053/j.nainr.2013.04.001

Pin, T., Eldridge, B., & Galea, M. P. (2007). A review of the effects of sleep position, play position, and equipment use on motor development in infants. *Developmental Medicine & Child Neurology, 49*(11), 858–867.

Piontelli, A. (2015). *Development of normal fetal movements: The last 15 weeks of gestation.* New York, NY: Springer. doi:10.1007/978-88-470-1402-2

Placksin, S. (2000). *Mothering the new mother: Women's feelings and needs after childbirth* (2nd ed.). New York, NY: NewMarket Press.

Planalp, E. M., & Braungart-Rieker, J. M. (2013). Temperamental precursors of infant attachment with mothers and fathers. *Infant Behavior and Development, 36*(4), 796–808. doi:10.1016/j.infbeh.2013.09.004

Poole, S., & Magilner, D. (2000). Crying complaints in the emergency department. In R. G. Barr, B. Hopkins, & J. A. Green (Eds.), *Crying as a sign, a symptom and a signal: Evolving concepts of crying behavior—Clinical, emotional and developmental aspects of infant and toddler crying* (pp. 96–105). London, UK: Cambridge University Press.

Prechtl, H. (1977). *The neurological examination of the full-term newborn infant* (2nd ed.). London, UK: Spastics International Medical Publications.

Pruett, K. (1997). How men and children affect each others' development. *Zero to Three, 18*(1), 1–10.

Ramey, C., & Ramey, S. (1999). *Right from birth: Building your child's foundation for life.* New York, NY: Goddard Press.

Rosenberg, R., Greening, D., & Windell, J. (2003). *Conquering postpartum depression: A proven plan for recovery.* Cambridge, MA: Perseus Books Group.

Runyan, D. K., Hennink-Kaminski, H. J., Zolotor, A. J., Barr, R. G., Murphy, R. A., Barr, M., . . . Nocera, M. (2009). Designing and testing a shaken baby syndrome prevention program—The Period of PURPLE Crying: Keeping babies safe in North Carolina. *Social Marketing Quarterly, 15*(4), 2–24. doi:10.1080/15245000903304635

Salls, J., Silverman, L., & Gatty, C. (2002). The relationship between infant sleep and play positioning to motor milestone achievement. *American Journal of Occupational Therapy, 56,* (5), 577– 580.

Sammons, W. (1999). *The self-calmed baby.* Boston, MA: Little, Brown.

Schaal, B., Orgeur, P., & Rognon, C. (1995). Odor sensing in the human fetus: Anatomical, functional, and chemoecologial bases. In J.-P. Lecanuet, N. A. Krasnegor, W. P. Fifer, & W. P. Smotherman (Eds.), *Fetal development: A psychobiological perspective* (pp. 205–237). Hillsdale, NJ: Erlbaum.

Schott, J. M., & Rossor, M. N. (2003). The grasp and other primitive reflexes. *Journal of Neurology, Neurosurgery, and Psychiatry, 74*(5), 558–560. doi:10.1136/jnnp.74.5.558

Sears, W., & Sears, M. (1996). *Parenting the fussy baby and high-needs child.* Boston, MA: Little, Brown.

Sears, W., & Sears, M. (2001). *The attachment parenting book: A common sense guide to understanding and nurturing your baby.* Boston, MA: Little, Brown.

Shahmoon-Shanok, R. (1990). Parenthood: A process marking identity and intimacy capacities. *Zero to Three, 21*(2), 1–9.

Shapiro, L. (2003). *The secret language of children: How to understand what your kids are really saying.* Naperville, IL: Sourcebooks.

Shelov, S., & Hannemann, R. (2004). *The American Academy of Pediatrics complete and authoritative guide to caring for your baby and young child, birth to age 5* (4th ed.) New York, NY: Bantam Books.

Slade, A., Cohen, L., Sadler, L., & Miller, M. (2009). The psychology and psychopathology of pregnancy. In C. Zeanah (Ed.), *Handbook of infant mental health* (3rd ed., (pp. 22–39). New York, NY: Guilford.

Smotherman, W., & Robinson, S. (1995). Tracing developmental trajectories into the prenatal period. In J-P. Lecanuet, N. A. Krasnegor, W. P. Fifer, & W. P. Smotherman (Eds.), *Fetal Development* (pp. 15–32). Hillsdale, NJ: Erlbaum.

Smyke, A. (1998). Theories of spoiling and fear of spoiling: Historical and contemporary perspectives. *The Signal Newsletter of the World Association for Infant Mental Health, 5*(4), 1–9.

Stone, R. (1996). *The healing art of storytelling.* New York, NY: Hyperion.

Swain, J., Lorberbaum, J., Kose, S., & Strathearn, L. (2007). Brain basis of early parent–infant interactions: Psychology, physiology, and in vivo functional neuroimaging studies. *Journal of Child Psychology and Psychiatry, 48*(3–4), 262–287.

Tajani, E., & Ianniruberto, A. (1990). The uncovering of fetal competence. In M. Papini, A. Pasquinelli, & E. A. Gidoni (Eds.), *Development handicap and rehabilitation: Practice and theory* (pp. 3–8). Amsterdam, the Netherlands: Elsevier.

Tallandini, M. (2015). Kangaroo mother care and mother premature infant. *Dyadic Interaction, 36*(2), 238–239. doi:10.1002/imhj.

Tedder, J. (1991). Using the Brazelton Neonatal Assessment Scale to facilitate the parent-infant relationship in a primary care setting. *Nurse Practitioner, 16*(3), 26–36.

Tedder, J. L. (2008). Give them the HUG: An innovative approach to helping parents understand the language of their newborn. *Journal of Perinatal Education, 17*(2), 14–20. doi:10.1624/105812408X298345

The New York Times. (2010, February 22). *The dangers of baby walkers.* Retrieved from http://consults.blogs.nytimes.com/2010/02/22/the-dangers-of-baby-walkers/?_r=0

Tikotzky, L., De Marcas, G., Har-Toov, J., Dollberg, S., Bar-Haim, Y., & Sadeh, A. (2010). Sleep and physical growth in infants during the first 6 months. *Journal of Sleep Research, 19*(1-Part-I), 103–110.

Torczynski, E. (1989). Normal development of the eye and orbit before birth: The development of the eye. In S. Isenberg (Ed.), *The eye in infancy* (pp. 9–30). Chicago, IL: Year Book Medical.

Trapanotto, M., Benini, F., Farina, M., Gobber, D., Magnavita, V., & Zacchello, F. (2004). Behavioural and physiological reactivity to noise in the newborn. *Journal of Paediatrics and Child Health, 40*(5-6), 275–281.

U.S. Department of Health and Human Services. (n.d.). *Breastfeeding—Best for baby. Best for mom*. www.womenshealth.gov/breastfeeding.

U.S. Department of Health and Human Services & Office of Disease Prevention and Health Promotion. (2012). *Healthy People 2020.* Washington, DC: Author.

Vergara, E., & Bigsby, R. (2004). *Developmental and therapeutic interventions in the NICU.* Baltimore, MD: Brookes.

Victoria, C. (1997). Pacifier use and short duration of breastfeeding: Cause, consequence or coincidence? *Pediatrics, 99*(3), 39–41.

Walton, G., Bower, N., & Bower, T. (1992). Recognition of familiar forms by newborns. *Infant Behavior and Development, 15*, 265–269.

White, C., Simon, M., & Bryan, A. (2002). Using evidence to educate birthing center nursing staff: About infant states, cues, and behaviors. *MCN: The American Journal of Maternal/Child Nursing, 27*(5), 294–298.

Willinger, M., Hoffman, H., & Hartford, R. (1994). Infant sleep position and risk for sudden infant death syndrome: Report of meeting held January 13 and 14, 1994, National Institutes of Health, Bethesda, MD. *Pediatrics, 93*(5), 814–819.

Wirth, F. (2001). *Prenatal parenting.* New York, NY: HarperCollins.

Wolff, P. (1959). Observations on human infants. *Psychosomatic Medicine, 221*, 110–118.

Woolridge, M. W. (1986). The "anatomy" of infant sucking. *Midwifery, 2*(4), 164–171. doi:10.1016/S0266-6138(86)80041-9

Worobey, J. (1985). A review of Brazelton-based interventions to enhance parent–infant interactions. *Journal of Reproductive and Infant Psychology, 18*(5) 64–73.

Younger, J. (2002). *New mother's guide to breastfeeding: American Academy of Pediatrics.* New York, NY: Bantam Books.

Younger Meek, J., & American Academy of Pediatrics. (2011). *New mother's guide to breastfeeding.* New York: Bantam Books.

Zachry, A. H., & Kitzmann, K. M. (2011). Caregiver awareness of prone play recommendations. *American Journal of Occupational Therapy, 65*(1), 101–105. doi:10.5014/ajot.2011.09100

Zelazny, S. (1999, April). *The relationship between infant positioning and motor skill acquisition.* Paper presented at the annual meeting of the American Occupational Therapy Association, Indianapolis, IN.

About the Author

Jolene Pearson, MS, PhD, IMH-E® (IV)

Dr. Pearson is an associate professor at Bethel University in St. Paul, MN, where she teaches courses in early education and development. She earned her bachelor's degree at the University of Minnesota, a master's degree from Wheelock College in Boston, MA, and her doctorate from the University of Minnesota in the Family, Youth and Community program. Dr. Pearson's research focuses on what students in BA/BS early childhood licensure programs learn about infants, toddlers, and parents.

She has been an adjunct faculty member and instructor at the University of Minnesota's Center for Early Education and Development, the University of St. Thomas, and St. Cloud State University, teaching courses in parent education, infant mental health, and early childhood special education.

Dr. Pearson is a certified Neonatal Behavioral Assessment Scale examiner and is licensed in the fields of parent education, early childhood education, and early childhood special education. She is endorsed as an infant health mentor by the Michigan Association for Infant Mental Health and is a member of the Minnesota Association for Infant and Early Childhood Mental Health.

Index

Page numbers of photographs appear in italics.